D1013092

Fractal Image Compression

——— **AK Peters Books in Computer Science and Related Areas** ———

Barnsley M., and Anson, L., *The Fractal Transform*

Barnsley M., and Hurd, L., *Fractal Image Compression*

Birmingham, W.P., Gupta, A.P., and Siewiorek, D.P., *Automating the Design of Computer Systems: The MICON Project*

Davis, P., *Spirals: From Theodorus to Chaos*

Flynn, A., and Jones, J., *Mobile Robots: Inspiration to Implementation*

Geometry Center, University of Minnesota, *Not Knot* (VHS video)

Hansen, V.L., *Geometry in Nature*

Healey G., *et al.* (eds.), *Physics-Based Vision: Principles and Practice, Color*

Hoschek, J., and Lasser, D., *Fundamentals of Computer-Aided Geometric Design*

Iterated Systemc, Inc., *Floppy Book: A P.OEM PC Book*

Iterated Systems, Inc., *SNAPSHOTS: True-Color Photo Images Using the Fractal Formatter*

Klinker, G.J., *A Physical Approach to Color Image Understanding*

Myers, B.A. (ed.), *Languages for Developing User Interfaces*

Parke, F.I., and Waters, K., *Computer Facial Animation*

Whitman, S., *Multiprocessor Methods for Computer Graphics Rendering*

Wolff, L., *et al.* (eds.), *Physics-Based Vision: Principles and Practice, Radiometry*

Wolff, L., *et al.* (eds.), *Physics-Based Vision: Principles and Practice, Shape Recovery*

Fractal Image Compression

Michael F. Barnsley

Iterated Systems, Inc.
Norcross, Georgia

Lyman P. Hurd

Iterated Systems, Inc.
Norcross, Georgia

Illustrations by Louisa F. Anson

AK Peters, Ltd.
Wellesley, Massachusetts

Editorial, Sales, and Customer Service Offices
AK Peters, Ltd.
289 Linden Street
Wellesley, MA 02181

Cover illustrations provided by Michael F. Barnsley, Iterated Systems, Inc.

Library of Congress Cataloging-in-Publication Data

Barnsley, M. F. (Michael Fielding), 1946-
    Fractal image compression / Michael F. Barnsley ; Lyman P. Hurd.
        p.   cm.
    Includes bibliographical references and index.
    ISBN 1-56881-000-8
    1. Image processing--Digital techniques--Mathematics.
    2. Fractals.   I. Title.
    TA1632.B353   1992
    621.36'7—dc20   92-39927
                                                                      CIP

Printed in the United States of America

96 95 94 93 92   10 9 8 7 6 5 4 3 2 1

Dedicated to Edward Barnsley and Christopher Wade

Contents

Acknowledgments

The fractal transform was discovered by the first author in March, 1988. The basic mathematics forms the core of US Patent # 5065447 jointly held with Alan Sloan, co-founder of Iterated Systems, Inc., who helped with its development.

In the early history of the development of fractal image compression, we would like to acknowledge Arnaud Jacquin, Andy Harrington, John Herndon, Els Withers, and John Elton.

Research in fractal image compression is ongoing at Iterated Systems. We would like to acknowledge discussions with research staff John Elton, Doug Hardin, Hawley Rising, Ning Lu, John Muller, Yaakov Shima, Els Withers, and Charles Moreman. The second author would particularly like to thank Steve Demko for teaching him the fractal transform and for innumerable insights along the way.

We would like to thank an anonymous referee for helpful suggestions in the information theory sections of the book. We thank Alice and Klaus Peters for sharing our vision.

1

Introduction

In December 1992, in time for Christmas, Microsoft Corporation published
a remarkable compact disk. It is entitled "Microsoft Encarta," and comes
in a delicate box with a picture of a bird's nest, eggs, and twigs on it. It
consists of a single shiny CD, and can be played on a personal computer
equipped with a standard compact disk drive.

Encarta is a multimedia encyclopedia, and it is quite unique. It contains an exhaustive collection of articles, animations, sounds, illustrations,
graphs, and photographs, as well as an atlas and a dictionary. It contains
seven hours of sound, 100 animations, and 800 color maps, with the ability
to zoom in on locations. There are also more than 7,000 photographs of
flowers, plants, people, places, clouds, spires, animals, and more. A green
banner of ferns lies above the pictures of the flowers. The pictures are of
high quality. All of this is encoded in less than 600 megabytes of data, laid
out as zeros and ones on the surface of the shiny compact disk! How is this
possible?

Fractal Image Compression is about the mathematical ideas that lie be-
hind the photographs and other pictures on Encarta. They are all fractals!
They are stored as highly compressed data files produced using fractal
image compression.

Fractal image compression involves three basic mathematical modeling
problems. The required models are (1) a mathematical model for real world
images, (2) a model for approximating model images by means of resolution

1

independent image approximants, which must be described by finite data strings, and (3) a computationally tractable model for the sources of the data strings, to enable the application of information theory to provide efficient representation of the image approximants. This book describes various models for each of these steps. It also includes C source code for applications of a number of these models. These applications clarify understanding of how the models work in a digital environment.

In Chapter 2, we describe the space $\Re$ of real world images. These are magical things indeed! They are endlessly stretchable and possess infinite detail. Fractal image compression puts them into computers and makes them reappear again at will. To start the process, we present various mathematical models for $\Re$. Some are provided by functions, others by subsets of three dimensional space, and yet others by measure theory. The chapter concludes with a discussion of how pictures are measured with the aid of scanners, digitizers, and quantizers. These measurements yield the long strings of zeros and ones that describe the colors and intensities at a large number of different locations in a picture. These strings are the input to fractal image compression systems.

In Chapter 3, we summarize the basic mathematics needed for understanding fractal image compression systems. This includes a low-level language for describing properties of images, namely topology on metric spaces. Topology is also the basis of generalized collage theorems, which are fundamental to fractal image compression. Relevant spaces and functions, affine transformations on the Euclidean plane, and the contraction mapping theorem are described.

Fractal image compression systems relate finite strings of zeros and ones to infinite images in a smooth and continuous manner. They make use of approximating entities (*image approximants*) which, on the one hand, represent the very members of the mathematical space we have chosen for making images, and, on the other hand, are controlled by finitely many parameters, as in model (2) above.

In this book, we consider two families of approximants: *iterated function system fractals*, which are dealt with in Chapter 4, and *fractal transform fractals*, which are considered in Chapter 6. Both types of approximants are specified by finite strings of zeros and ones. Also, they consist of infinitely stretchable images with endless detail. Thus, they are ideal for approximating real world images.

In Chapter 4, we introduce the theory of iterated function systems (IFS theory), and the approximation of real world images by IFS fractals. To do this, we describe the Hausdorff space $\mathcal{H}$, contraction mappings on $\mathcal{H}$, and iterated function systems. Then we describe the photocopy machine algorithm for computing IFS fractals, and introduce the collage theorem; this leads into a methodology for fractal image compression. More elaborate systems are introduced based on the use of IFS's with probabilities, whose attractors can be computed using the grayscale photocopy machine algorithm. The chapter concludes with a brief description of a fractal image compression system [Monroe and Dudbridge], which is based on IFS fractals.

A fundamental part of the fractal image compression story is the modeling problem (3) above. A methodology is needed to connect the strings of zeros and ones that describe fractal approximants to *information theory*. Information theory considers the mathematical modeling of pure discrete symbolic data to describe it in the most efficient manner; it seeks the greatest economy in number of symbols required to communicate the strings. It involves the study of coding schemes for encrypting finitely generated Markov sources. Here, we are awed by a beautiful realization, that IFS theory, that is, fractal theory itself, provides not only the right answer to the image description problem, but also it yields efficient compression of the data used to describe the fractals themselves. In many circumstances, IFS theory yields optimal compression of strings of symbols whose frequencies of occurrence are known.

In Chapter 5, we consider discrete spaces and information theory, and the optimal compression of discrete data generated by Markov sources. We introduce information sources, Markov sources, codes, and the Kraft–McMillan inequality. This leads us to the concept of the entropy of a source. We treat compression using Shannon–Fano codes and Huffman codes, and we build up intuition as we advance. With this basic material in mind, we review the concept of addresses on IFS fractals. This elucidates the last section of the chapter, where we tie together arithmetic compression and IFS fractals.

In Chapter 6, we present the fractal transform and the approximation of real world images by fractal transform fractals. This involves the introduction of the fascinating subject of *local iterated function systems, (local IFS)*. We start the chapter with a general description of fractal image compression methodology. Then we introduce local IFS, and give an example of a corresponding collage theorem. This example relates to binary images such as drawings transmitted by fax. We show how attractors of local IFS can be computed using an escape time algorithm, similar to the ones used to compute pictures of Julia sets. This leads us to a formal description of an automatic fractal image compression system for binary, black-and-white images, known as the *black and white fractal transform*. We then turn our attention to the application of local IFS theory to the automatic compression of grayscale images. We describe a simple, computationally feasible process called the *grayscale fractal transform*. We illustrate the corresponding compressed formulas, fractal transform codes, and the corresponding fractals, known as *FT fractals*. We conclude the chapter with a detailed model digital implementation in C, to illustrate the inner workings of such a system.

Since this book is all about fractal image compression, it seems appropriate, by way of counterpoint, to provide the reader with an understanding of how a non-fractal image compression system works. Thus, we have included the Appendix on the current JPEG Discrete Cosine Transform (DCT) system, which includes specific implementation information.

Digital computation devices for the process of fractal image compression, based on material in this book, may be covered by U.S. Patents, Numbers 5,065,447 and 4,941,193, related international patents, and other patents pending in the U.S. and other countries. For further information, contact

Licensing Department
Iterated Systems, Inc.
5550-A Peachtree Parkway
Norcross, GA 30092

2

Formulation of Mathematical Models for Real World Images

The poet's eye, in a fine frenzy rolling,
Doth glance from heaven to earth, from earth to heaven;
And, as imagination bodies forth
The forms of things unknown, the poet's pen
Turns them to shapes, and gives to airy nothing
A local habitation and a name.

— William Shakespeare [A Midsummer Night's Dream]

2.1. Goals of This Chapter

In this chapter, we introduce the space $\Re$ of real world images, and we discuss various mathematical models for $\Re$. We also discuss the acquisition of image data via scanners, the representation of color, and digitization.

Real world images are fascinating as mathematical entities. For example, they have this astonishing property: if one clips out a part of a real world image and stretches it the size of the original, then one has another real world image. Thus, $\Re$ is naturally broken into "worlds" — the members of an image world are all of the members of $\Re$ that can be accessed from one member of $\Re$. This property is reminiscent of the situation one finds when playing with a computer program, such as [LC] or [DFDS], where one can explore, seemingly forever, a single fractal. So it is too with a single real world image.

The goal of this book is the study of approximation methods for approaching real world images by means of approximants, such as IFS fractals and FT fractals, and the succinct description of these approximants using information theory. The starting place is $\Re$.

2.2.   Description and Properties of Real World Images

We begin by describing the concept of *real world images*. These are the objects for which we will make mathematical models. They capture intuitive feelings that we have about the visual world. These feelings relate to the way we interact visually with the physical world; we can look closely at one thing, and from far away at another. It seems as though we can see all of the scene that is in front of us, as though it is all there, in an instant, encompassed by our mind. Images feel as though they are analog entities that belong to an infinitely divisible world. These feelings are not exactly correct; they do not fit precisely with reality, but they allow our brains to cope with the complexity of what they perceive. These feelings, and others that we are going to describe, are true more or less, over a range of scales, and to an approximation and they contain valid information about the nature of the physical world; but the physical observable world itself is subtly different from these illusions. It is an endless vista that we can neither define nor even grasp. What we can grasp is the concept of real world images.

By a real world image, we mean an idealized entity that does not really exist, just as a mathematical line or triangle does not exist. It comes closest to existence in our imagination, where it is a seeming continuum, which can be stretched endlessly, and explored in infinite detail. Picture a beach and blue sea, with colored parasols, clouds, and sky. Imagine looking ever closer at the sand until you can see the grains of sand, or look far out to sea, towards the horizon where the tiny shape of a ship can be seen, and look closer at it, until you can see the portholes and the gulls upon the railings, or look up in your picture at the intricate coruscations and crenations in edges of the clouds, present in greater and greater abundance the closer you look. However, a real world image cannot be defined as a physical object, such as an actual photograph, or the actual pattern of light that falls upon the retina of the eye. A number of physical principles conspire to make the tangible existence of an image of infinite resolution an idealization. A real world image can never be realized because of the trembling of the atoms of which objects are made, the Heisenberg Uncertainty Principle, the finite wavelengths of light particles, and quantization effects.

What is a real world image? Roughly, it is any image that we could see, or imagine seeing somewhere. One way to think of a real world image is to consider it to be a high-quality, sharply focused, instantaneously snapped photograph taken somewhere in or near the world. It might be taken from far away, from an aircraft high up, or from the surface of the moon looking back at the earth or out into space, depicting billions of stars. It might be a close-up of a beautiful face on the front of a magazine. It might be of a blade of grass, or a scarf, or a fern, or a close-up view of the structure of a gnat's wing, seen through an electron microscope. It might be a picture of a football game. It might be a picture of a painting, of a black-and-white photograph, of a page from a newspaper, of a floor show at a computer graphics conference, with lots of artificial pictures on screens of computers. It might depict a technical drawing for a new chip, or an architect's blueprint for a house. It might show a landscape with mountains, clouds and flowers, or a single flower. A real world image might show a gallery full of photographs, or the reflected image of itself, seen within a mirror. These are the objects for which we form mathematical models.

Before going on to gather the properties of our real world images, we comment on the perception of the physical observable universe by the mind. These ideas are the philosophy of Immanuel Kant (1724–1804), and are well summarized in [PFS], from which the following passage is quoted, with some omissions:

> Any empirical researcher, any natural scientist, takes as his field of investigation some aspect or selection of natural objects and events, located in space and occurring in time. The scientist's business is to discover the laws of working which govern the behavior and account for the characteristics of his selected objects. But those general features which constitute the very framework of such enquiries — the spatio-temporality of nature and the existence of discoverable law — are alike attributed by Kant to the constitution of the human mind. Empirical enquiry can yield us knowledge only of appearances — of the appearances that things present to beings constituted as we are. Of things as they are in themselves, experience and scientific investigation can yield no knowledge at all.

> *Sir Peter Strawson 1987*

Let $\Re$ denote the set of all real world images. What can we say about a member $\mathcal{I}$ of $\Re$. For brevity, we refer to $\mathcal{I}$ as an *image*.

Property (i) Any real world image $\mathcal{I} \in \Re$ has a *support*, and *physical dimensions*, which can be described as follows. The support of an image is a set $\Box \subset \mathbb{R}^2$, where $\mathbb{R}^2$ denotes the Euclidean plane. $\Box$ is defined by

$$\Box = \{(x, y) \in \mathbb{R}^2 : a \leq x \leq b, \ c \leq y \leq d\},$$

where $a < b$ and $c < d$ are real constants. Here, the physical dimensions of $\mathcal{I}$ are $(b - a)$ units and $(d - c)$ units, where *units* refers to physical units such as meters or inches, for example. We say that $\Box$ is the *support* of the image $\mathcal{I}$.

The set $\Box \subset \mathbb{R}^2$, together with its physical dimensions $(b - a)$ units, and $(d - c)$ units, provides the physical extent of the image. We require

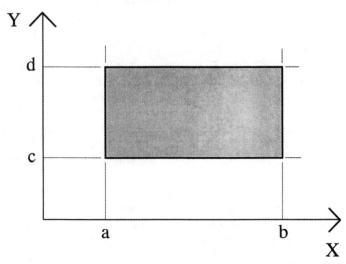

Figure 2.1. A real world image has a support $\square = \{(x,y) \in \mathbb{R}^2 : a \leq x \leq b, \ c \leq y \leq d\}$. We think of the support of an image as being a sheet of paper on which the image resides.

the existence of physical dimensions in order to allow the setting of a baseline in size and scale, and to enable $\Re$ to make contact with the physical world. Physical objects have physical dimensions, and at some point in the development of the theory one will want to tie back to such objects.

A real world image possesses the geometry and topology of its support $\square$. The support of an image is made of that imagined, axiomatic substance, the Euclidean plane. It can be continuously deformed and stretched endlessly, via the rules of topology and real analysis. The concept of the support of an image is illustrated in Fig. 2.1.

A *point* in an image means a point in its support. Every point in the support of an image is a point in the image. The distance d between a pair of points (x_1, y_1) and (x_2, y_2) in the support of an image is measured using the Euclidean metric,

$$d = \sqrt{(x_1 - x_2)^2 + (y_1 - y_2)^2}.$$

We imagine the support of an image to be the sheet of paper or the photographic film on which the image resides. A *region within an image* means the part of the image that is associated with a region within its support. A *subset of an image* means the part of an image associated with a subset of its support; and so on.

Figure 2.2. Let $\mathcal{I} \in \Re$. Then $\mathcal{I}$ possesses chromatic attributes. Every measurable set in the support of $\mathcal{I}$ is associated with sets of numbers that represent its colors and light intensities.

The support of an image, $\square \subset \mathbb{R}^2$, together with the Euclidean metric, is an example of a *metric space*. The *topology* of this space provides information about the nature of real world images. Topological properties and classifications of subsets of the support of an image, such as boundary, interior, openness, closedness, connectedness, and compactness, are important, since they are preserved by transformations of the support that provide equivalent metrics. Topology provides the basis for the description of many properties of images, as well as underpinning much of the mathematical superstructure. Topology of metric spaces is discussed in Chapter 3.

Property(ii) Let $\mathcal{I} \in \Re$. Then $\mathcal{I}$ possesses *chromatic attributes*. These provide the frequencies (colors) and intensities of light associated with subsets of the image. They may be modeled by real valued functions, or real valued Borel measures supported on the support of the image. Every measurable set in the support of $\mathcal{I}$ can be associated with a collection of numerical attributes that describe various averages, over the set and over ranges of frequencies, of intensities of light associated with the set. This idea is illustrated in Fig. 2.2.

In Section 2.3, we discuss mathematical models for assigning chromatic attributes to real world images. Here, we are mainly concerned with the general description of the properties of $\Re$. However, to explain the property of resolution independence, we provide some specific modeling illustrations here.

Of particular importance in connection with digital imaging applications is the case where the support of an image is broken up by a grid of lines into an array of rectangular subsets, called *pixels*. Each pixel, which is itself a member of $\Re$, has its own chromatic attributes. In digital imaging, these are modeled by a finite set of truncated real numbers, representing for example the red, green, and blue intensities of light associated with the pixel.

Real world images can be modeled to be pure black-and-white, as, for example, one thinks of a fax document or a page of print; they can be modeled with only a few colors as in a comic book, or with a great range of colors as in the best photographs and prints; they can be modeled to be grayscale, as in an old movie or in a grayscale photograph.

If $\mathcal{I}$ is modeled to be a pure black-and-white image, then each point in its support $\Box$ might be associated with either a zero or a one, depending on whether the point is black or white, respectively. If it is to be modeled as a grayscale image, then each point in $\Box$ might be associated with a numerical value that represents the intensity of light at that point in the image. This task is not as easy as it appears at first thought, because of the possible presence of point sources of light, and the possible presence of light sources reflected by sets of measure zero. The existence of such sources is posited by the desire to model $\Re$ by mathematically complete spaces.

However if one assigns chromatic attributes to an image, it must be done in such a manner that averages and/or other small sets of values can be assigned to various regions and subsets in an image. For example, one wants to be able to say that the sky is blue and that a certain pixel in an image has a certain intensity, and so on.

Property(iii)   Let $\mathcal{I} \in \Re$. Then $\mathcal{I}$ is *resolution independent*. This means that $\mathcal{I}$ can be described at finite, arbitrarily high resolutions. Numerical values can be assigned to pixels, representing their colors and intensities. This can be done, however finely the pixels are defined, both spatially and in terms of their image attributes, such as color and intensity values. It can be done in a consistent manner. There is no logical contradiction between the interpretation of an image described at two different resolutions. This idea is illustrated in Fig. 2.3. We have to go to another level of refinement in the mathematical modeling process to determine just how numerical values are attached to $\Box$ to provide it with numerical attributes at any desired resolution. Examples are provided in Section 2.3.

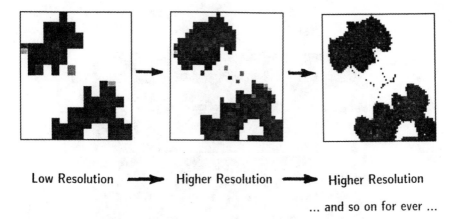

Figure 2.3. The same image at three different resolutions. Any image $\mathcal{I}$ in the set of real world images is *resolution independent*. It can be defined at finite, albeit arbitrarily high, resolutions.

Property (iv) The set $\Re$ of all real world images is *closed under the clipping operation*, as follows. Let $\mathcal{I} \in \Re$. Choose any rectangular region within the support of $\mathcal{I}$, with sides parallel to the sides of the support of $\mathcal{I}$, and use this to define a new image $\tilde{\mathcal{I}}$. Then $\tilde{\mathcal{I}} \in \Re$. This idea is illustrated in Fig. 2.4. The property of being closed under the clipping operation expresses the fundamental idea that any real world image, no matter how small, contains information and is a valid image in its own right. This property together with the next one express critical structural ingredients of a mathematically rich theory of images.

Property (v) Let $\mathcal{I} \in \Re$. Let $\tilde{\mathcal{I}}$ denote the result of either *isotropically stretching or isotropically shrinking* $\mathcal{I}$. Then $\tilde{\mathcal{I}} \in \Re$; that is, $\Re$ is closed under isotropic stretching and shrinking. This idea is illustrated in Fig. 2.5.

This property asserts, in particular, that it is possible to stretch an image isotropically. That the stretching is isotropic means that it applies equally in all directions. The property does not specify how stretching (or shrinking) is applied to an image; in particular, it does not make precise how the chromatic attributes of the stretched image are specified. This specification is dependent on the mathematical model that is made for $\Re$.

The way in which one thinks of the stretching process on an image has implications on how one models the assignment of chromatic attributes to a stretched image. We take note of the following examples of how images are

Member of the space

New member of the space ℜ

Figure 2.4. The set ℜ of all real world images is closed under the clipping operation. If one chooses any rectangular region within a real world image, of the same proportions as the original image, and stretches it, or "blows it up," to the size of the original, then the result is another real world image. This expresses the idea that there is no limit to the magnifiability of real world images; no loss of detail is imposed by the physical laws of optics, the construction of cameras, or the fineness of the chemical emulsion used on the film that captures the imagined images.

The same figure, of a butterfly both stretched and shrunk.

Figure 2.5. Butterfly is shown both stretched and shrunk. $\Re$ is closed under isotropic stretching and shrinking.

stretched in the real world, and what happens to their chromatic attributes. One way of stretching an image is with the aid of a magnifying glass. In this case, there is loss of brightness because the number of photons emitted per unit area of the original image remains constant, but they are spread over a larger area in the magnified image. For this reason, systems for magnifying images usually include a means for providing increased illumination to their subjects, to maintain the sense that the image is of consistent coloration and brightness after magnification. Another example is presented by slide projectors, which project color images onto screens: if the brightness of the light reflected from a screen is to remain constant when the distance between the screen and the projector is doubled, then power of the bulb in the projector must be increased by a factor of four because the area of the images increases by a factor of four. In this case, the natural choice of stretched image is the one whose rate of photon emission is scaled up in proportion to the increase in area. Yet another example is provided by our own everyday experience of viewing objects from different distances. If the distance between an observer and a picture hanging on a wall is halved, then the area of the image falling on the observer's retina is increased by a factor of four. However, the number of photons falling on the observer's retina is also increased by a factor of four. Everything balances out and overall the brightness of colors in the image remains constant. This is our typical experience in the physical observable world, and thus is the way that we expect that brightness in images should scale.

A white Sierpinksi Triangle
on a black background, and
three copies of the same,
making a "stretched"
Sierpinski Triangle.

Figure 2.6.

The preceding discussion works well for regions of constant color, but more complex effects can be envisaged. For example, suppose that one is so far away from sources of light, that they appear to be point sources, perhaps bright fireflies on a dark night; then double the distance between the observer and the sources. The brightness of the sources will decrease by a factor of four, the distances between the sources will decrease by a factor of two, but the physical dimensions of each source will seem to be the same; namely, points. In such cases one can use Borel measures to model the chromatic attributes of the image. Another example is provided by a picture of a Sierpinski triangle. One way of stretching it to twice its linear dimensions is with the aid of three duplicate copies of the original, as illustrated in Fig. 2.6. Then we deduce the curious fact that the total light emitted and/or reflected by the Sierpinski triangle (imagine that it is white on a black background) is tripled when its linear dimensions are doubled. Thus, a Sierpinski triangle of twice the size, viewed from twice as far away, appears fainter than the original at the original viewing distance. Another way in which one can think of stretching an image is to leave the optical system alone, and to physically stretch the image: for example, the image may be embedded in a colorful sheet of rubber; then when the rubber is stretched, the image is stretched, while color intensities remain constant. We conclude that care needs to be taken regarding the definition of the process of stretching a mathematical model for a real world image. Examples of stretching models for real world images are given in Section 2.3.

We may also choose to endow real world images with the following properties.

Property (vi)   Let $\mathcal{I} \in \Re$. Let $\tilde{\mathcal{I}}$ denote the result of reflecting $\mathcal{I}$ in an axis parallel to one of the sides of its support. Then $\tilde{\mathcal{I}} \in \Re$; that is, $\Re$ is closed under reflection. This idea is illustrated in Fig. 2.7.

Property (vii)   Let $\mathcal{I} \in \Re$. Let $\tilde{\mathcal{I}}$ denote the result of clipping a rotated rectangular region of $\mathcal{I}$. Then $\tilde{\mathcal{I}} \in \Re$; that is, $\Re$ is closed under such rotation operations. This idea is illustrated in Fig. 2.8.   Isotropic stretching and shrinking of an image are examples of *similitudes* of the image. Similitudes, rotations, and reflections are examples of affine transformations, and are described in Chapter 3.   Properties (v), (vi), and (vii) together can be generalized to the following property.

Property (viii) $\Re$ is closed under the application of arbitrary invertible affine transformations, applied to clipped parallelograms within images, and chosen so as to yield rectangular images, as illustrated in Fig. 2.9.

For simplicity, we restrict the following discussion, for the remainder of Section 2.2, to consideration of implications of Properties (iv) and (v) taken together. Essentially, the same discussion can be made if one replaces Property (v) by Properties (v) and (vi); or by Properties (vi) and (vii); or by Property (viii).

Properties (iv) and (v) taken together express the fact that real world images have the following astonishing property. If one chooses any rectangular region within a real world image, of the same proportions as the original image, and stretches it or "zooms it up" to the size of the original, then the result is another real world image. This suggests that nontrivial mathematical models for real world images will be inherently rich in mathematical and visual properties. For example, any real world image gives rise to the collection of real world images that can be derived from it by clipping and zooming. This allows the definition of an order relation and an equivalence class structure on $\Re$.

Definition *Let $\mathcal{I}$ and $\mathcal{H}$ be members of $\Re$. Then we say that $\mathcal{H}$ is derived from $\mathcal{I}$ if and only if $\mathcal{H}$ can be obtained from $\mathcal{I}$ by clipping and stretching (or shrinking), using Properties (iv) and (v). We use the notation $\mathcal{H} < \mathcal{I}$ to mean $\mathcal{H}$ is derived from $\mathcal{I}$.*

Figure 2.7. The reflection of a real world image is another real world image.

Figure 2.8. The result of clipping a rotated rectangle out of the middle of a real world image will produce another real world image.

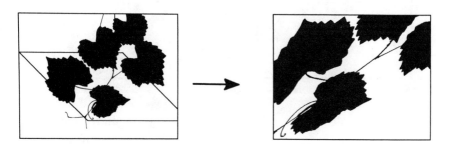

Figure 2.9. An invertible affine transformation is applied to a clipped parallelogram within an image, and yields a rectangular image.

Definition *Let $S \subset \Re$ denote a set of real world images. Define $\mathcal{W}(S) \subset \Re$ by*

$$\mathcal{W}(S) = \{\mathcal{H} \in \Re : \mathcal{H} < \mathcal{I} \ \text{for some} \ \mathcal{I} \in S\}.$$

Then we say that $\mathcal{W}(S)$ is the set or world *of images generated by S, using Properties (iv) and (v).*

Definition *We say that two images, $\mathcal{I}$ and $\mathcal{H}$ in $\Re$, are* equivalent, *under Properties (iv) and (v), if and only if $\mathcal{I} < \mathcal{H}$ and $\mathcal{H} < \mathcal{I}$. We use the notation $\mathcal{H} \sim \mathcal{I}$ to mean that the two images $\mathcal{I}$ and $\mathcal{H}$ are equivalent.*

It is straightforward to show that the definition of equivalence here indeed provides an *equivalence relation* [JG] on the space $\Re$. It follows that $\Re$ is partitioned by this relation into *equivalence classes*. Each equivalence class is represented by a representative element. We use the notation $\mathcal{E}(\mathcal{I})$ to denote the equivalence class associated with $\mathcal{I} \in \Re$. Let $\mathcal{I}, \mathcal{H} \in \Re$. Then $\mathcal{I} < \mathcal{H}$ if and only if $\mathcal{P} < \mathcal{Q}$ for all $\mathcal{P} \in \mathcal{E}(\mathcal{I})$ and $\mathcal{Q} \in \mathcal{E}(\mathcal{H})$. This means that our partial ordering can be lifted to the equivalence class structure; that is, we can make the definition that $\mathcal{E}(\mathcal{I}) < \mathcal{E}(\mathcal{H})$ if and only if $\mathcal{I} < \mathcal{H}$.

One can also show the following. Let $\mathcal{J}, \mathcal{H} \in \Re$, let $\mathcal{W}(\mathcal{J})$ denote the set of images generated by $\mathcal{J}$, and let $\mathcal{E}(\mathcal{H})$ denote the equivalence class of $\mathcal{H}$. Then $\mathcal{E}(\mathcal{H}) \cap \mathcal{W}(\mathcal{J})$ is either empty or equal to $\mathcal{E}(\mathcal{H})$. It follows that

$$\mathcal{W}(\mathcal{J}) = \bigcup_{\mathcal{H} \in T} \mathcal{E}(\mathcal{H}),$$

for some set $T \subset \Re$.

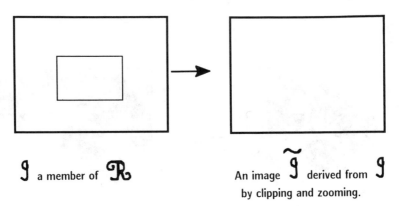

$\mathcal{G}$ a member of $\mathfrak{R}$

An image $\tilde{\mathcal{G}}$ derived from $\mathcal{G}$
by clipping and zooming.

Figure 2.10. All images that can be derived from $\mathcal{U}$ look the same as $\mathcal{U}$ and so $||\mathcal{W}(\mathcal{U})|| = 1$.

Let $|A|$ denote the number of elements of the set A. For $\mathcal{J} \in \mathfrak{R}$, let $||\mathcal{W}(\mathcal{J})||$ denote the number of equivalence classes in $\mathcal{W}(\mathcal{J})$, that is,

$$||\mathcal{W}(\mathcal{J})|| = \text{Min} \ \{|T| : T \subset \mathfrak{R} \ \text{such that} \ \mathcal{W}(\mathcal{J}) = \bigcup_{\mathcal{H} \in T} \mathcal{E}(\mathcal{H})\};$$

that is, $||\mathcal{W}(\mathcal{J})||$ is equal to the number of distinct equivalence classes it contains, from which it follows that $||\mathcal{W}(\mathcal{J})|| \geq 1$ for all $\mathcal{J} \in \mathfrak{R}$. There exist images for which equality is attained here. If $\mathcal{U}$ is an image of constant uniform chromatic attributes, as illustrated in Fig. 2.10, then all images that can be derived from $\mathcal{U}$ look the same as $\mathcal{U}$, providing we model stretching in such a way that this is the case, and so $||\mathcal{W}(\mathcal{U})|| = 1$.

Now we restrict attention to the case where $||\mathcal{W}(\mathcal{J})|| < \infty$; that is, we define $\mathcal{F} \subset \mathfrak{R}$ by

$$\mathcal{F} = \{\mathcal{J} \in \mathfrak{R} : ||\mathcal{W}(\mathcal{J})|| < \infty\}.$$

Then, for example, $\mathcal{U} \in \mathcal{F}$. Then for any $\mathcal{J} \in \mathcal{F}$, we can diagram the equivalence class structure of $\mathcal{W}(\mathcal{J})$, as illustrated in Figs. 2.11 and 2.12. Here, for simplicity, we treat images as identical if the only differences between them occur on the boundary of $\square$.

$\mathcal{F}$ is a collection of images for which it is likely to be possible to develop a complete theory of image complexity, independent of image resolution. We believe this because $\mathcal{F}$ includes many of the IFS fractals and FT fractals, and yet it seems to be theoretically manageable. It also seems to be a space rich in content and depth, and quite sufficient for approximating $\mathfrak{R}$.

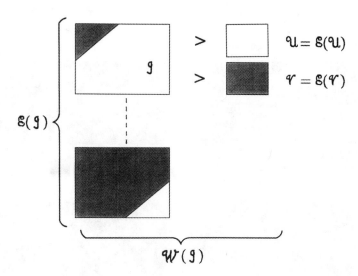

Figure 2.11. Diagram of the equivalence class structure of $\mathcal{W}(\mathcal{J})$, when $\mathcal{J} \in \mathcal{F}$ is two colors bounded by a sloping line. In this case $\mathcal{W}(\mathcal{J}) = \mathcal{E}(\mathcal{J}) \cup \mathcal{E}(\mathcal{U}) \cup \mathcal{E}(\mathcal{V})$ and $\|\mathcal{W}(\mathcal{J})\| = 3$. Notice that $\mathcal{E}(\mathcal{J})$ has infinitely many elements. How would $\mathcal{E}(\mathcal{J})$ look if general affine transformations were allowed?

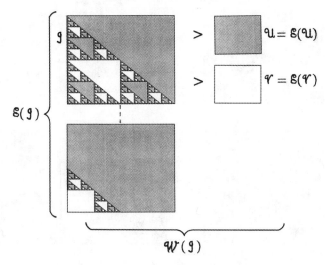

Figure 2.12. Diagram of the equivalence class structure of $\mathcal{W}(\mathcal{J})$, when $\mathcal{J} \in \mathcal{F}$ is two colors bounded by a Sierpinski triangle. In this case, $\mathcal{W}(\mathcal{J}) = \mathcal{E}(\mathcal{J}) \cup \mathcal{E}(\mathcal{U}) \cup \mathcal{E}(\mathcal{V})$ and $\|\mathcal{W}(\mathcal{J})\| = 3$. Notice that $\mathcal{E}(\mathcal{J})$ has infinitely many elements. How would $\mathcal{E}(\mathcal{J})$ look if general affine transformations were allowed?

Figure 2.13. Some members of a world of images, $\mathcal{W}(\mathcal{I})$, where $\mathcal{I}$ is a Bavarian castle.

Figure 2.14. Members of a world of images, $\mathcal{W}(\mathcal{I})$, where $\mathcal{I}$ is a single fractal image.

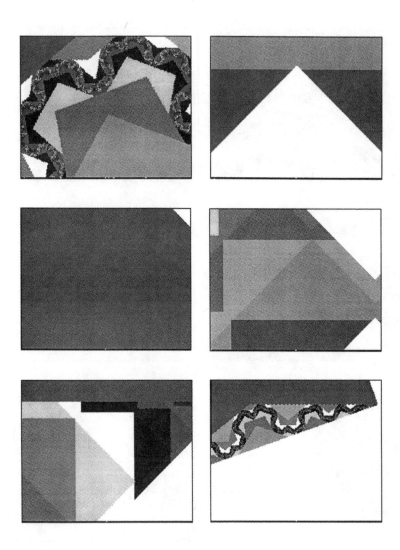

Figure 2.15. Members of a world of images, $\mathcal{W}(\mathcal{I})$, where $\mathcal{I}$ is a single fractal image.

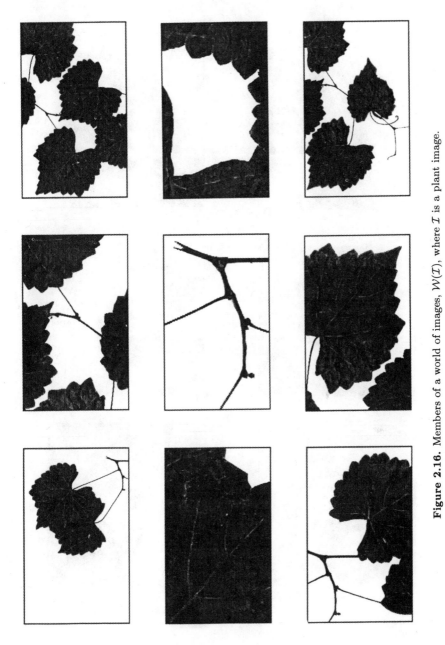

Figure 2.16. Members of a world of images, $\mathcal{W}(\mathcal{I})$, where $\mathcal{I}$ is a plant image.

Figure 2.17. Members of a world of images, $\mathcal{W}(\mathcal{I})$, where $\mathcal{I}$ is an image of a plant, and arbitrary affine transformations are admitted.

Examples:

(i) Let $\mathcal{I} \in \mathfrak{R}$. Then $\mathcal{I} < \mathcal{I}$.

(ii) Let $S \subset \mathfrak{R}$ and let $\mathcal{W}(S)$ denote the set of images generated by S. Then $\mathcal{W}(\mathcal{W}(S)) = \mathcal{W}(S)$.

(iii) Some members of the world of images generated from a Bavarian castle are illustrated in Fig. 2.13.

(iv) Two worlds of images generated by *The Desktop Fractal Design System* [DFDS] are illustrated in Figs. 2.14 and 2.15.

(v) A world of images generated by a plant image is illustrated in Fig. 2.16. Think of them all on an equal footing.

(vi) A world of images generated from a plant image, by allowing arbitrary affine transformations, is illustrated in Fig. 2.17.

It is important to distinguish the space of real world images from *visual space*, which was defined by Ewald Hering. Visual space is a mathematical model for the space in which real world objects appear, as received and processed by the human visual system. It consists of a three-dimensional manifold. It is not a Euclidean space, since the sun and moon vary in apparent size with elevation. We refer to [RG] for references and more information on how scientists and philosophers understand the relationship between the physical observable universe and that which we think we see. We mention that the formal spaces of mathematics are analytical structures of relationships developed from axioms which merely need to satisfy the condition of not containing internal contradictions. Attempts to express the properties of visual space in formal mathematical terms — for example, postulating a hyperbolic metric for visual space — have generally not met with much success [GW]. In our formulation of the space of real world images, we have drawn attention to a simpler problem, the modeling of pictures or images, as they seem in our minds, illuminated by our imaginations, rather than objects as they are received and processed by the human visual system.

2.3. Mathematical Models for Real World Images

Mathematical models for $\mathfrak{R}$ are needed, to enable us to handle images in practice. Here, we give some examples. The descriptions of these examples require some concepts from measure theory and integration theory that are dealt with in [FE], for example. However, all readers should read the models and will undoubtedly grasp a good intuitive sense of what is meant, even without additional reading. There are various ideas also mentioned, such as affine transformations, that are discussed in the next chapter. The purpose of this section is to exemplify the structure of possible mathematical models for $\Re$, not to make a definitive list.

Model (i) $\Re$ is modeled by $\Re_i$, which uses only the colors black and white to represent real world images. One thinks of such images as fax documents, dark silhouettes on white backgrounds, the outlines cast at dusk by tree shapes against the sky, and other imagined images seen by strange black-and-white eyesight. Any member $\mathcal{J}$ of $\Re_i$ is represented by its support $\square$ together with the characteristic function $\chi_A : \square \to \{0,1\}$ of some Borel measurable subset $A \subset \square$. The set A, "drawn" on $\square$, provides a black picture on a white background. "0" signifies the color white, and "1" signifies the value black. The function $\chi_A(x)$ is defined by

$$\chi_a(x) = \left\{ \begin{array}{ll} 1 & \text{when } x \in A, \\ 0 & \text{when } x \notin A. \end{array} \right.$$

χ_A provides the chromatic attributes of the image.

   In this model, any real world image is completely specified by its support $\square$ together with a Borel subset $A \subset \square$; and conversely, any pair

$$\{\square, A \subset \square : A \text{ is a Borel subset of } \mathbb{R}^2\}$$

defines a member of $\Re_i$.

   We require that the set A, and hence also the function $\chi_A : \square \to \{0,1\}$, be Borel measurable in order that it be possible to evaluate integrals over measurable subsets of the image. This in turn allows us to define, in a consistent manner, finite resolution approximations to the image, as is required by the resolution independence property (Property (iii)) of $\Re$. For example, we can define the finite, arbitrarily high resolution digital approximation models for $\mathcal{J}$ by assigning the value 0 or 1 to a pixel $P \subset \square$ according to whether the number

$$\frac{\int_P \chi_A(x) \ dx}{\int_P dx}$$

is less than 0.5 or greater than or equal to 0.5. This defines a finite resolution (digital) approximation $\tilde{A}$ to A, as illustrated in Fig. 2.18. We use the notation $\tilde{A} = \mathcal{P}_{m \times n}(A)$ in the case where the pixels P are defined by partitioning $\square$ into an array of m pixels horizontally and n pixels vertically. Then, in this model, $\mathcal{P}_{m \times n} : \Re_i \to \Re_i$ is a projection

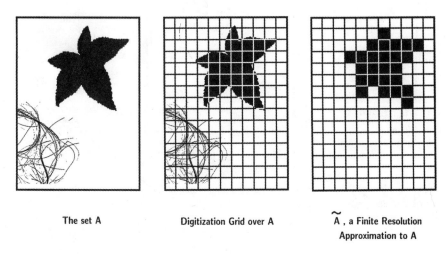

The set A   Digitization Grid over A $\widetilde{A}$, a Finite Resolution
                                                                       Approximation to A

Figure 2.18. The finite resolution approximation $\tilde{A}$ to A is obtained by overlaying an array of pixels on the image A, and recording as black those pixels whose average color is closer to black than white.

operator that takes the space of real world images into itself. We have $\mathcal{P}_{m\times n}(\mathcal{P}_{m\times n}(A)) = \mathcal{P}_{m\times n}(A)$ for all Borel subsets A of $\square$. We say that the finite resolution models $\{\mathcal{P}_{m\times n}(A); m, n = 1, 2 \ldots\}$ are consistent because if one forms a sufficiently high-resolution digital approximation to A, say, $\mathcal{P}_{m'\times n'}(A)$, where m' is an integer much larger than m and n' is an integer much larger than n, and one makes the same approximation to $\mathcal{P}_{m\times n}(A)$, namely, $\mathcal{P}_{m'\times n'}(\mathcal{P}_{m\times n}(A))$, then the result is approximately the same; that is, holding m and n fixed,

$$d(\mathcal{P}_{m'\times n'}(A), \mathcal{P}_{m'\times n'}(\mathcal{P}_{m\times n}(A))) \to 0$$

as m' and n' tend to infinity together.

Here, d represents any appropriate metric on the space $\Re_i$, for comparing images with the same support, such as

$$d(A, B) = \int_{\square} |\chi_A(x) - \chi_B(x)| dx.$$

Any image $\mathcal{J}$ in $\Re_i$, associated with a Borel set A as before, is stretched (shrunk) to produce a new image $\mathcal{H} \in \Re_i$ by mapping the support of $\mathcal{J}, \square \subset \mathbb{R}^2$, into another larger (smaller) region $\square \subset \mathbb{R}^2$ whose physical

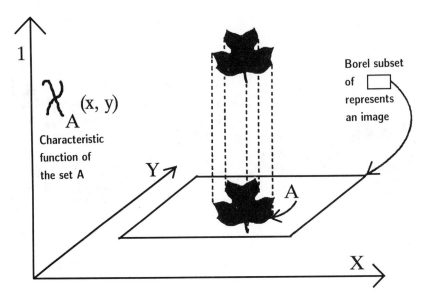

Figure 2.19. Real world images are modeled by $\Re_i$ which uses Borel subsets of $\square$ to represent binary images.

dimensions are a constant factor $s > 0$ larger (smaller) than those of $\square$. If the origin of coordinates is taken to be the lower left-hand corner of the support, then the chromatic attributes of $\mathcal{H}$ are provided by $\chi(x) = \chi_A(x/s)$ for all $x = (x, y) \in \square$. $\Re_i$ is illustrated in Fig. 2.19.

Model (ii)   In this case, $\Re$ is modeled by $\Re_{ii}$. The chromatic attributes of an image in $\Re_{ii}$ are represented with the aid of an interval I of real numbers, such as $[0, 255] \subset \mathbb{R}$, specifying possible grayscale intensities, and a function $f : \square \to I$. The function $f(x, y)$ provides the intensity or brightness of the image at the point (x, y) in the image. An integrability and/or continuity class to which f is supposed to belong can be specified to sharpen the model. For example, one might use functions that belong to $\ell^1(\square), \ell^2(\square)$, or $\ell^\infty(\square)$; or one might require the functions to obey a certain Hölder condition, or to be piecewise continuous. The function f provides the chromatic attributes of the image.

In $\Re_{ii}$, any image is completely specified by its support $\square$ together with a function $f : \square \to I$; and conversely, any function

$$f : \square \to I,$$

with some side constraint such as $f \in \ell^1(\square)$, defines a member of $\Re_{ii}$.

Finite, arbitrarily high-resolution approximation models for $\mathcal{J} \in \Re_{ii}$ can be obtained by assigning the value

$$f(P) = \frac{\int_P f(x) \ dx}{\int_P dx}$$

to the pixel P, for each $P \in \square$.

Any image $\mathcal{J}$ in $\Re_{ii}$, with chromatic attributes provided by f as just shown, is stretched (shrunk) to produce a new image $\mathcal{H} \in \Re_{ii}$ by mapping the support of $\mathcal{J}$, $\square \subset \mathbb{R}^2$ into another larger (smaller) region $\square \subset \mathbb{R}^2$ whose physical dimensions are a constant factor $s > 0$ larger (smaller) than those of $\square$. The chromatic attributes of $\mathcal{H}$ are provided by $g(x,y) = f(x/s, y/s)$ for all $(x,y) \in \square$.

In $\Re_{ii}$, the distance between two images $\mathcal{J}$ and $\mathcal{H}$ with the same support can be measured with the distance function corresponding to the chosen space, such as $\ell^1(\square)$, or $\ell^2(\square)$, or $\ell^\infty(\square)$. For example, we can define

$$d(\mathcal{J}, \mathcal{H}) = \int_\square |f(x) - g(x)| \ dx,$$

where $f : \square \to I$ and $g : \square \to I$ are the chromatic functions for the two images. $\Re_{ii}$ is illustrated in Fig. 2.20.

Model (iii)   In this case, $\Re$ is modeled by $\Re_{iii}$. An image in $\Re_{iii}$ is represented with the aid of a real-valued normalized Borel measure μ supported on $\square$. The total amount of light emitted by a Borel measurable subset $A \subset \square$ is

$$\int_A d\mu.$$

In this model, it is not possible, in general, to describe the intensity of light associated with a single point in the image.

In $\Re_{iii}$, any image is completely specified by its support $\square$ together with a normalized Borel measure μ; and conversely, any Borel measure supported on $\square$, normalized so that

$$\int_\square d\mu = 1,$$

defines a member of $\Re_{iii}$.

Finite, arbitrarily high-resolution approximation models for $\mathcal{J} \in \Re_{iii}$ can be obtained by assigning the value

$$f(P) \int_P d\mu$$

to the pixel P, for each $P \in \square$.

Any image $\mathcal{J}$ in $\Re_{iii}$, with chromatic attributes provided by a μ as just shown, is stretched (shrunk) to produce a new image $\mathcal{H} \in \Re_{iii}$ by mapping the support of $\mathcal{J}$, $\square \subset \mathbb{R}^2$ into another larger (smaller) region $\square \subset \mathbb{R}^2$ whose physical dimensions are a constant factor $s > 0$ larger (smaller) than those of $\square$. The chromatic attributes of $\mathcal{H}$ are provided by the measure ν, where $\nu(B) = \mu(s^{-1}B)$ for all Borel subsets $B \subset \square$, and here s^{-1} denotes the affine mapping on $\mathbb{R}^2$ that takes $\square$ to $\square$.

In $\Re_{iii}$, the distance between two images $\mathcal{J}$ and $\mathcal{H}$, with the same support, can be measured with the distance function d defined by

$$d(\mathcal{J}, \mathcal{H}) = \int_{\square} |d\mu(x) - d\nu(x)|,$$

where μ and ν are the measures associated with the two images.

$\Re_{iii}$ is illustrated in Fig. 2.21.

Model (iv) In this case, $\Re$ is modeled by $\Re_{iv}$. The chromatic attributes of an image in $\Re_{iv}$ are represented with the aid of an interval I of real numbers, such as $[0, 255] \subset \mathbb{R}$, representing possible intensities, and three functions $f_r : \square \rightarrow I, f_g : \square \rightarrow I, f_b : \square \rightarrow I$, where $f_r(x,y), f_g(x,y), f_b(x,y)$ provide the intensity of the red, green, and blue components of the image at the point (x, y) in the support of the image. One needs to specify an integrability class for these functions.

In $\Re_{iv}$, the distance between two images $\mathcal{J}$ and $\mathcal{H}$, with the same support can be measured with the distance function corresponding to the chosen space, such as $\ell^1(\square)$, or $\ell^2(\square)$, or $\ell^\infty(\square)$. For example, we can define

$$d(\mathcal{J}, \mathcal{H}) = \int_{\square} |f_r(x) - g_r(x)|\, dx + \int_{\square} |f_g(x) - g_g(x)|\, dx$$
$$+ \int_{\square} |f_b(x) - g_b(x)|\, dx,$$

where f and g are the chromatic functions for the two images.

The rest of the structure and treatment of this model follows similar lines to those of $\Re_{ii}$.

$\Re_{iv}$ is illustrated in Fig. 2.22.

Many other mathematical models for $\Re$ are possible and useful. In Model (iv), one can instead describe the grayscale intensity and certain chromaticity values of the image, such as is used in the (Y, U, V) representation system or in the (H, I, Q) image representation system. One can also use surfaces in real three-dimensional space to represent the brightness of color components of an image as a function of position. The collection of surfaces taken together can be treated as a single geometrical entity that is used to model

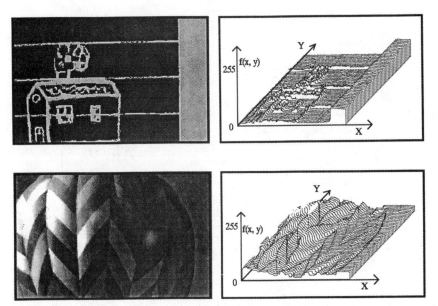

Figure 2.20. Real world images are modeled by $\Re_{ii}$ which uses real valued functions $f : \square \to [0, 255]$ to represent grayscale images.

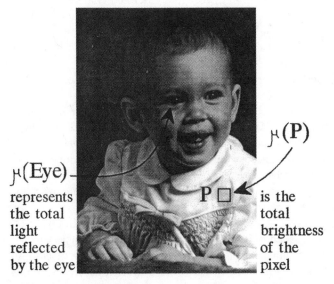

μ(Eye) represents the total light reflected by the eye

μ(P)

P $\square$ is the total brightness of the pixel

Figure 2.21. Real world images are modeled in $\Re_{iii}$, which uses normalized Borel measures μ supported on $\square$ to represent grayscale images.

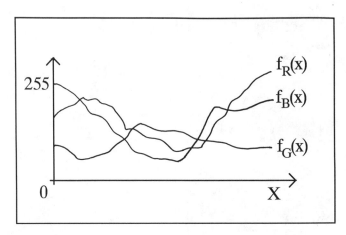

Figure 2.22. In $\Re_{iv}$, three functions are used to represent the red, green, and blue intensities.

an image; or again, one can use Borel measures to represent the distribution of photon brightness in an image, for each different color component of the image.

In each case, the underlying mathematical entity, which is used to make the model for $\Re$, is of an infinitely finely defined character — every region in the image, however small and precisely specified it may be, is associated with numbers that describe its optical characteristics.

Once a mathematical model for the "pictures" of $\Re$ has been formed, whether this be by means of functions in a particular function class, appropriate measures, or subsets of three-dimensional space, for example, the next step is to go to strings of zeros and ones. We need to be able to approximate our mathematical "pictures," that is, our measures or functions lying in this or that special space, in a methodical manner; to enable us to connect the finite strings of zeros and ones to the infinite images in a smooth and continuous manner. We desire to introduce families of approximating entities that on the one hand lie in, approximate, or model the very members of the mathematical space we have chosen for making images, and on the other hand are controlled by finitely many parameters. They should be such that their own associated approximation theory has characteristics, such as the rate of convergence with increasing elaborateness of approximant, and a growth rate of complexity of computation of approximants, that are good with respect to the chosen image metric (distance) and image function class. In particular, *these approximants must have good properties with respect to those images in the chosen mathematical model(s) for $\Re$ that fit most comfortably with the class of real world* *images with which we are most accustomed, and with the way our visual system deals with these images.*

Our choice for making approximants to mathematical models for images consists of two classes: (a) *IFS fractals* and (b) *FT fractals*. Both approximation families satisfy the basic requirements of providing resolution independent models that are attached to finite strings of zeros and ones. Also, both approximation families are consistent with the properties of $\Re$. Of particular importance is the fact that each class of approximants provides resolution independent images, and that these images tend to have constant information density — clipping and zooming do not decrease the information content.

2.4. Scanning and Digitizing

Often it is convenient to think of data as a function. With sound or radio waves, the function expresses intensity or amplitude in terms of time. For still images, the free variable is spatial. For video, both time and space are varied. When the domain and range of such a function are defined as intervals of real numbers, and the function can attain all of the values in its range, the data is said to be *analog*. When the domains and ranges consist of finite sets of possible values, represented by integers, the data is said to be *digital*.

A scanner converts analog image data, focused light reflected off pictures, into digital data. A scanner can be modeled as a function from $\Re$, the space of real world images, into the space of digital images. The conversion is achieved by sampling an optical image at a grid of locations, corresponding to pixels, with the aid of one or more charge coupled devices (CCDs). A CCD converts chromatic attributes of one or an array of pixel-sized regions into electrical charges that are converted into truncated real numbers, quantized that is, by means of analog-to-digital converters. Because the resolution of the digitizing scanner, both spatially and in the range of intensity and color values that it can output, is usually much lower than the resolution of the scanned image, which is determined by physical characteristics of lenses and the wavelength of light, for example, the ranges of values and available selection of sampling locations can be treated as continuous intervals. Hence, we say that the input image data to the scanner is analog, while the output image data is digital.

The input analog image $\mathcal{I}$ can be described using mathematical models for the space of real world images, and we say that $\mathcal{I} \in \Re$. The output of the scanner is a member of the space of digital images.

Resolution 951 x 1360   Resolution 94 x 136   Resolution 951 x 1360
64 gray levels   64 gray levels   4 gray levels

Figure 2.23. This figure illustrates the effect on an image of varying resolution and bits per pixel.

Analog data has the property that the information it contains is potentially infinite. Nature exhibits all of the colors of a rainbow, which are described by an interval of radiation frequencies, and infinitely many values seem to be possible. Current computer monitors display $2^8 = 256$, $2^{15} = 32,768$ or $2^{24} = 16,777,216$ colors. Similarly, the spatial components of an image are continuous. At some point in the acquisition of a digital image, a spatial resolution (pixel width and height) and a number of values (pixel depth) are imposed on the image. Each of these choices involves the introduction of errors.

While our primary focus is images, analog voice or radio signals can be digitized also. To digitize a time-varying function, the number of samples per second (sampling rate) must be chosen as well as the number of distinct function values the function is allowed to take at each sample (sampling resolution). For images, these two variables are called resolution (width and height) and bits per pixel (depth). Fig. 2.23 shows the effect on an image of varying resolution and bits per pixel.

Deviation from the original introduced by sampling at a finite instead of infinite number of points is called *sampling error*. Deviation introduced by coercing the function values at each of the sampled data points to finitely many values is called *quantization error*.

If converting an analog signal to a digital signal introduces so many sources of error, why do it? Digital data is easier to store, transmit, and manipulate. Using error correcting codes, digital signals can be transmitted with arbitrarily high fidelity even over an unreliable communication channel. A digital signal can be copied exactly without attenuation of the original. Being in digital form, the image can be subjected to transformations that would be impractical to realize on an analog signal.

There are a couple of reasons why we want to examine an image before digitization. One concerns the description of errors. The aim of image compression is fidelity to the analog image, not to its digital representation; this fact is the principal difference between image compression and more general digital compression. In particular, fractal image compression allows images to be output at higher resolution than they are input. The other reason relates to sampling rate. which we discess next.

One method for digitizing an image is to sample it at a grid of discrete points. To understand the errors introduced in this process, we examine its inverse. Given a discrete sequence of data points, how difficult is it to interpolate the missing data? The answer depends on the type of function we are using to fit the data.

As an illustration, suppose that we want to fit the data with a real valued function taking the form

$$f(x) = \cos(\omega x).$$

We are not given the real number ω, but we are told the values of $f(x)$ at a discrete sequence of equally spaced points,

$$y_n = f(n\Delta x).$$

A problem arises because the determination of ω is not unique. One can easily check that if ω is a solution to the problem, so is $\omega + (2\pi m)/\Delta x$ for any integer m.

The number $f_s = (2\pi)/\Delta x$ is the *sampling frequency*. The higher this frequency, the more accurate our reconstruction. How high is high enough? If the sampling frequency is f_s, we must be able to constrain ω to lie between $-f_s/2$ and $f_s/2$. Put the other way around, if $|\omega| < f_{max}$, the sampling frequency should be chosen to be at least twice this rate. The frequency $f_{nyq} = 2f_{max}$ is called the *Nyquist* rate.

General signals are more complicated than a single sinusoid, but for various models they can be built up from a sum of curves of this form. For example, according to Fourier theory, functions f in appropriate integrability classes can be represented in terms of their Fourier transforms $\hat{f}(\omega)$:

$$f(x) = \int_{-\infty}^{\infty} \hat{f}(\omega)\cos(\omega x)\ d\omega.$$

The coefficient $\hat{f}(\omega)$ applies to the component of f with frequency ω.

The squared magnitude of the coefficient $\hat{f}(\omega)$, as a function of ω, is called the *power spectrum* $P(\omega)$ of f. If there is a cutoff frequency ω_M such that $P(\omega) = 0$ for $|\omega| > \omega_M$, the signal is called *band-limited*. The Nyquist theorem says that if a band-limited signal is sampled at a rate greater than $2\omega_M$, the Nyquist rate, the function f can be uniquely recovered from the sampled values. Conversely, sampling below the Nyquist rate (under-sampling) can cause spurious low-frequency artifacts.

What if the signal we wish to sample is not band-limited? To avoid aliasing, the frequency components above half the sampling rate must be filtered out before the data is sampled. We do not discuss the details of analog filter construction except to note the following limitations. The design of filters is of necessity imperfect. There are always consequences in lower frequencies of removing high-frequency data. One ubiquitous source of high-frequency data in images is edges. The lack of high-frequency data is especially noticeable when one tries to reconstruct the image at high resolution, using Fourier methods [KGB].

Exercises

1. A turbine turning at a rate ω is illuminated by a strobe with a variable flashing rate.

(a) Show that if the strobe frequency is greater than 2ω, one perceives the correct motion.

(b) Show that if the strobe light is between ω and 2ω, the turbine appears to be going backwards.

(c) Show that if the strobe rate is less than ω, the apparent motion is slowed down.

(d) What does one see when the strobe frequency is precisely 2ω?

2. Phone lines sample voices at 8,000 samples per second with 8 bits per sample. What range of frequencies does this allow? How does this compare with the dynamic range of a human voice? How long a conversation could you fit on a 1.2 MB diskette?

3. Audio compact disks have a sampling rate of 44,100 samples per second and a sampling resolution of 16 bits per sample. What frequency range does this allow? How much space is required to represent a five-minute song at CD quality? How much space would the same song require at phone line quality?

One way in which images are acquired is by the human eye. It is a type of image scanner. Here, we note some facts about the resolution and visual acuity of the eye, and the rate at which it acquires information.

Calculations are based on the central 2° region, the fovea of the eye. [HJ] calculates the number of points that can be resolved within the fovea to be about 10^4. The information capacity of the whole retina is thought to be about 10 times that of the fovea. [HJ] assumed that, at the limit of resolution, a person could distinguish black from white but not discriminate any intermediate shade of gray. He thus associated one bit of information with each small area, a cell or pixel, surrounding one of the resolved points.

[RWD1] has calculated the information capacity of the retina from measurements of the variation of contrast sensitivity with number of lines per degree of visual angle for targets that were sinusoidal gratings. This calculation yields a value of 5×10^5 bits per second, though the method includes capacity in terms of targets with different shades of gray.

When working near the limit of resolution, contrast discrimination is poor. For the central region, the flicker-fusion frequency is about 50 cycles per second, so that the information capacity is about 50×10^4 bits per second. These estimates exclude color information, but it is unlikely that the additional information due to color is more than about 20 percent, making 6×10^5 bits in all [RWD2].

At low illumination, approximately one bit of information is received for each photon absorbed by a cone cell in the foveal region. In daylight the efficiency drops to approximately 10^4 bits per photon. At low illuminations, therefore, purely physical considerations determine efficiency, but at higher levels, the properties of the visual system as a whole must be taken into account. The relevant properties, according to [RWD1], are (i) the aperture and quality of the lens of the eye, (ii) the number and spacing of the photon detectors, (iii) the number of associated nerve fibers, and (iv) the neural processes by which information is transformed so that it is most readily assimilated by the higher centers of the brain.

Properties (i), (ii), and (iii) are matched in such a way that each by itself would give a limit of about 10^4 resolved points in the fovea. The neural processes include an edge-sharpening device (*lateral inhibition*), an arrangement by which an object appears to be about the same size over a range of distances, (*size constancy scaling*), and other manipulations of the information. Loss of information as a result of these processes is estimated to be as low as 20%.

[RWD2] ascribes the information transfer rate provided by the eye to the evolutionary process for higher animals. Decisions vital to survival had to be based on visual information. A wide variety of situations were encountered, so a vast information capacity was needed. Yet the amount used in making a decision had to be limited to the minimum required to make a correct decision. This limited amount had to be processed to yield an action as quickly as possible. If too little information was processed, a wrong decision was more likely, while too much information processed meant that a decision came too late. Either way, the the animal was less likely to survive. Those species that did survive usually had a large visual information capacity but were able to select from a small number of bits for processing towards an action decision.

The mind is naturally able to achieve scaling very rapidly, as in size constancy scaling, and in the effect whereby the moon appears larger when near the horizon. The mind is also good at tracking moving objects. Thus, it appears that affine transformations hold a special position both in the world and in the inner workings of the mind.

2.5. Quantization, Scan Order, and Color

To represent a continuous signal in digital form, first the data is sampled at discrete intervals. The next step is to map each of the values at the sample points to one of a fixed number of values. This process is called *quantization*. The error introduced by quantizing will depend on the specific signal, but often one makes the assumption that the data values are distributed uniformly between quantized values. The average error arrived at this way is one quarter the distance between levels; the maximum error is half the distance between levels.

The prevalent form of output for digital images is the computer monitor; the discussion would be different if one concentrated on printers. For images, the pixel values are a function of luminosity. We must pick quantization levels. A natural choice might be to find the lowest and highest intensity values occurring in the images we wish to display and choose two equally spaced intensity values between the two extremes. However, equally spaced intensity levels do not translate to equally spaced perceived brightness. The eye's response to light appears to be roughly logarithmic. So instead we choose to make uniform the changes in logarithm. Each intensity level maintains a constant ratio with the previous one.

The smallest perceivable change in intensity is about 1 percent. Given 256 quantization levels (8 bits per pixel), we choose a lowest intensity I_0 and represent the remaining intensities by the rule

$$I_n = (1.01)^n I_0.$$

The brightest pixels are roughly 12 times as bright as the dimmest — $(1.01)^{255} \simeq 12.6$.

One side effect of this scheme for representing pixel brightness is that negative pixel values make physical sense. Since this scale is logarithmic, the cutoffs at each end are arbitrary. While there is no physically sensible interpretation of a negative intensity, translated onto this scale, a pixel value of negative one represents a pixel with 99% (100/101) of the intensity level zero. This observation will simplify the discussion later, when we apply affine transformations to pixel values. While in practice pixel values are truncated to a fixed range, the theory makes sense for arbitrarily large positive and negative numbers.

Exercises

1. Later we apply affine transformations to the brightness levels in images. What is the effect on intensity of translating the brightness (pixel value) by a constant?

2. To what mathematical operation does the contrast knob on a monitor correspond? What about the brightness knob?

After sampling and quantizing, we are left with an array of values. We need to read them off in a fixed pattern to produce a one-dimensional stream of data for input into a digital computing environment. How this is done is often dependent on how the data will be used. For example, one may want to use the data in a block by block manner rather than in a pixel by pixel manner. One then is still left with the problem of ordering the blocks. A general principle for compressing a stream of data is to pick an ordering that minimizes the variation in the data. The way in which this is accomplished is to try to make the scan order reflect the geometry of the image; nearby pixels in the image should go to nearby pixels in the ordering.

One possible ordering is to read the pixels from left to right, top to bottom (or sometimes bottom to top). This is called *scanline order*; see Fig. 2.24. Pixels are ordered in the way that they are output to a non-interlaced monitor. At the end of each scanline, two pixels are adjacent in the ordering that were not adjacent in the image.

The discontinuity at the end of a scanline can be removed by flipping every other line, scanning first left to right then right to left, as shown in Fig. 2.25. All pixels are spatially next to their neighbors in the sequence. Most vertical correlations between pixels are ignored in this scheme.

Figure 2.26 shows a different approach to the ordering of pixels. Here, an attempt is made to preserve as much of the two-dimensional information as possible. The resultant path is known as a *Hilbert curve*. Like the preceding example, adjacent pixels in the ordering always correspond to adjacent pixels in the image. However, there is no longer a preferred direction. This ordering is only defined when the resolution of the digital image has width and height that are powers of two; it has the property that the first quarter of the image corresponds to the first quarter of the pixels in the

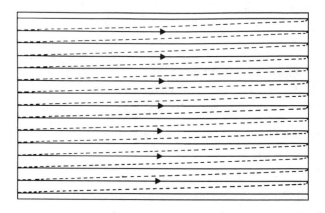

Figure 2.24. One possible ordering is to read the pixels from left to right, top to bottom. At the end of each scanline, two pixels are adjacent in the ordering that were not adjacent in the image.

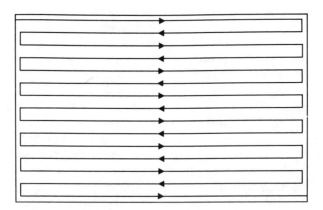

Figure 2.25. The discontinuity at the end of a scanline can be removed by flipping every other line, scanning first left to right, then right to left. All pixels are spatially next to their neighbors in the scanning sequence, but most vertical correlations are ignored.

Figure 2.26. This figure illustrates image scanning order using a Hilbert curve. Adjacent pixels in the ordering correspond to adjacent pixels in the image.

scanning sequence, the second quarter to the second quarter, ..., the first sixteenth of the image corresponds to the first sixteenth of the pixels in the sequence, and so on.

Exercises

1. Consider the image that consists of a rectangle divided by a line parallel to one of the sides of the rectangle, which is black on one side of the line and white on the other. How will the files yielded by the three different types of scanning order considered earlier look?

2. Determine the rule underlying the Hilbert curve ordering in Fig. 2.26. Specifically, if an image has 2^m pixels on a side (2^{2m} total pixels), find a function that will list the pixels in scan order. If $m = 2$, the answer is given by $(0,0), (1,0), (1,1), (0,1)$.

3. Show that by passing to the infinite limit, the Hilbert curve can be used to describe a continuous function $h : [0,1] \to [0,1] \times [0,1]$ from the unit interval to the unit square. Show that h is *onto* (every point in the square is visited at least once,) but that it is not invertible because some points are visited more than once.

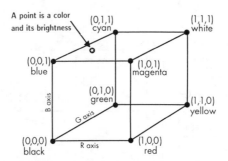

Figure 2.27. Colors are often represented by a cube in color space. Each point in this space corresponds to a different color.

To this point, we have not said much about color, although this is essential in applications. Here, we consider the digital representation of color. More information can be found in [FVD].

Physically, light is made up of an infinite spectrum of frequencies. To specify a color of light would require giving an intensity value to each frequency, or a large subset thereof. This would make the description of color images highly impractical. The situation is simplified by restricting attention not to physical color but to perceived color; moreover, this is consistent with our understanding of $\Re$.

Color vision is usually explained in terms of Helmholtz's tri-stimulus theory. The eye is sensitive to combinations of intensities from three additive primary colors: red, green, and blue. Again, pixel values represent a logarithm, and 24 bits, or 8 bits for each of these intensities, seems to exhaust the range of distinguishable colors. Colors are often represented by a cube in color space. One can normalize the length of each axis to one. See Fig. 2.27.

Figure 2.28 shows a color image separated into R, G, and B components.

The (R, G, B) system will form the basis for our discussion of color, but it is not always the most convenient coordinate system to use. There are two other coordinate systems that are commonly used, that can be defined in terms of R, G, and B. Each of these coordinate systems is related to (R, G, B) by a linear transformation, as follows.

Figure 2.28. A color image separated into its red, green, and blue components. See color Plate 1 for a full color version of this image.

$$\begin{bmatrix} Y \\ I \\ Q \end{bmatrix} = \begin{bmatrix} 0.299 & 0.587 & 0.114 \\ 0.596 & -0.275 & -0.321 \\ 0.212 & -0.528 & 0.311 \end{bmatrix} \begin{bmatrix} R \\ G \\ B \end{bmatrix}$$

$$\begin{bmatrix} Y \\ U \\ V \end{bmatrix} = \begin{bmatrix} 0.299 & 0.587 & 0.114 \\ -0.147 & -0.289 & 0.436 \\ 0.615 & -0.515 & -0.100 \end{bmatrix} \begin{bmatrix} R \\ G \\ B \end{bmatrix}$$

In each case, the grayscale component of the information is separated out from the color information. The Y vector represents a weighted sum of the three intensities meant to model perceived brightness. Thus, the Y component is often called the *luminance*. The remaining two components determine the color characteristics, called *hue* and *saturation* in the case of the (Y, I, Q) system. These two components collectively are known as the *chrominance*. Together, the luminance and chrominance provide the chromatic attributes of the image in this type of model for $\Re$. Another reason for using the (Y, I, Q) basis comes from the fact that the variance of the chrominance data tends to be less than that of the luminance data. By separating the components in this way, it is possible to conserve bandwidth. Bearing this in mind, North American color television signals assign 4 MHz to Y, 1.5 MHz to I, and 0.6 MHz to Q.

The (Y, U, V) basis is defined similarly and forms the basis for color separation in European television. The (Y, U, V) basis is also used in commercial digital image compression schemes such as the JPEG standard, described in the Appendix.

Other color coordinates used in computer graphics are the HSV (*H*ue, *S*aturation, and *V*alue) and the HSL (*H*ue, *S*aturation, and *L*ightness) systems [FVD]. The relation between these coordinate systems and the R, G, B basis is nonlinear, and therefore they are not usually associated with standard compression methods. The hue in these systems is an angular variable and corresponds to color. The other two coordinates determine the brightness and amount of white. The hue of a shade of gray is not defined.

Printers use a subtractive system and much printing is done in a basis consisting of Cyan, Magenta, Yellow, (and Black.) This is known as the $CMY(K)$ system. The black component is the sum of the Cyan, Magenta, and Yellow components. Fig. 2.29 shows an image separated into its printing components.

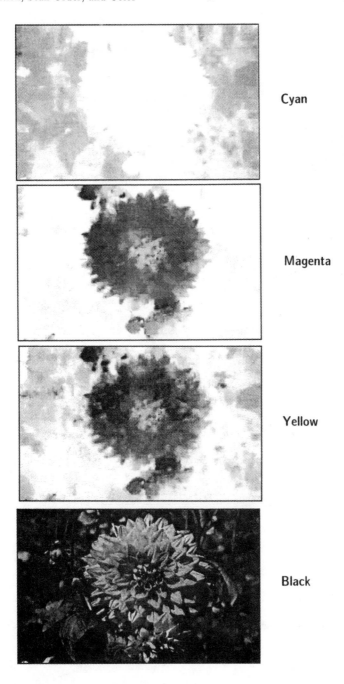

Figure 2.29. An image separated into its cyan, magenta, yellow, and black components. See color Plate 1 for a full color version of this image.

Exercises

1. Assuming that R, G, B takes values between 0 and 255, what are the maximum and minimum possible values for Y, U, and V ? What about Y, I, and Q ?

2. How many bits of precision in Y, U, V are required if the transformation $(R, G, B) \rightarrow (Y, U, V)$ is to be lossless? Conversely, assuming that R, G, B, Y, U, and V are represented with 8 bits each, determine the average error due to rounding in the conversions. Here, the averages can be taken over the R, G, B cube.

2.6. References

[FE] M. Barnsley, *Fractals Everywhere*. Academic Press, Boston (1988).

[DFDS] Michael F. Barnsley, *The Desktop Fractal Design System (IBM PC and MacIntosh Software)*. Academic Press, San Diego (1992).

[KGB] K. G. Beauchamp, *Transforms for Engineers: A Guide to Signal Processing*. Oxford University Press, London (1987).

[RWD2] R.W. Ditchburn and A.E. Drysdale, *Vision Research*, 13, 2435 (1973).

[RWD1] R.W. Ditchburn, "Visual Information Rate" in [RG], pp.795–796.

[FVD] James D. Foley, Andries van Dam, Steven K. Feiner, and John F. Hughes, *Computer Graphics: Principles and Practice (2nd ed.)*. Addison-Wesley, Reading, MA (1990).

[JG] J. A. Green, *Sets and Groups, Library of Mathematics* (Editor: Walter Ledermann). Routledge and Kegan Paul, London (1965).

[RG] Richard L. Gordon, *The Oxford Companion to the Mind*. Oxford University Press, London (1987).

[HJ] H. Jacobson, *Science*, 113, 292. (1951)

[LC] Kevin D. Lee, Yosef Cohen, *Fractal Attraction (MacIntosh Software)*. Academic Press, San Diego (1992).

[PFS] Sir Peter Strawson, "Immanuel Kant" in [RG], pp .406–408.

[GW] Gerald Westheimer, "Visual Space" in [RG], p.796.

3

Mathematical Foundations for
Fractal Image Compression I

What immortal hand or eye
Dare frame thy fearful symmetry?

— *William Blake*

3.1. Goals of This Chapter

The purpose of this chapter is to provide basic notation, definitions, and information relating to topology and geometry. This material is fundamental to the subject of fractal image compression. The material summarized in this chapter is covered in greater detail in [FE]. See also [BM] and [HW].

The support of an image, $\square \subset \mathbb{R}^2$, together with the Euclidean metric, is an example of a *metric space*. The *topology* of this space provides information about the nature of real world images. Topological properties and classifications of subsets of the support of an image, such as boundary, interior, openness, closedness, connectedness, and compactness, are important, since they are preserved by transformations of the support, which provide equivalent metrics. Topology provides the basis for the description of many properties of images, as well as underpinning much of the mathematical superstructure.

The geometrical concept of affine transformations is introduced. Affine transformations are needed both in the application of IFS theory, and in the application of *local IFS theory*, to image compression.

3.2. Spaces, Mappings, and Transformations

We begin by giving some definitions. Throughout, we use *space* to mean a set with some structure on it. Examples of spaces are the real line $\mathbb{R}$, the Euclidean plane $\mathbb{R}^2$, three-dimensional space $\mathbb{R}^3$, the unit interval $[0,1]$, the unit square $\square \subset \mathbb{R}^2$, and code space Σ. One way a space can have structure is for it to have a metric.

Definition *A* metric space $(\mathbf{X}, d)$ *is a space, or a set,* $\mathbf{X}$ *together with a real-valued function* $d : \mathbf{X} \times \mathbf{X} \to \mathbb{R}$, *which measures the* distance *between pairs of points* x *and* y *in* $\mathbf{X}$. *Suppose that* d *has the following properties:*

(i) $d(x,y) = d(y,x), \quad \forall\, x,y \in \mathbf{X}$.
(ii) $0 < d(x,y) < \infty, \quad \forall\, x,y \in \mathbf{X}, \quad x \neq y$.
(iii) $d(x,x) = 0, \quad \forall\, x \in \mathbf{X}$.
(iv) $d(x,y) \leq d(x,z) + d(z,y), \quad \forall\, x,y,z \in \mathbf{X}$.

Then d *is called a* metric *on the space* $\mathbf{X}$.

Examples:

(i) $(\mathbb{R},\, d(x,y) = |x - y|,\, \forall\, x,y \in \mathbb{R})$. This is the real line with the Euclidean metric.

(ii) $(\mathbb{R}^2,\, d(x,y) = \sqrt{(x_1 - y_1)^2 + (x_2 - y_2)^2},\quad \forall\, x,y \in \mathbb{R}^2)$. This is the Euclidean plane with the Euclidean metric.

(iii) $(\mathbb{R}^2,\, d(x,y) = |x_1 - y_1| + |x_2 - y_2|,\quad \forall\, x,y \in \mathbb{R}^2)$. This is the Euclidean Plane with the Manhattan metric.

(iv) $(\mathbb{R}^2,\, d(x,y) = \max\{|x_1 - y_1|, |x_2 - y_2|\},\quad \forall\, x,y \in \mathbb{R}^2)$.

(v) (Σ, d) is a metric space, where the metric d is defined on code space Σ by

$$d(\sigma, \omega) = d(\sigma_1 \sigma_2 \sigma_3 \ldots, \omega_1 \omega_2 \omega_3 \ldots) = \sum_{i=1}^{\infty} \frac{|\sigma_i - \omega_i|}{(N+1)^i}.$$

Definition *Let* $\mathbf{X}$ *be a space. A* transformation, map, *or* mapping *on* $\mathbf{X}$ *is a function* $f : \mathbf{X} \to \mathbf{X}$. *If* $S \subset \mathbf{X}$, *then* $f(S) = \{f(x) : x \in S\}$. *The function* f *is* one-to-one *if* $x,y \in \mathbf{X}$ *with* $f(x) = f(y)$ *implies* $x = y$. *It is* onto *if* $f(\mathbf{X}) = \mathbf{X}$. *It is called* invertible *if it is one-to-one and onto:*

in this case, it is possible to define a transformation $f^{-1} : \mathbf{X} \to \mathbf{X}$, called the inverse *of f, by $f^{-1}(y) = x$, where $x \in \mathbf{X}$ is the unique point such that $y = f(x)$.*

Definition *Let $f : \mathbf{X} \to \mathbf{X}$ be a transformation on a space. The* forward iterates *of f are transformations $f^{\circ n} : \mathbf{X} \to \mathbf{X}$ defined by $f^{\circ 0}(x) = x$, $f^{\circ 1}(x) = f(x)$, $f^{\circ(n+1)}(x) = f \circ f^{(n)}(x) = f(f^{(n)}(x))$ for $n = 0, 1, 2, \ldots$. If f is invertible, then the* backward iterates *of f are transformations $f^{\circ(-m)}(x) : \mathbf{X} \to \mathbf{X}$ defined by*

$$f^{\circ(-1)}(x) = f^{-1}(x), \quad f^{\circ(-m)}(x) = (f^{\circ m})^{-1}(x)$$

for $m = 1, 2, 3, \ldots$.

Examples:

(i) Let $f : \mathbf{X} \to \mathbf{X}$ be an invertible transformation. Then one can readily show that

$$f^{\circ m} \circ f^{\circ n} = f^{\circ(m+n)} \text{ for all integers } m \text{ and } n.$$

(ii) If $f : \mathbf{X} \to \mathbf{X}$ is not invertible, this relationship holds for all nonnegative integers m and n.

3.3.   Affine Transformations in ℝ

Affine transformations in ℝ are transformations $f : \mathbb{R} \to \mathbb{R}$ of the form

$$f(x) = a \cdot x + b, \, \forall\, x \in \mathbb{R},$$

where a and b are real constants. Given the interval $I = [0, 1]$, $f(I)$ is a new interval of length $|a|$. The transformation f rescales by a. The left endpoint 0 of the interval is moved to b, and $f(I)$ lies to the right or left of b as a is positive or negative, respectively.

   The action of an affine transformation on all of ℝ can be described as follows. The whole line is stretched away from the origin if $|a| > 1$, or contracted towards it if $|a| < 1$; and it is flipped through $180°$ about O if $a < 0$. It is *translated*, that is, shifted as a whole, by an amount b. The shift is to the left if $b < 0$, and to the right if $b > 0$. Notice that if $f : [0, 1] \to [0, 1]$ and $g : [0, 1] \to [0, 1]$ are affine transformations on the interval $[0, 1] \subset \mathbb{R}$, then so is $f \circ g$.

Examples:

(i) Define $f : \mathbb{R} \to \mathbb{R}$ by $f(x) = 2 \cdot x + 3$. Then f is an affine transformation.

(ii) If $f : \mathbb{R} \to \mathbb{R}$ is an invertible affine transformation, then so is f^{on} : $\mathbb{R} \to \mathbb{R}$, for any integer n.

3.4. Construction of the Classical Cantor Set Using Two Affine Transformations on $\mathbb{R}$

With the aid of two affine transformations on the space $[0, 1] \subset \mathbb{R}$, one can construct an example of an IFS fractal, namely, the *classical Cantor set* $\mathcal{C}$. First, we describe $\mathcal{C}$ by means of a construction.

$\mathcal{C}$ is a subset of the metric space $[0,1]$, which is obtained by successive deletion of middle third open subintervals, as follows. We construct a nested sequence of closed intervals

$$I_0 \supset I_1 \supset I_2 \supset I_3 \supset I_4 \supset I_5 \supset I_6 \supset I_7 \ldots \supset I_N \supset \ldots,$$

where:

$I_0 = [0, 1]$,

$I_1 = [0, \frac{1}{3}] \cup [\frac{2}{3}, \frac{3}{3}]$,

$I_2 = [0, \frac{1}{9}] \cup [\frac{2}{9}, \frac{3}{9}] \cup [\frac{6}{9}, \frac{7}{9}] \cup [\frac{8}{9}, \frac{9}{9}]$,

$I_3 = [0, \frac{1}{27}] \cup [\frac{2}{27}, \frac{3}{27}] \cup [\frac{6}{27}, \frac{7}{27}] \cup [\frac{8}{27}, \frac{9}{27}] \cup [\frac{18}{27}, \frac{19}{27}] \cup [\frac{20}{27}, \frac{21}{27}] \cup [\frac{24}{27}, \frac{25}{27}] \cup [\frac{26}{27}, \frac{27}{27}]$,

$I_4 = I_3$ minus the middle open third of each interval in I_3,

$\vdots$

$I_N = I_{N-1}$ minus the middle open third of each interval in I_{N-1}.

This construction is illustrated in Fig. 3.1. The Cantor set $\mathcal{C}$ is defined:

$$\mathcal{C} = \bigcap_{n=0}^{\infty} I_n.$$

$\mathcal{C}$ contains the point $x = 0$, so it is nonempty. $\mathcal{C}$ is a perfect set (see Section 3.8) that contains uncountably many points. $\mathcal{C}$ is an example of an *IFS fractal* in the space $[0, 1] \subset \mathbb{R}$.

We consider $\mathcal{C}$ in the metric space $(\mathcal{C}, \text{Euclidean})$. A transformation $f_1 : \mathcal{C} \to \mathcal{C}$ is defined by $f_1(x) = \frac{1}{3}x$. This transformation is one-to-one but not onto. Another affine transformation that maps $\mathcal{C}$ one-to-one into $\mathcal{C}$ is $f_2(x) = \frac{1}{3}x + \frac{2}{3}$, and $\mathcal{C} = f_1(\mathcal{C}) \cup f_2(\mathcal{C})$; that is, $\mathcal{C}$ is the union of two affine transformations of itself.

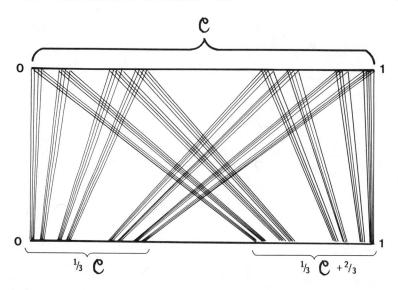

Figure 3.1. This figure shows how the classical Cantor set $\mathcal{C}$ is taken to itself by the application of two affine transformations.

3.5. Affine Transformations in the Euclidean Plane

Definition *A transformation* $w : \mathbb{R}^2 \to \mathbb{R}^2$ *of the form*

$$w(x, y) = (ax + by + e, cx + dy + f), \tag{3.1}$$

where $a, b, c, d, e,$ *and* f *are real numbers, is called a (two-dimensional) affine transformation.*

We use the following equivalent notations:

$$w(x) = w \begin{pmatrix} x \\ y \end{pmatrix} = \begin{pmatrix} a & b \\ c & d \end{pmatrix} \begin{pmatrix} x \\ y \end{pmatrix} + \begin{pmatrix} e \\ f \end{pmatrix} = \mathbf{A}x + \mathbf{T}.$$

Here,

$$\mathbf{A} = \begin{pmatrix} a & b \\ c & d \end{pmatrix}$$

is a 2×2 real matrix and $\mathbf{T}$ is the column vector

$$\begin{pmatrix} e \\ f \end{pmatrix},$$

which we do not distinguish from the coordinate pair $(e, f) \in \mathbb{R}^2$. Such transformations have important geometrical and algebraic properties. The reader is assumed to be familiar with matrix multiplication.

The matrix $\mathbf{A}$ can always be written in the form

$$
\begin{pmatrix} a & b \\ c & d \end{pmatrix} = \begin{pmatrix} r_1 \cos \theta_1 & -r_2 \sin \theta_2 \\ r_1 \sin \theta_1 & r_2 \cos \theta_2 \end{pmatrix},
$$

where (r_1, θ_1) are the polar coordinates of the point (a, c) and $(r_2, (\theta_2 + \frac{\pi}{2}))$ are the polar coordinates of the point (b, d). That is,

$$
r_1 = \sqrt{a^2 + c^2}, \quad \theta_1 = \tan^{-1}(c/a) \text{ if } a \neq 0,
$$

$$
\theta_1 = \frac{\pi}{2} \text{ if } a = 0 \text{ and } c \geq 0,
$$

$$
\theta_1 = \frac{3\pi}{2} \text{ if } a = 0 \text{ and } c < 0;
$$

$$
r_2 = \sqrt{b^2 + d^2}, \quad \theta_2 = \tan^{-1}(b/d) \text{ if } d \neq 0,
$$

$$
\theta_2 = \frac{\pi}{2} \text{ if } d = 0 \text{ and } b \leq 0,
$$

$$
\theta_2 = \frac{3\pi}{2} \text{ if } d = 0 \text{ and } b < 0.
$$

The linear transformation

$$
\begin{pmatrix} x \\ y \end{pmatrix} \rightarrow \mathbf{A} \begin{pmatrix} x \\ y \end{pmatrix}
$$

in $\mathbb{R}^2$ maps any triangle with a vertex at the origin to another triangle with a vertex at the origin, provided that $ad - bc \neq 0$, as illustrated in Fig. 3.2.

The general affine transformation $w(x) = \mathbf{A}x + \mathbf{T}$ in $\mathbb{R}^2$ consists of a linear transformation $\mathbf{A}$ followed by a *translation* specified by the vector $\mathbf{T}$. One can always find an affine transformation that maps a given triangle, with vertices at $(x_1, x_2), (y_1, y_2)$, and (z_1, z_2) to another specified triangle, e.g., with vertices at $(\tilde{x}_1, \tilde{x}_2), (\tilde{y}_1, \tilde{y}_2)$, and $(\tilde{z}_1, \tilde{z}_2)$. The necessary coefficients a, b, c, d, e, and f are obtained by solving the set of linear equations:

$$
\begin{array}{rcrcrcl}
x_1 a &+& x_2 b &+& e &=& \tilde{x}_1, \\
y_1 a &+& y_2 b &+& e &=& \tilde{y}_1, \\
z_1 a &+& z_2 b &+& e &=& \tilde{z}_1, \\
x_1 c &+& x_2 d &+& f &=& \tilde{x}_2, \\
y_1 c &+& y_2 d &+& f &=& \tilde{y}_2, \\
z_1 c &+& z_2 d &+& f &=& \tilde{z}_2.
\end{array}
$$

Plate 1. Compressed Zinnia
This Zinnia image was used as the basis for the RGB and CMY(K) separations shown in Figs. 2.28 and 2.29. The Zinnia photograph was scanned to create a 640 by 400 resolution, 768 KByte, 24-bit Targa file. This was compressed to a 14,930 byte fractal image format (FIF) file using Images Incorporated. This FIF file was decompressed to a 24-bit Targa file which was then printed on a SONY UP-D700 digital color printer to create the image shown here.

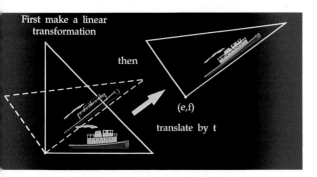

Plate 2. Affine Transformations
An affine transformation consists of a linear transformation followed by a translation. The ship is rotated, stretched and then moved.

Plate 3. **Four IFS Attractors** A beautiful image created from the harmonious combination of four IFS attractors.

Plate 4. **A Snowflake** A simple IFS creates a complex snowflake.

Plate 5. **Birds and Trees** An example of an image computed using VRIFS (see Chapter 4). It is made of a number of segments, each of which is made using a vector recurrent IFS with probabilities. The grayscale values for each segment are mapped into color values using a lookup table which has been adjusted interactively at the end of the process to make the image look as much like the original as possible.

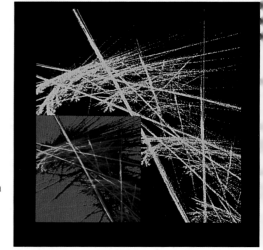

Plate 6. **Color version of the image shown in Fig. 4.25** This plate illustrates a measure $\mu \in P$, which is a fixed point of the Markov operator M associated with an IFS of affine maps. Computed using VRIFS.

Plate 7. **Color version of the image shown in Fig. 4.26** This plate illustrates a measure $\mu \in P$, which is a fixed point of the Markov operator M associated with an IFS of affine maps, where the maps have been carefully chosen to create the image of a root. Computed using VRIFS.

Plate 8. **Color version of the image shown in Fig. 4.28** This plate illustrates a measure $\mu \in P$, which is a fixed point of the Markov operator M with condensation. Look at Fig. 4.28 to see how the maps were constructed to create this image. Computed using VRIFS.

Plate 9. **Original Hibiscus Image** An original photograph was scanned at 100 dpi on an HP ScanJet IIc. This produced a 505 by 510 resolution, 24-bit image requiring 772,668 bytes of disk storage. Plates 9, 10, 11, and 12 were all printed on a Mitsubishi S340 color sublimation printer from 24-bit Targa files created using Images Incorporated.

Plate 10. **Hibiscus—Compression Ratio 9:1** Images Incorporated was used to compress the original file down to an 84,435 byte FIF file. At this compression ratio it is almost impossible to distinguish the decompressed image from the original.

Plate 11. **Hibiscus—Compression Ratio 46:1** Images Incorporated was used to compress the original file down to a 16,869 byte FIF file. At this compression ratio you lose most of the fine vein structure in the leaves and petals.

Plate 12. **Hibiscus—Compression Ratio 67:1** Images Incorporated was used to compress the original file down to an 11,608 byte FIF file. At this compression ratio you lose all the fine vein structure, and the pollen on the stamens and the highlights on the petals are blurred.

Plate 13. Original Gecko Image
The original gecko image is a 640 by 400 resolution, 24-bit image requiring 768 Kbyte of disk storage. This image was printed on a Mitsubishi S340 color sublimation printer from a 24-bit Targa file.

Plate 14. Gecko—Compression Ratio 156:1 The original gecko image shown in Plate 13 was compressed down to a 19,645 byte FIF file by using the fractal transform compression (FTC) II board and POEM compression driver software. This FIF file was decompressed to an image with 1280 by 800 resolution (twice that of the original), thus giving an effective compression ratio of 156:1.

Plate 15. Gecko—Compression Ratio 625:1 Now we use the same 19,645 byte FIF file and we 'zoom' in on the detail in one quarter of the original. The image shown here (one quarter of the original picture) has a resolution of 1280 by 800 pixels, giving an effective compression ratio of 625:1.

Plate 16. Gecko—Compression Ratio 2500:1 Finally, using the same 19,645 byte FIF file, we 'zoom' in once again. This small section (one eighth the area of the original picture) has a resolution of 1280 by 800 pixels, giving an effective compression ratio of 2500:1. Just think, in this image 2500 pixels requires three bytes of data from the FIF file, whereas in the original image, three bytes of data are required for just one pixel.

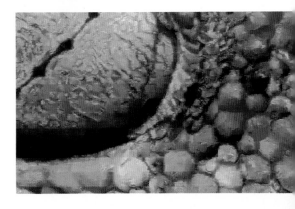

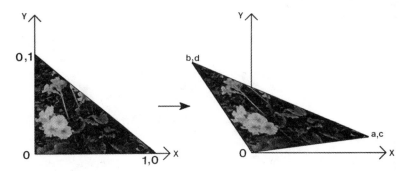

Figure 3.2. This figure illustrates a linear transformation in $\mathbb{R}^2$. It maps any triangle with a vertex at the origin to another triangle with a vertex at the origin, provided that $ad - bc \neq 0$.

This idea is illustrated in Fig. 3.3.

The *inverse* of the affine transformation $w(x,y) = (ax+by+e, cx+dy+f)$ is represented by the affine transformation

$$w^{-1}(x,y) = (d \cdot x - b \cdot y - d \cdot e + b \cdot f, -c \cdot x + a \cdot y + c \cdot e - a \cdot f) \div \alpha,$$

when $\alpha = (a \cdot d - b \cdot c) \neq 0$.

The affine transformation $w : \mathbb{R}^2 \to \mathbb{R}^2$, defined by $w(x,y) = (x,y)$, is called the *identity map*. See Fig. 3.4.

An affine transformation $w : \mathbb{R}^2 \to \mathbb{R}^2$ of the special form $w(x,y) = (r_1 x, r_2 y)$, where r_1 and r_2 are positive constants, is called a *dilation*. See Fig. 3.5.

The two affine transformations, $w(x,y) = (x, -y)$, and $w(x,y) = (-x, y)$, are examples of *reflections*, the first corresponding to reflection in the second coordinate axis, and the second to reflection in the first coordinate axis. See Fig. 3.6.

Affine transformations of the special form $w(x+f, y+g) = (x+f, y+g)$, where f and g are real constants, are called *translations*. See Fig. 3.7.

An affine transformation $w : \mathbb{R}^2 \to \mathbb{R}^2$ is called a *similitude* if it is an affine transformation having one of the special forms,

$$w\begin{pmatrix} x \\ y \end{pmatrix} = \begin{pmatrix} r\cos\theta & -r\sin\theta \\ r\sin\theta & r\cos\theta \end{pmatrix} \begin{pmatrix} x \\ y \end{pmatrix} + \begin{pmatrix} e \\ f \end{pmatrix},$$

$$w\begin{pmatrix} x \\ y \end{pmatrix} = \begin{pmatrix} r\cos\theta & r\sin\theta \\ r\sin\theta & -r\cos\theta \end{pmatrix} \begin{pmatrix} x \\ y \end{pmatrix} + \begin{pmatrix} e \\ f \end{pmatrix},$$

for some translation $(e, f) \in \mathbb{R}^2$, some real number $r \neq 0$, and some angle θ, $0 \leq \theta < 2\pi$. θ is called the rotation angle, while r is called the *scale factor* or *scaling*. See Fig. 3.8.

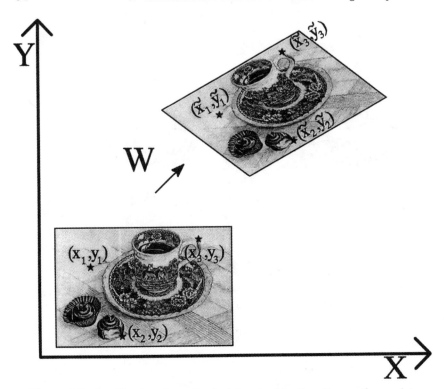

Figure 3.3. An affine transformation is determined by its action on three points.

Linear transformations of the special form

$$\mathbf{A}\begin{pmatrix} x \\ y \end{pmatrix} = \begin{pmatrix} \cos\theta & -\sin\theta \\ \sin\theta & \cos\theta \end{pmatrix}\begin{pmatrix} x \\ y \end{pmatrix}$$

are called *rotations*. See Fig. 3.9.

A linear transformation of one of the special forms,

$$w(x,y) = (x + by, y), \quad \text{or} \quad w(x,y) = (x, cx + y),$$

where b and c are real constants, is called a *skew*, or *shear transformation*. In each case, one of the two coordinates is left unchanged, as is the case when a deck of cards is sheared. See Fig. 3.10.

If $w_1 : \mathbb{R}^2 \to \mathbb{R}^2$ and $w_2 : \mathbb{R}^2 \to \mathbb{R}^2$ are both affine transformations, then so is $w_3 = w_1 \circ w_2$. Thus, we can compose affine transformations to make new affine transformations. This leads to the question of finding a set of elementary affine transformations out of which all affine transformations can be constructed by composition.

Before and After

$$\mathfrak{G} = w\,(\mathfrak{G})$$

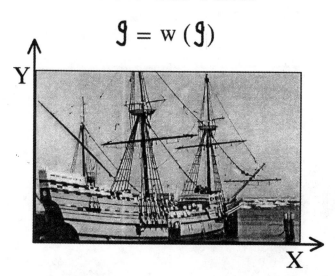

Figure 3.4. This figure illustrates an affine transformation $w : \mathbb{R}^2 \to \mathbb{R}^2$ defined by $w(x,y) = (x,y)$. It is called the identity map. Really.

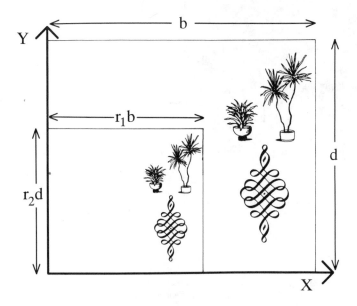

Figure 3.5. This figure illustrates an affine transformation $w : \mathbb{R}^2 \to \mathbb{R}^2$ of the special form $w(x,y) = (r_1 x, r_2 y)$, where r_1 and r_2 are positive constants. It is called a *dilation*.

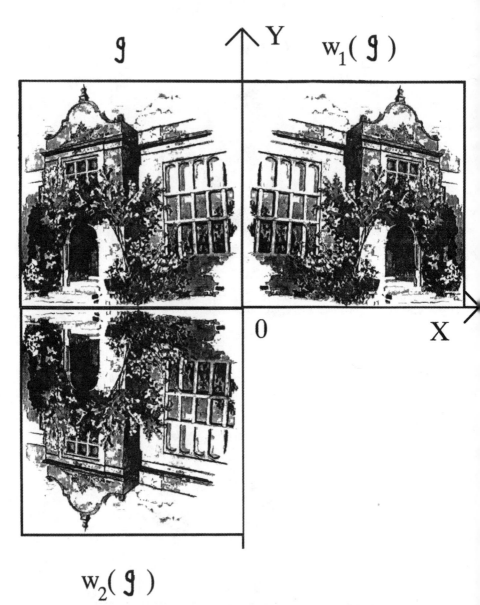

Figure 3.6. This figure illustrates the affine transformations $w_1(x,y) = (-x,y)$, and $w_2(x,y) = (x,-y)$, which are examples of *reflections*.

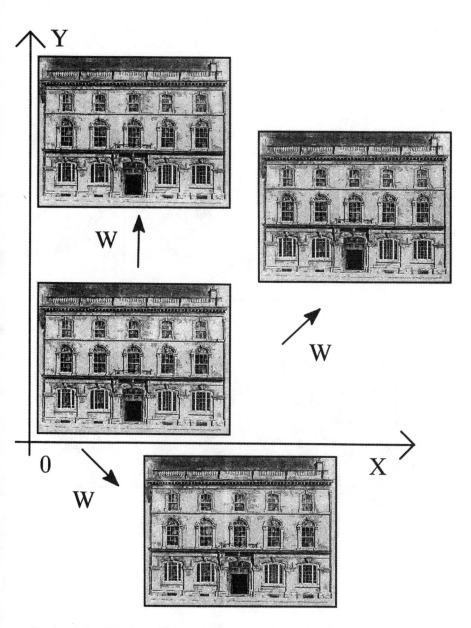

Figure 3.7. This figure illustrates affine transformations of the special form $w(x + f, y + g) = (x + f, y + g)$, where f and g are real constants. They are called *translations*.

Figure 3.8. This figure illustrates the special forms of affine transformations called *similitudes*.

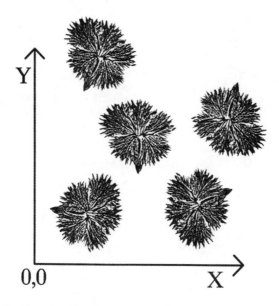

Figure 3.9. This figure illustrates the special form of linear transformations called *rotations*.

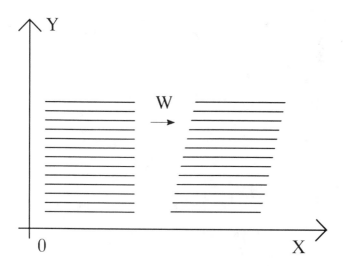

Figure 3.10. This figure illustrates a linear transformation of the special form $w(x, y) = (x + by, y)$, where b is a real constant. It is an example of a *shear transformation*.

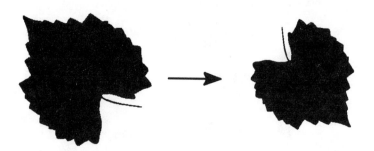

Figure 3.11. When det $\mathbf{A} < 0$, the leaf L is "flipped over" by the transformation.

The most general affine transformation can be built up by composing a translation with a linear transformation. The most general linear transformation can be obtained by composing a dilation with a rotation and a skew.

Let S be a region in $\mathbb{R}^2$ bounded by a polygon or other "nice" boundary. Let $w : \mathbb{R}^2 \to \mathbb{R}^2$ be an affine transformation, $w(x) = \mathbf{A}x + \mathbf{T}$, as in Eq. (3.1). The determinant of $\mathbf{A}$, $\det(\mathbf{A})$, is given by the formula $\det(\mathbf{A}) = a \cdot d - b \cdot c$. One can show that

$$(\text{area of } w(S)) = |\det(\mathbf{A})| \cdot (\text{area of } S).$$

When det $\mathbf{A} < 0$, S is "flipped over" by the transformation. See Fig. 3.11.

3.6.   Affine Transformations in Three-Dimensional Real Space

The most general affine transformation $w : \mathbb{R}^3 \to \mathbb{R}^3$ can be expressed in the matrix notation

$$w \begin{bmatrix} x \\ y \\ z \end{bmatrix} = \begin{bmatrix} a & b & t \\ c & d & u \\ r & s & p \end{bmatrix} \begin{bmatrix} x \\ y \\ z \end{bmatrix} + \begin{bmatrix} e \\ f \\ q \end{bmatrix},$$

where $a, b, c, d, e, f, p, q, r, s, t, u$, are real constants, and $(x, y, z) \in \mathbb{R}^3$; that is,

$$w(x, y, z) = (a \cdot x + b \cdot y + t \cdot z + e, c \cdot x + d \cdot y + u \cdot z + f, r \cdot x + s \cdot y + p \cdot z + q).$$

We will also denote this transformation by $w(x) = \mathbf{A}x + \mathbf{T}$ in the obvious notation. Provided that the matrix of the determinant of the matrix $\mathbf{A}$ is

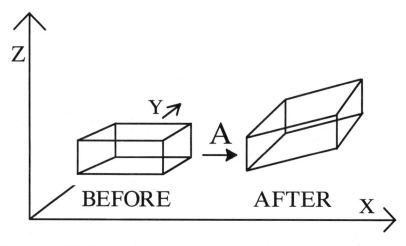

Figure 3.12. This figure shows the relationship between two tetrahedra that determine an affine transformation.

nonzero, the transformation is invertible. It maps tetrahedra into tetrahedra. A tetrahedron is determined by four non-coplanar points. Conversely, two tetrahedra can be used to specify an affine transformation in three dimensions. Notice that an affine transformation in three dimensions can produce the mirror image of a set.

Of particular interest to us is the case of affine transformations $v : \mathbb{R}^3 \to \mathbb{R}^3$ of the special form

$$v(x, y, z) = (w(x, y), pz + q),$$

where $w : \mathbb{R}^2 \to \mathbb{R}^2$ is an affine transformation in two dimensions. Any line segment parallel to the z-axis is mapped to a line segment parallel to the z-axis. Any triangle lying in a plane perpendicular to the z-axis is transformed into a new triangle lying in a plane perpendicular to the z-axis.

We illustrate three-dimensional affine transformations in Figs. 3.12 to 3.15. Figure 3.12 illustrates how two tetrahedra can determine an affine transformation in three dimensions. Figure 3.13 shows affine transformation of the special form $(w(x, y), pz + q)$. Such transformations play a special role in fractal transform image compression. Figure 3.14 shows three-dimensional affine transformations used to generate a fractal fern using an iterated function system. The IFS is defined in terms of these transformations. Figure 3.15 shows the effect of certain three-dimensional affine transformations on three-dimensional lettering, produced by a computer drawing program.

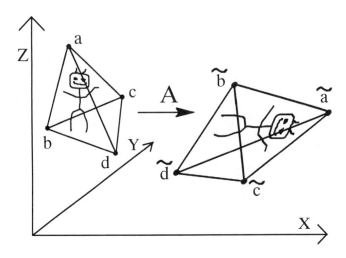

Figure 3.13. This figure illustrates affine transformations of the special form $(x, y, z) \rightarrow (w(x, y), pz + q)$, where w is an affine transformation in two dimensions. Points that lie "one above the other" or are "vertically aligned" remain so after transformation. This type of affine transformation is used in applications of the fractal transform.

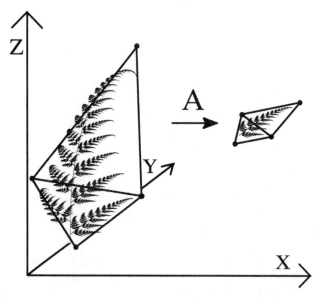

Figure 3.14. This illustration shows an affine transformation in three dimensions acting upon a fractal fern. The tetrahedron defined by the tips of three fronds and the base is taken into a tetrahedron that is defined by a single primary frond.

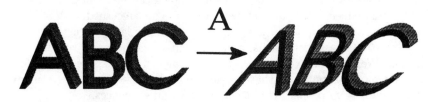

Figure 3.15. This figure shows affine transformations in 3D using 3D lettering, as produced by a computer drawing program.

3.7. Norms on Linear Transformations on $\mathbb{R}^2$

In both of the metric spaces $(\mathbb{R}^2, d)$ and $(\mathbb{R}^3, d)$, we define the *norm* of a point $x \in \mathbb{R}^2$ to be $||x|| = d(x, O)$, where O denotes the origin.

Let **A** denote a linear transformation on either of these spaces; that is, either

$$\mathbf{A}(x, y) = (ax + by, cx + dy)$$

or

$$\mathbf{A}(x, y, z) = (ax + by + tz, cx + dy + uz, rx + sy + pz),$$

where $a, b, c, d, t, u, r, s, p$ are real constants. Then we define the *norm of the linear transformation* **A** by

$$||\mathbf{A}|| = \max \left\{ \frac{||\mathbf{A}x||}{||x||} : x \in \mathbb{R}^2, \, x \neq 0 \right\}$$

when this maximum exists. One can show that $||\mathbf{A}||$ is well-defined when d is the Euclidean metric, for example. Also, when $||\mathbf{A}||$ exists, we have

$$||\mathbf{A}x|| \leq ||\mathbf{A}|| \, ||x|| \text{ for all } x \in \mathbb{R}^2 (\text{or } \mathbb{R}^3).$$

3.8. Topological Properties of Metric Spaces and Transformations

Here, we describe a number of topological properties of certain subsets of a metric space, certain sequences of points in a metric space, and of certain functions that act upon metric spaces, which are needed elsewhere in this presentation. They are readily accessible in the context of metric space theory, and are presented in some detail in [FE].

The properties of sets are those such as openness, closedness, compactness, boundedness, and completeness; we are also concerned with Cauchy sequences, and continuous functions. These properties are treated in the form of statements, definitions, and theorems, together with relevant examples. We begin with the concept of equivalent metric spaces. Transformations on a metric space that provide equivalent metrics preserve many of the topological properties of their subsets and sequences.

Definition *Two metrics d_1 and d_2 on a space X are* equivalent *if there exist constants $0 < c_1 < c_2 < \infty$ such that*

$$c_1 d_1(x,y) \leq d_2(x,y) \leq c_2 d_1(x,y), \quad \forall \ (x,y) \in X \times X.$$

Examples:

(i) The Manhattan and Euclidean metrics are equivalent on $\square \subset \mathbb{R}^2$.

(ii) Let Σ denote code space on N symbols. One can define two different metrics d_1 and d_2 on Σ by

$$d_1(\sigma, \omega) = d(\sigma_1\sigma_2\sigma_3\ldots, \omega_1\omega_2\omega_3\ldots) = \sum_{i=1}^{\infty} \frac{|\sigma_i - \omega_i|}{(N+1)^i},$$

and

$$d_2(\sigma, \omega) = d(\sigma_1\sigma_2\sigma_3\ldots, \omega_1\omega_2\omega_3\ldots) = \left| \sum_{i=1}^{\infty} \frac{\sigma_i - \omega_i}{(N+1)^i} \right|.$$

Then the two metrics are equivalent.

Definition *Two metric spaces $(\mathbf{X}_1, d_1)$ and $(\mathbf{X}_2, d_2)$ are* equivalent *if there is an invertible function $h : \mathbf{X}_1 \rightarrow \mathbf{X}_2$, such that the metric $\tilde{d}_1$ on $\mathbf{X}_1$ defined by*

$$\tilde{d}_1(x,y) = d_2(h(x), h(y)), \quad \forall \ x,y \in \mathbf{X}_1$$

is equivalent to d_1.

Examples:

(i) The two metric spaces (Σ, d_1) and (Σ, d_2), described earlier, are equivalent. In this case, $\Sigma = \mathbf{X}_1 = \mathbf{X}_2$, and the invertible function $h : \mathbb{R} \rightarrow \mathbb{R}$ is simply the identity map $h(x) = x, \ \forall \ x \in \Sigma$.

(ii) If $\mathbf{X}_1 = [1, 2]$ and $\mathbf{X}_2 = [0, 1]$, d_1 denotes the Euclidean metric and $d_2(x,y) = 2 \cdot |x - y|$ in $\mathbf{X}_2$, then $(\mathbf{X}_1, d_1)$ and $(\mathbf{X}_2, d_2)$ are equivalent metric spaces.

(iii) ($\square$, Euclidean) and ($\square$, Manhattan) are equivalent metric spaces.

(iv) Let $w : \mathbb{R}^2 \to \mathbb{R}^2$ be an invertible affine transformation. Let d_1 denote the Euclidean metric on $\mathbb{R}^2$ and let $d_2(x, y) = d_1(w(x), w(y))$. Then $(\mathbb{R}^2, d_1)$ and $(\mathbb{R}^2, d_2)$ are equivalent metrics.

(v) Let $w : \mathbb{R}^3 \to \mathbb{R}^3$ be an invertible affine transformation. Let d_1 denote the Euclidean metric on $\mathbb{R}^3$ and let $d_2(x, y) = d_1(w(x), w(y))$. Then $(\mathbb{R}^3, d_1)$ and $(\mathbb{R}^3, d_2)$ are equivalent metrics.

Definition *A function $f : \mathbf{X} \to \mathbf{Y}$ from a metric space $(\mathbf{X}, d)$ into a metric space $(\mathbf{Y}, e)$ is* continuous *if, for each $\epsilon > 0$ and $x \in \mathbf{X}$, there is a $\delta > 0$ so that*

$$d(x, y) < \delta \Rightarrow e(f(x), f(y)) < \epsilon.$$

Examples:

(i) Affine transformations on $\mathbb{R}^n$ for $n = 1, 2$, and 3, with the Euclidean metric, are examples of continuous functions.

(ii) The shift transformation $S : \Sigma \to \Sigma$, on code space, with the code space metric, is an example of a continuous function. This function is defined by

$$S(x_1 x_2 x_3 x_4 \ldots) = x_2 x_3 x_4 x_5 \ldots$$

(iii) If $f : \mathbf{X} \to \mathbf{Y}$ is continuous, with respect to the metric d_1 on $\mathbf{X}$, and if d_2 is an equivalent metric to d_1 on $\mathbf{X}$, then f is continuous with respect to the metric d_2 on $\mathbf{X}$. Similarly, if the metric on $\mathbf{Y}$ is changed to an equivalent metric, then the continuity of f is preserved.

Definition *A sequence of points $\{x_n\}_{n=1}^{\infty}$ in a space $\mathbf{X}$ is a function $f : \mathbb{Z}^+ \to \mathbf{X}$, where $\mathbb{Z}^+$ denotes the set of all positive integers, and $f(n) = x_n$ for all $n \in \mathbb{Z}^+$. A sequence of positive integers $\{n_i\}_{i=1}^{\infty}$ is an order-preserving function $g : \mathbb{Z}^+ \to \mathbb{Z}^+$ such that $g(i) = n_i$ for all $i \in \mathbb{Z}^+$. We say that $g : \mathbb{Z}^+ \to \mathbb{Z}^+$ is order-preserving when it has the property "$m < n \Rightarrow g(m) < g(n)$, $\forall \; m, n \in \mathbb{Z}^+$.". A subsequence $\{x_{n_i}\}_{i=1}^{\infty}$ is a function of the form $f \circ g : \mathbb{Z}^+ \to \mathbf{X}$ with f and g as before, where x_{n_i} denotes the point $f(g(i))$.*

Definition *A sequence $\{x_n\}_{n=1}^{\infty}$ of points in a metric space $(\mathbf{X}, d)$ is called a* Cauchy sequence *if, for any given number $\epsilon > 0$, there is an integer $N > 0$ such that*

$$d(x_n, x_m) < \epsilon \quad \text{for all} \quad n, m > N.$$

Definition *A sequence* $\{x_n\}_{n=1}^{\infty}$ *of points in a metric space* $(\mathbf{X}, d)$ *is said to* converge *to a point* $x \in \mathbf{X}$ *if, for any given number* $\epsilon > 0$, *there is an integer* $N > 0$ *such that*

$$d(x_n, x) < \epsilon \ \text{ for all } \ n > N.$$

In such a case, the sequence is said to be convergent. The point $x \in \mathbf{X}$, to which such a sequence converges, is called the *limit* of the sequence. We use the notation: $x = \lim_{n \to \infty} x_n$.

Theorem *If a sequence of points* $\{x_n\}_{n=1}^{\infty}$ *in a metric space* $(\mathbf{X}, d)$ *converges to a point* $x \in \mathbf{X}$, *then* $\{x_n\}_{n=1}^{\infty}$ *is a Cauchy sequence.*

Example:

(i) If $(\mathbf{X}, d_1)$ and $(\mathbf{X}, d_2)$ are two equivalent metric spaces, then $\{x_n\}_{n=1}^{\infty}$ is a Cauchy sequence in the first space if, and only if, it is a Cauchy sequence in the second space. In other words, the property of being a Cauchy sequence is preserved between equivalent metric spaces.

Definition *A metric space* $(\mathbf{X}, d)$ *is* complete *if every Cauchy sequence* $\{x_n\}_{n=1}^{\infty}$ *in* $\mathbf{X}$ *has a limit* $x \in \mathbf{X}$.

Examples:

(i) $(\mathbb{R}, \text{Euclidean metric})$ is a complete metric space.

(ii) $(\mathbb{R}^2, \text{Euclidean metric})$ is a complete metric space.

(iii) $(\square, \text{Euclidean metric})$ is a complete metric space.

(iv) $(\Sigma, \text{code space metric})$ is a complete metric space.

(v) Let $(\mathbf{X}_1, d_1)$ and $(\mathbf{X}_2, d_2)$ be equivalent metric spaces. Then $(\mathbf{X}_1, d_1)$ is complete if and only if $(\mathbf{X}_2, d_2)$ is complete.

Definition *Let* $S \subset \mathbf{X}$ *be a subset of a metric space* $(\mathbf{X}, d)$. *A point* $x \in \mathbf{X}$ *is called a* limit point *of* S *if there is a sequence* $\{x_n\}_{n=1}^{\infty}$ *of points* $x_n \in S\{x\}$ *such that* $\lim_{n \to \infty} x_n = x$.

Definition *Let* $S \subset \mathbf{X}$ *be a subset of a metric space* $(\mathbf{X}, d)$. *The* closure *of* S, *denoted* $\overline{S}$, *is defined to be* $\overline{S} = S \cup \{\text{limit points of } S\}$.

Definition S *is* closed *if it contains all of its limit points; that is,* $S = \overline{S}$.

Figure 3.16. This figure illustrates in a fanciful manner the topological properties of open and closed sets. We think of the petals of the flowers in the foreground as defining closed subsets of the support of the image. This is because it seems strange for a petal not to have an edge. We think of the background of the image as being an open set because the boundaries of it, such as the edges of the flowers, do not belong to it. Recall that we have chosen to define the support of an image, $\Box \subset \mathbb{R}^2$, as open in our axiomatic description of the space of real world images $\Re$.

Definition *Let $S \subset \mathbf{X}$ be a subset of a metric space $(\mathbf{X}, d)$. S is* open *if for each $x \in S$, there is an $\epsilon < 0$ such that $B(x, \epsilon) = \{y \in \mathbf{X} : d(x, y) \le \epsilon\} \subset S$. This definition is equivalent to: S is* open *if it is not closed.*

Figure 3.16 illustrates the topological properties of open and closed.

Definition *S is* perfect *if it is equal to the set of all its limit points.*

Examples:

(i) The Cantor set $\mathcal{C}$ with the Euclidean metric is closed and perfect.

(ii) The subset $S = \{x = 1/n : n = 1, 2, 3, \ldots\}$ is closed in $((0,1]$, Euclidean), but not in $([0,1]$, Euclidean).

(iii) $S = [0, 1]$ is a closed, perfect subset of $(\mathbb{R}$, Euclidean).

(iv) $S = \Sigma$ is a closed, perfect subset of $(\Sigma$, code space metric).

(v) If S is a subset of a complete metric space $(\mathbf{X}, d)$, then (S, d) is a metric space. (S, d) is complete if, and only if, S is closed in $\mathbf{X}$.

Definition *Let $S \subset \mathbf{X}$ be a subset of a metric space $(\mathbf{X}, d)$. S is* compact *if every infinite sequence $\{x_n\}_{n=1}^{\infty}$ in S contains a subsequence having a limit in S.*

Definition *Let $S \subset \mathbf{X}$ be a subset of a metric space $(\mathbf{X}, d)$. S is* bounded *if there is a point $a \in \mathbf{X}$ and a number $R > 0$ so that $d(a, x) < R$, $\forall x \in \mathbf{X}$.*

Definition *Let $S \subset \mathbf{X}$ be a subset of a metric space $(\mathbf{X}, d)$. S is* totally bounded *if, for each $\epsilon > 0$, there is a finite set of points $\{y_1, y_2, \ldots y_n\} \subset S$ such that whenever $x \in \mathbf{X}$, $d(x, y_i) < \epsilon$ for some $y_i \in \{y_1, y_2, \ldots, y_n\}$.*

Theorem *Let $(\mathbf{X}, d)$ be a complete metric space. Let $S \subset \mathbf{X}$. Then S is compact if and only if it is closed and totally bounded.*

Examples:

(i) If S is a closed subset of a complete metric space $(\mathbf{X}, d)$, then (S, d) is a complete metric space.

(ii) If $(\mathbf{X}_1, d_1)$ and $(\mathbf{X}_2, d_2)$ are equivalent metric spaces, and a transformation $\theta : \mathbf{X}_1 \to \mathbf{X}_2$ provides this equivalence and $S \subset \mathbf{X}_1$ is closed, then it can be shown that $\theta(S) = \{\theta(s) : s \in S\}$ is closed.

(iii) If $(\mathbf{X}, d)$ is a metric space, then $\mathbf{X}$ is open.

(iv) If $(\mathbf{X}, d)$ is a metric space, then "$S \subset \mathbf{X}$ is open" is the same as "$\mathbf{X} \setminus S$ is closed."

(v) Every closed, bounded subset of $(\mathbb{R}^2$, Euclidean) is compact. In particular, every metric space of the form (closed bounded subset of $\mathbb{R}^2$, Euclidean) is a complete metric space.

(vi) Let $(\mathbf{X}, d)$ be a metric space. Let $f : \mathbf{X} \to \mathbf{X}$ be continuous. Let A be a compact nonempty subset of $\mathbf{X}$. Then $f(A)$ is a compact nonempty subset of $\mathbf{X}$.

(vii) Let $S \subset (\mathbf{X}_1, d_1)$ be open, and let $(\mathbf{X}_2, d_2)$ be a metric space equivalent to $(\mathbf{X}_1, d_1)$, the equivalence being provided by a function $h : \mathbf{X}_1 \to \mathbf{X}_2$. Then $h(S)$ is an open subset of $\mathbf{X}_2$.

(viii) The Cantor set $\mathcal{C}$ is closed and compact.

(ix) If two spaces are equivalent, then the following topological properties of sets are preserved: openness, closedness, boundedness, completeness, compactness, and perfection.

Definition *Let* $S \subset \mathbf{X}$ *be a subset of a metric space* $(\mathbf{X}, d)$. *A point* $x \in \mathbf{X}$ *is a* boundary point *of* S *if for every number* $\epsilon > 0, B(x, \epsilon)$ *contains a point in* $\mathbf{X} \setminus S$ *and a point in* S.

Definition *The set of all boundary points of* S *is called the* boundary *of* S, *and is denoted* ∂S.

Definition *Let* $S \subset \mathbf{X}$ *be a subset of a metric space* $(\mathbf{X}, d)$. *A point* $x \in S$ *is called an* interior point *of* S *if there is a number* $\epsilon > 0$ *such that* $B(x, \epsilon) \subset S$.

Definition *The set of interior points of* S *is called the* interior *of* S, *and is denoted* S^0.

Examples:

(i) Let S be a subset of a metric space $(\mathbf{X}, d)$. Then $\partial S = \partial(\mathbf{X} \setminus S)$ and $\partial \mathbf{X} = \emptyset$.

(ii) The properties of being a boundary of a set, and of being the interior of a set, are preserved under metric equivalence.

(iii) Let $(\mathbf{X}, d)$ be the real line with the Euclidean metric. Let S denote the set of all rational points in $\mathbf{X}$, that is, the real numbers that can be written p/q, where p and q are integers with $q \neq 0$. Then $\partial S = \mathbf{X}$.

(iv) Let S be a closed subset of a metric space. Then $\partial S \subset S$.

(v) Let S be an open subset of a metric space. Then $\partial S \cap S = \emptyset$.

(vi) Let S be an open subset of a metric space. Then $S^0 = S$. Also, if $S^0 = S$, then S is open.

(vii) Let S be a closed subset of a metric space. Then $S = S^0 \cup \partial S$.

(viii) The property of being the interior of a set is invariant under metric equivalence.

(ix) Show that the boundary of a set S in a metric space divides the space into two disjoint open sets whose union, with the boundary ∂S, is the whole space.

(x) Let S be a subset of a compact metric space. Then ∂S is compact.

Definition *A metric space* $(\mathbf{X}, d)$ *is* connected *if the only two subsets of* $\mathbf{X}$ *that are simultaneously open and closed are* $\mathbf{X}$ *and* $\emptyset$. *A subset* $S \subset \mathbf{X}$ *is* connected *if the metric space* (S, d) *is connected.*

Definition S *is* disconnected *if it is not connected.*

Definition S *is* totally disconnected *provided that the only nonempty connected subsets of S are subsets consisting of single points.*

Examples:

(i) The properties of being connected and disconnected are invariant under metric equivalence.

(ii) The metric space $(\square$, Euclidean) is connected.

(iii) The metric space $(\mathbf{X} = (0,1) \cup \{2\}$, Euclidean) is disconnected.

(iv) The metric space $(\Sigma$, code space metric) is totally disconnected.

3.9. Contraction Mapping Theorem — Key to Fractal Image Compression

Definition *Let* $f : \mathbf{X} \to \mathbf{X}$ *be a transformation on a space. A point* $x_f \in \mathbf{X}$ *such that* $f(x_f) = x_f$ *is called a* fixed point *of the transformation.*

Figures 3.17, and 3.18 illustrate fixed points of affine transformations. A transformation $T : \Sigma \to \Sigma$ on code space is defined by

$$T(\sigma_1 \sigma_2 \sigma_3 \sigma_4 \sigma_5 \ldots) = \sigma_2 \sigma_3 \sigma_4 \sigma_5 \sigma_6 \ldots$$

and is called a *shift operator.*

The transformation $T^{\circ n}$, for any $n \in \{0, 1, 2, 3, \ldots\}$, acts according to

$$T^{\circ n}(\sigma_1 \sigma_2 \sigma_3 \sigma_4 \sigma_5 \ldots) = \sigma_{n+1} \sigma_{n+2} \sigma_{n+3} \sigma_{n+4} \sigma_{n+5} \sigma_{n+6} \cdots.$$

When code space is built up from the two symbols $\{0, 1\}$, the fixed points of $T^{\circ 3}$ are

000000000000000000000000000000000000000000000000000000000 ...
111111111111111111111111111111111111111111111111111111111 ...
011011011011011011011011011011011011011011011011011011011110 ...
100100100100100100100100100100100100100100100100100100100 ...
001001001001001001001001001001001001001001001001001001010 ...

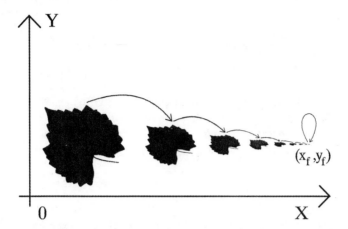

Figure 3.17. This figure illustrates how a contractive affine transformation has a fixed point. Repeated application of the affine transformation w to the first leaf produces a trail of leaves, each smaller than the last. The end of the trail is the fixed point $(x_f, y_f) = w(x_f, y_f)$.

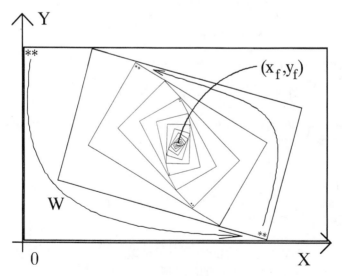

Figure 3.18. This figure illustrates the fixed point of an affine transformation, $(x_f, y_f) = w(x_f, y_f)$.

Definition *A transformation* $f : \mathbf{X} \to \mathbf{X}$ *on a metric space* $(\mathbf{X}, d)$ *is called* **contractive** *or a* **contraction mapping** *if there is a constant* $0 \leq s < 1$ *such that*

$$d(f(x), f(y)) \leq s \cdot d(x, y) \, \forall \, x, y \in \mathbf{X}.$$

Any such number s *is called a* contractivity factor *for* f.

Theorem (The Contraction Mapping Theorem)
Let $f : \mathbf{X} \to \mathbf{X}$ *be a contraction mapping on a complete metric space* $(\mathbf{X}, d)$. *Then* f *possesses exactly one fixed point* $x_f \in \mathbf{X}$, *and moreover for any point* $x \in \mathbf{X}$, *the sequence* $\{f^{\circ n}(x) : n = 0, 1, 2, \ldots\}$ *converges to* x_f; *that is,*

$$\lim_{n \to \infty} f^{\circ n}(x) = x_f, \text{for each } x \in \mathbf{X}.$$

Proof. Let $x \in \mathbf{X}$. Let $0 \leq s < 1$ be a contractivity factor for f. Then

$$d(f^{\circ n}(x), \, f^{\circ m}(x)) \leq s^{m \wedge n} \, d(x, f^{\circ |n-m|})(x)) \tag{3.2}$$

for all $m, n = 0, 1, 2, \ldots$, where we have fixed $x \in \mathbf{X}$. The notation $m \wedge n$ denotes the minimum of the pair of numbers m and n. In particular, for $k = 0, 1, 2, \ldots$, we have

$$
\begin{aligned}
d(x, f^{\circ k}(x)) &\leq d(x, f(x)) + (f(x), f^{\circ 2}(x)) + \ldots + d(f^{\circ (k-1)}((x), f^{\circ k}(x)), \\
&\leq (1 + s + s^2 + \ldots s^{k-1}) d(x, f(x)), \\
&\leq (1 - s)^{-1} d(x, f(x)),
\end{aligned}
$$

so substituting into Eq. (3.2), we now obtain

$$d(f^{\circ n}(x), f^{\circ m}(x)) \leq s^{m \wedge n} \cdot (1 - s)^{-1} \cdot (d(x, f(x)),$$

from which it immediately follows that $\{f^{\circ n}(x)\}_{n=0}^{\infty}$ is a Cauchy sequence. Since $\mathbf{X}$ is complete, this Cauchy sequence possesses a limit $x_f \in \mathbf{X}$, and we have

$$\lim_{n \to \infty} f^{\circ n}(x) = x_f.$$

Now we shall show that x_f is a fixed point of f. Since f is contractive, it is continuous, and hence

$$f(x_f) = f(\lim_{n \to \infty} f^{\circ n}(x)) = \lim_{n \to \infty} f^{\circ (n+1)}(x) = x_f.$$

Finally, can there be more than one fixed point? Suppose there are. Let x_f and y_f be two fixed points of f. Then $x_f = f(x_f)$, $y_f = f(y_f)$, and

$$d(x_f, y_f) = d(f(x_f), f(x_f)) \leq sd(x_f, y_f),$$

whence $(1 - s)\, d(x_f, y_f) \leq 0$, which implies $d(x_f, y_f) = 0$, and hence $x_f = y_f$. This completes the proof.

Examples:

(i) Let $w : \square \to \square$ be a contraction mapping on $(\square,$ Euclidean$)$. Then there is a point x_f in $\square$ that is left unmoved by the transformation. When you move this page further away, keeping your eyes and head steady, so that the page is mapped inside the page, on your retina, there is a point that does not move — for example, a letter or a word seems to be in almost the same location.

(ii) The affine transformation $f : \mathbb{R} \to \mathbb{R}$ defined by $f(x) = \frac{1}{2}x + \frac{1}{2}$ is a contraction mapping, with contractivity factor $s = 0.5$ and fixed point $x_f = 1.0$. Hence, we have

$$\lim_{n \to \infty} f^{on}(x) = 1 \text{ for each } x \in \mathbb{R}.$$

In particular, we deduce that

$$\frac{1}{2} + (\frac{1}{2} + (\frac{1}{2} + (\frac{1}{2} + (\frac{1}{2} + (\frac{1}{2} + (\frac{1}{2} + (\frac{1}{2} + (\frac{1}{2} + (\ldots)))))))))) = 1.$$

(iii) The affine transformation $w : \mathbb{R}^2 \to \mathbb{R}^2$ defined by $w(x) = \mathbf{A}x + \mathbf{T}$ is a contraction, where

$$\mathbf{A} = \begin{pmatrix} \frac{1}{2}\cos 120° & -\frac{1}{2}\sin 120° \\ \frac{1}{2}\sin 120° & \frac{1}{2}\cos 120° \end{pmatrix} \quad \text{and} \quad \mathbf{T} = \begin{pmatrix} \frac{1}{2} \\ 0 \end{pmatrix}.$$

The contractivity factor is $s = 0.5$. As in example (ii), we deduce that

$$\mathbf{T} + \mathbf{A}(\mathbf{T} + \mathbf{A}(\mathbf{T} + \mathbf{A}(\mathbf{T} + \mathbf{A}(\mathbf{T} + \mathbf{A}(\mathbf{T} + \mathbf{A}(\mathbf{T} + +(\ldots))))))))x = x_f.$$

(iv) Let $(\mathbf{X}, d)$ be a compact metric space, and let $f : \mathbf{X} \to \mathbf{X}$ be a contraction mapping. Then one can show that $\{f^{on}(\mathbf{X})\}_{n=0}^{\infty}$ is a Cauchy sequence of points in $(\mathcal{H}(\mathbf{X}), h)$, and $\lim_{n \to \infty} f^{on}(\mathbf{X}) = \{x_f\}$, where x_f is the fixed point of f. $(\mathcal{H}(\mathbf{X}), h)$ is defined in Chapter 4.

(v) The transformations $T : \Sigma \to \Sigma$ on code space Σ defined by

$$T(\sigma_1 \sigma_2 \sigma_3 \sigma_4 \sigma_5 \ldots) = 1\sigma_1 \sigma_2 \sigma_3 \sigma_4 \sigma_5 \sigma_6 \ldots,$$

where "1" is one of the symbols, is a contraction mapping with respect to the code space metric. Its fixed point is

$$1111111111111111111111111111111111111111\ldots$$

3.10.   References

[FE] Michael Barnsley, *Fractals Everywhere*. Academic Press, Boston (1988).

[HW] Hermann Weyl, *Symmetry in The World of Mathematics* (Editor: James R. Newman). Simon & Schuster, New York (1956).

[BM] Bert Mendelson, *Introduction to Topology*, Blackie and Son Limited, London (1963).

4

Fractal Image Compression I: IFS Fractals

4.1. Goals of This Chapter

The purpose of this chapter is to present the basic theory of *iterated function systems (IFS theory)*, and the application of this theory to fractal image compression. We describe the Hausdorff space $\mathcal{H}$, contraction mappings on $\mathcal{H}$, and the definition of an IFS. We focus on IFS's made of affine transformations, and on the resulting IFS fractals. Such IFS fractals can be used as approximants for real world images; they have the property that they are themselves models for real world images, and, at the same time, they are fully defined by finite strings of zeros and ones; they are thus suitable for compression. IFS fractals can be used to approximate real world images in particular because they can be controlled as approximating entities with the aid of the collage theorem.

We consider the approximation of black-and-white (binary) images using attractors of iterated function systems of affine transformations. We also consider the compression of real world images, represented by the space $\mathcal{P}$ of normalized Borel measures supported on $\square$, using IFS fractals. IFS fractals generated by affine transformations are suitable for this task because of the remarkable fact that an explicit moment theory is available for them.

Both IFS theory and FT theory provide means to associate finite strings of symbols with resolution independent images. They provide fundamental

Figure 4.1. Some members of the space $\mathcal{H}(\Box)$.

mechanisms used in fractal image compression. The material in this chapter is an introduction to fractal image compression. It also serves as the basis for making a connection between *IFS fractals* and *code space*, which is needed elsewhere in this book.

4.2. Spaces of Images — the Hausdorff Space $\mathcal{H}$

We describe a convenient space $\mathcal{H}$ where one can study important subsets of metric spaces such as ($\Box$, Euclidean). We restrict attention to complete metric spaces, since this is the only case needed for the study of fractal image compression. We have in mind the case where $(\mathbf{X}, d)$ is $\mathbb{R}^2$ with the Euclidean metric; but the general construction is useful also. In particular, when we wish to discuss drawings, pictures, and other "black on white" subsets of $\mathbb{R}^2$, it is convenient to use the metric space $(\mathcal{H}(\mathbb{R}^2), h(\text{Euclidean}))$. By way of an intuitive introduction, some elements of this space are illustrated in Fig. 4.1.

Definition *Let $(\mathbf{X}, d)$ be a complete metric space. Then $\mathcal{H}(\mathbf{X})$ denotes the space whose points are the compact subsets of $\mathbf{X}$, other than the empty set.*

Definition *Let $(\mathbf{X}, d)$ be a complete metric space, $x \in \mathbf{X}$, and $B \in \mathcal{H}(\mathbf{X})$.*

Define

$$d(x, B) = \min\{d(x, y) : y \in B\}.$$

$d(x, B)$ *is called the* distance *from the point x to the set B.*

Definition *Let $(\mathbf{X}, d)$ be a complete metric space. Let A and B belong to $\mathcal{H}(\mathbf{X})$. Define*

$$d(A, B) = \max\{d(x, B) : x \in A\}.$$

$d(A, B)$ *is called the* distance *from the set $A \in \mathcal{H}(\mathbf{X})$ to the set $B \in \mathcal{H}(\mathbf{X})$.*

Lemma *Let $(\mathbf{X}, d)$ be a complete metric space. If A, B, and C belong to $\mathcal{H}(\mathbf{X})$, then*

$$d(A \cup B, C) = d(A, C) \vee d(B, C),$$

where $x \vee y$ means the maximum of x and y.

Definition *Let $(\mathbf{X}, d)$ be a complete metric space. Then the* Hausdorff distance *between the points A and B in $\mathcal{H}(\mathbf{X})$ is defined by*

$$h(A, B) = d(A, B) \vee d(B, A).$$

We also call h the Hausdorff metric *on $\mathcal{H}$.*

Lemma *Let $(\mathbf{X}, d)$ be a complete metric space. Then for all A, B, C, D in $\mathcal{H}(\mathbf{X})$,*

$$h(A \cup B, C \cup D) \leq h(A, C) \vee d(B, D).$$

Lemma *Let $(\mathbf{X}, d)$ be a complete metric space. Let A and B be in $\mathcal{H}(\mathbf{X})$. Let $\epsilon > 0$. Then*

$$h(A, B) \leq \epsilon \iff A \subset B + \epsilon \text{ and } B \subset A + \epsilon,$$

where $A + \epsilon = \{x \in \mathbf{X} : d(x, A) \leq \epsilon\}$.

The preceding results, which are presented in greater detail in [FE], are useful in proving the following central theorem. This theorem allows us to assert the existence of IFS fractals.

Theorem *Let $(\mathbf{X}, d)$ be a complete metric space. Then $\mathcal{H}(\mathbf{X}, h)$ is a complete metric space. Moreover, if $\{A_n \in \mathcal{H}(\mathbf{X}) : n = 1, 2, \ldots\}$ is a Cauchy sequence, then*

$$A = \lim_{n \to \infty} A_n \in \mathcal{H}(\mathbf{X})$$

can be characterized as

$$A = \{x \in \mathbf{X} : \exists \ a \ Cauchy \ sequence \ \{x_n \in A_n\} \ convergent \ to \ x\}.$$

Proof. See [FE] and references therein.

Let $(\mathbf{X}, d)$ be a metric space and let $(\mathcal{H}(\mathbf{X}), h(d))$ denote the associated Hausdorff space, with the Hausdorff metric $h(d)$ described before. We use the notation $h(d)$ to show that d is the underlying metric for the Hausdorff metric h.

4.3. Contraction Mappings on the Space $\mathcal{H}$

Lemma *Let $w : \mathbf{X} \to \mathbf{X}$ be a contraction mapping on the metric space $(\mathbf{X}, d)$. Then w is continuous.*

Proof. Let $\epsilon > 0$ be given. Let $s > 0$ be a contractivity factor for w. Then

$$d(w(x), w(y)) \le s \, d(x, y) < \epsilon$$

whenever $d(x, y) < \delta$, where $\delta = \epsilon/s$. This completes the proof.

Lemma *Let $w : \mathbf{X} \to \mathbf{X}$ be a continuous mapping on the metric space $(\mathbf{X}, d)$. Then w maps $\mathcal{H}(\mathbf{X})$ into itself.*

Proof. Let S be a nonempty compact subset of $\mathbf{X}$. Then clearly $w(S) = \{w(x) : x \in S\}$ is nonempty. We want to show that $w(S)$ is compact. Let $\{y_n = w(x_n)\}$ be an infinite sequence of points in S. Then $\{x_n\}$ is an infinite sequence of points in S. Since S is compact, there is a subsequence $\{x_{N_n}\}$ that converges to a point $\hat{x} \in S$; but then the continuity of w implies that $\{y_{N_n} = f(x_{N_n})\}$ is a subsequence of $\{y_n\}$ that converges to $\hat{y} \in w(S)$. This completes the proof.

The following lemma tells us how to make a contraction mapping on $(\mathcal{H}(\mathbf{X}), h)$ out of a contraction mapping on $(\mathbf{X}, d)$.

Lemma *Let $w : \mathbf{X} \to \mathbf{X}$ be a contraction mapping on the metric space $(\mathbf{X}, d)$ with contractivity factor s. Then $w : \mathcal{H}(\mathbf{X}) \to \mathcal{H}(\mathbf{X})$ defined by*

$$w(B) = \{w(x) : x \in B\}, \ \forall \, B \in \mathcal{H}(\mathbf{X})$$

is a contraction mapping on $(\mathcal{H}(\mathbf{X}), h(d))$ with contractivity factor s.

Proof. From Lemma 1, it follows that $w : \mathbf{X} \to \mathbf{X}$ is continuous. Hence, by Lemma 2, w maps $\mathcal{H}(\mathbf{X})$ into itself. Now let $B, C \in \mathcal{H}(\mathbf{X})$. Then

$$
\begin{aligned}
d(w(B), w(C)) &= \max\{\min\{d(w(x), w(y)) : y \in C\} : x \in B\} \\
&\leq \max\{\min\{s \cdot d(x, y) : y \in C\} : x \in B\} \\
&= s \cdot d(B, C).
\end{aligned}
$$

Similarly, $d(w(C), w(B)) \leq s \cdot d(C, B)$. Hence,

$$
\begin{aligned}
h(w(B), w(C)) &= d(w(B), w(C)) \vee d(w(C), w(B)) \\
&\leq s \cdot d(B, C) \vee d(C, B) \leq s \cdot d(B, C).
\end{aligned}
$$

This completes the proof.

The next lemma provides a fundamental method for combining contraction mappings on $(\mathcal{H}(\mathbf{X}), h)$ to produce new contraction mappings on $(\mathcal{H}(\mathbf{X}), h)$. This method is distinct from the obvious one of composition.

Lemma *Let $(\mathbf{X}, d)$ be a metric space. Let $\{w_n : n = 1, 2, \ldots, N\}$ be contraction mappings on $(\mathcal{H}(\mathbf{X}), h)$. Let the contractivity factor for w_n be denoted by s_n for each n. Define $W : \mathcal{H}(\mathbf{X}) \to \mathcal{H}(\mathbf{X})$ by*

$$
\begin{aligned}
W(B) &= w_1(B) \cup w_2(B) \cup \ldots \cup w_N(B) \\
&= \bigcup_{n=1}^{N} w_n(B), \quad \text{for each } B \in \mathcal{H}(\mathbf{X}).
\end{aligned}
$$

Then W is a contraction mapping with contractivity factor $s = \max\{s_n : n = 1, 2, \ldots, N\}$.

Proof. We demonstrate the claim for $N = 2$. An inductive argument then completes the proof. Let $B, C \in \mathcal{H}(\mathbf{X})$. We have

$$
\begin{aligned}
h(W(B), W(C)) &= h(w_1(B) \cup w_2(B), w_1(C) \cup w_2(C)) \\
&\leq h(w_1(B), w_1(C)) \vee h(w_2(B), w_2(C)) \\
&\leq s_1 h(B, C) \vee s_2 h(B, C) \leq s h(B, C).
\end{aligned}
$$

This completes the proof.

4.4. Iterated Function Systems

The name *iterated function system* was coined in [BD]. There are many other relevant references, including [M1], [MW], [DS], [H], [K1], and [K2].

Definition *A (hyperbolic)* iterated function system *consists of a complete metric space* $(\mathbf{X}, d)$ *together with a finite set of contraction mappings* $w_n :$ $\mathbf{X} \to \mathbf{X}$, *with respective contractivity factors* s_n, *for* $n = 1, 2, \ldots, N$. *The abbreviation "IFS" is used for "iterated function system." The notation for this IFS is* $\{\mathbf{X}; w_n, n = 1, 2, \ldots, N\}$ *and its contractivity factor is* $s = \max\{s_n : n = 1, 2, \ldots, N\}$.

We put the word *hyperbolic* in parentheses in this definition because it is usually dropped in practice. Moreover, we will sometimes use the nomenclature IFS to mean simply a finite set of maps acting on a metric space, with no particular conditions imposed upon the maps.

The following theorem summarizes the main facts so far about a hyperbolic IFS.

Theorem (The IFS Theorem) *Let* $\{\mathbf{X}; w_n, n = 1, 2, \ldots, N\}$ *be a hyperbolic iterated function system with contractivity factor* s. *Then the transformation* $W : \mathcal{H}(\mathbf{X}) \to \mathcal{H}(\mathbf{X})$ *defined by*

$$W(B) = \bigcup_{n=1}^{N} w_n(B),$$

for all $B \in \mathcal{H}(\mathbf{X})$, *is a contraction mapping on the complete metric space* $(\mathcal{H}(\mathbf{X}), h(d))$ *with contractivity factor* s; *that is*

$$h(W(B), W(C)) \leq s \cdot h(B, C)$$

for all $B, C \in \mathcal{H}(\mathbf{X})$. *It has a unique fixed point,* $A \in \mathcal{H}(\mathbf{X})$, *which obeys*

$$A = W(A) = \bigcup_{n=1}^{N} w_n(A),$$

and is given by $A = \lim_{n \to \infty} W^{\circ n}(B)$ *for any* $B \in \mathcal{H}(\mathbf{X})$.

Proof. See [FE].

Definition *The fixed point* $A \in \mathcal{H}(\mathbf{X})$ *described in the IFS Theorem is called the* attractor *of the IFS.*

Many examples of iterated function systems and their attractors can be found in the literature. We note in particular the following sources: [AH], [B], [BD], [BJMRS], [BAS], [BEHL], [BS], [CEJ], [D], [DFDS], [FE], [GE], [HD], [H], [PJS], [M1], [M2], [MMC], and [MW]. See also the next sections.

A simple example of an IFS is $\{\mathbb{R}; w_1(x) = 0, w_2(x) = \frac{2}{3}x + \frac{1}{3}\}$. Its attractor consists of a countable increasing sequence of real points $\{x_n : n = 0, 1, 2, \ldots\}$ together with $\{0\}$, where

$$x_n = \frac{2^n}{3^{n+1}}.$$

A different type of example of an IFS involves code space. Let (Σ, d) be the code space of three symbols $\{0, 1, 2\}$, with metric

$$d(x, y) = \sum_{n=1}^{\infty} \frac{|x_n - y_n|}{4^n}.$$

Define $w_1 : \Sigma \to \Sigma$ by $w_1(x) = 0x_1x_2x_3\ldots$ and $w_2(x) = 2x_1x_2x_3\ldots$. Then w_1 and w_2 are both contraction mappings. The attractor of the IFS $\{\Sigma; w_1, w_2\}$ is a subset of Σ with a structure similar to that of the classical Cantor set $\mathcal{C}$. If we include in the IFS a third transformation defined by $w_3(x)1x_1x_2x_3\ldots$, the attractor becomes the whole space Σ.

$\star$ The rest of this section, which deals with another method for making contraction mappings on $\mathcal{H}(\mathbf{X})$, can be omitted on a first reading.$\star$

Definition *Let* $(\mathbf{X}, d)$ *be a metric space and let* $C \in \mathcal{H}(\mathbf{X})$. *Define a transformation* $w_0 : \mathcal{H}(\mathbf{X}) \to \mathcal{H}(\mathbf{X})$ *by* $w_0(B) = C$ *for all* $B \in \mathcal{H}(\mathbf{X})$. *Then* w_0 *is called a* condensation transformation *and* C *is called the associated* condensation set.

Observe that a condensation transformation $w_0 : \mathcal{H}(\mathbf{X}) \to \mathcal{H}(\mathbf{X})$ is a contraction mapping on the metric space $(\mathcal{H}(\mathbf{X}), h(d))$, with contractivity factor equal to zero, and that its unique fixed point is the condensation set.

Definition *Let* $\{\mathbf{X}; w_1, w_2, \ldots, w_N\}$ *be a hyperbolic IFS with contractivity factor* $0 \leq s < 1$. *Let* $w_0 : \mathcal{H}(\mathbf{X}) \to \mathcal{H}(\mathbf{X})$ *be a condensation transformation. Then* $\{\mathbf{X}; w_0, w_1, \ldots, w_N\}$ *is called a (hyperbolic) IFS with condensation, with contractivity factor* s.

The IFS Theorem can be generalized to the case of an IFS with condensation.

Theorem (The IFS Condensation Theorem)
Let $\{\mathbf{X}; w_n : n = 0, 1, 2, \ldots, N\}$ *be a hyperbolic iterated function system with condensation, with contractivity factor* s. *Then the transformation*

$W : \mathcal{H}(\mathbf{X}) \to \mathcal{H}(\mathbf{X})$ *defined by*

$$W(B) = \bigcup_{n=0}^{N} w_n(B), \quad \forall B \in \mathcal{H}(\mathbf{X}),$$

is a contraction mapping on the complete metric space $(\mathcal{H}(\mathbf{X}), h(d))$ *with contractivity factor* s; *that is*

$$h(W(B), W(C)) \le s \cdot h(B, C), \quad \forall B, C \in \mathcal{H}(\mathbf{X}).$$

Its unique fixed point $A \in \mathcal{H}(\mathbf{X})$ *obeys*

$$A = W(A) = \bigcup_{n=0}^{N} w_n(A)$$

and is given by $A = \lim_{n \to \infty} W^{\circ n}(B)$ *for any* $B \in \mathcal{H}(\mathbf{X})$.

Proof. See [FE].

4.5. Iterated Function Systems of Affine Transformations in $\mathbb{R}^2$

Consider the IFS $\{\mathbb{R}^2; w_1, w_2, w_3\}$, where the w_i are affine transformations in $\mathbb{R}^2$:

$$w_1 \begin{bmatrix} x \\ y \end{bmatrix} = \begin{bmatrix} 0.5 & 0 \\ 0 & 0.5 \end{bmatrix} \begin{bmatrix} x \\ y \end{bmatrix} + \begin{bmatrix} 0 \\ 0 \end{bmatrix},$$

$$w_2 \begin{bmatrix} x \\ y \end{bmatrix} = \begin{bmatrix} 0.5 & 0 \\ 0 & 0.5 \end{bmatrix} \begin{bmatrix} x \\ y \end{bmatrix} + \begin{bmatrix} 100 \\ 0 \end{bmatrix},$$

$$w_3 \begin{bmatrix} x \\ y \end{bmatrix} = \begin{bmatrix} 0.5 & 0 \\ 0 & 0.5 \end{bmatrix} \begin{bmatrix} x \\ y \end{bmatrix} + \begin{bmatrix} 30 \\ 30 \end{bmatrix}.$$

The attractor of this IFS is a Sierpinski triangle with vertices at the points (0,0), (200, 0) and (60, 60), as illustrated in Fig. 4.2.

The notation for an IFS of affine maps using matrices is inefficient. Let us agree to write

$$w_i(x) = w_i \begin{bmatrix} x \\ y \end{bmatrix} = \begin{bmatrix} a_i & b_i \\ c_i & d_i \end{bmatrix} \begin{bmatrix} x \\ y \end{bmatrix} + \begin{bmatrix} e_i \\ f_i \end{bmatrix} = A_i x + t_i.$$

Then the IFS $\{\mathbb{R}^2; w_1, w_2, w_3\}$, can be expressed as shown in Table 4.1.

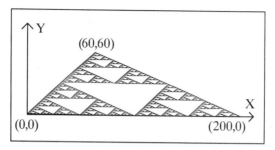

Figure 4.2. Sierpinski triangle with vertices at the points (0,0), (200, 0), and (60, 60).

Table 4.1 also provides a number p_i associated with w_i for $i = 1, 2, 3$. These numbers can be interpreted as probabilities. In the more general case of the IFS $\{\mathbf{X}; w_n : n = 1, 2, \ldots, N\}$, there would be N such numbers $\{p_i : i = 1, 2, \ldots N\}$, which obey

$$p_1 + p_2 + p_3 + \ldots + p_N = 1 \quad \text{and } p_i > 0 \ \text{ for } i = 1, 2, \ldots N.$$

These numbers are related to the measure theory of IFS attractors, and play a role in the computation of images of the attractor of an IFS attractor using the random iteration algorithm [FE], and also using the grayscale photocopy machine algorithm, which is described later in this chapter. They play no role in the photocopy machine algorithm as applied to "black-and-white" images. In connection with the random iteration algorithm, their values can be taken to be

$$p_i \approx \frac{|\det A_i|}{\sum_{i=1}^{N} |A_i|} = \frac{|a_i d_i - b_i c_i|}{\sum_{i=1}^{N} |a_i d_i - b_i c_i|} \quad \text{for } i = 1, 2, \ldots N.$$

Here, the symbol $\approx$ means *approximately equal to*. If, for some i, $\det A_i = 0$, then p_i should be assigned a small positive number, such as 0.001. Other situations should be treated empirically. We refer to the data in Table 4.1 as an IFS *code*. Other IFS codes are given in Tables 4.2, 4.3, and 4.4.

Table 4.1. IFS code for a Sierpinski triangle.

w	a	b	c	d	e	f	p
1	0.5	0	0	0.5	0	0	0.33
2	0.5	0	0	0.5	100	0	0.33
3	0.5	0	0	0.5	30	30	0.34

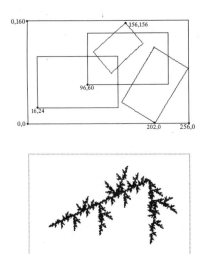

Figure 4.3. Attractor of an IFS computed with the aid of the random iteration algorithm. The IFS code is

a	b	c	d	e	f
0.50	0.00	0.00	0.50	16	24
0.21	−.33	0.33	0.21	202	0
0.50	0.00	0.00	0.50	96	60
−.20	0.18	−.18	−.20	156	156

The attractor of an IFS can be computed with the aid of the random iteration algorithm [FE]. In Figs. 4.3 to 4.7, we show a number of different IFS's of affine transformations, together with their attractors. In each case, the affine transformations that constitute the IFS are represented by their action on a rectangle in $\mathbb{R}^2$ with corners at the points $(0, 0)$, $(0, 160)$, $(256, 0)$ and $(256, 160)$. These images were all computed using the *Desktop Fractal Design System* [DFDS1], which makes use of the random iteration algorithm.

In Figs 4.8 to 4.11, we show a number of different IFS's of affine transformations, each with a condensation set, and the corresponding attractor. These images were computed using the *Desktop Fractal Design System, version 2.0* [DFDS2].

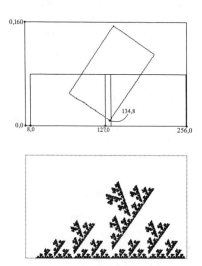

Figure 4.4. Attractor of an IFS computed with the aid of the random iteration algorithm. The IFS code is

a	b	c	d	e	f
0.50	0.00	0.00	0.50	8	0
0.50	0.00	0.00	0.50	127	0
0.28	−.40	0.40	0.28	134	8

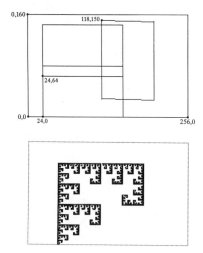

Figure 4.5. Attractor of an IFS computed with the aid of the random iteration algorithm. The IFS code is

a	b	c	d	e	f
0.00	0.53	−.48	0.00	118	150
0.50	0.00	0.00	0.50	24	0
0.50	0.00	0.00	0.50	24	64

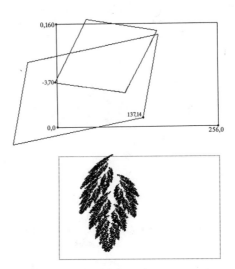

Figure 4.6. Attractor of an IFS computed with the aid of the random iteration algorithm. The IFS code is

a	b	c	d	e	f
0.44	0.32	−.07	0.61	−3	70
−.82	0.16	−.16	−.81	137	14

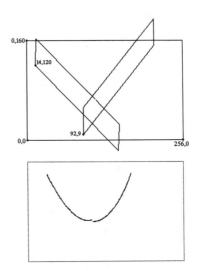

Figure 4.7. Attractor of an IFS computed with the aid of the random iteration algorithm. The IFS code is

a	b	c	d	e	f
0.53	0.01	−.54	0.27	14	120
−.46	0.00	−.56	0.92	92	9

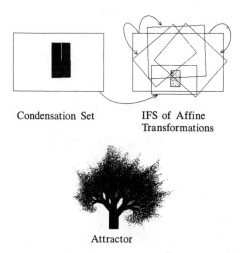

Condensation Set   IFS of Affine
Transformations

Attractor

Figure 4.8. An IFS with condensation and its attractor.

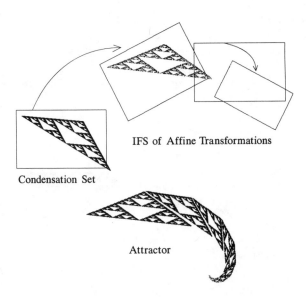

IFS of Affine Transformations

Condensation Set

Attractor

Figure 4.9. IFS with condensation and its attractor.

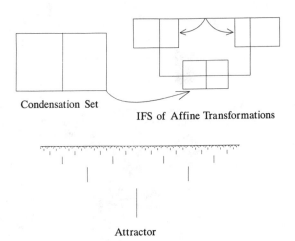

Condensation Set

IFS of Affine Transformations

Attractor

Figure 4.10. IFS with condensation and its attractor.

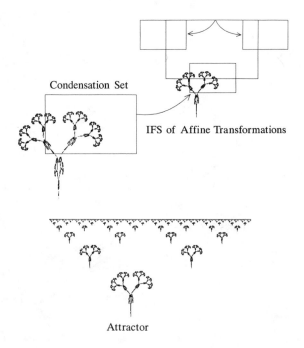

Condensation Set

IFS of Affine Transformations

Attractor

Figure 4.11. IFS with condensation and its attractor.

4.6. The Photocopy Machine Algorithm for Computing the Attractor of an IFS

According to the IFS theorem, in Section 4.4, we have the following result, which suggests methods for constructing the attractor of an IFS. Let $\{\mathbb{R}^2; w_1, w_2, \ldots, w_N\}$ be a hyperbolic IFS. Choose a compact set $A_0 \subset \mathbb{R}^2$. Then we can compute successively $A_n = W^{\circ n}(A)$ according to

$$A_{n+1} = \bigcup_{j=1}^{N} w_j(A_n) \text{ for } n = 1, 2, \ldots;$$

that is, we can construct a sequence $\{A_n : n = 0, 1, 2, 3, \ldots\} \subset \mathcal{H}(\mathbb{R}^2)$. According to the IFS theorem, the sequence $\{A_n\}$ converges to the attractor of the IFS in the Hausdorff metric. This provides a procedure for calculating successive approximations for the attractor of the IFS.

One way of putting this procedure into practice, in the case where the w_n are similitudes, is with the aid of a photocopy machine, as follows. Figure 4.12(a) shows a rectangular piece of paper with three rectangles drawn on it, each smaller rectangle being a copy of the boundary of the sheet of paper scaled down by a factor 0.4096. Eight identical copies of this sheet of paper are made; we refer to these as the master sheets. Next, three copies of a page of text, also shrunk by a factor 0.4096, are produced and glued to one of the master sheets, one small page of text in each rectangle, as shown in Fig. 4.12(b). Three copies of the resulting image are now made, also shrunk down by a factor 0.4096, and pasted into the rectangles marked on a second master sheet, as illustrated in Fig. 4.12(c). The process is repeated over and over, resulting in the sequence of images shown in Figs. 4.12(b)–(h). The image is changed successively by less and less — that is, the process appears to produce a convergent sequence of images, in line with our theoretical promise. The *final* image is essentially unchanged when put through the process again — it represents a *fixed picture*, the attractor, for the transformation process. It is the *fractal* defined by the three affine transformations on the master sheet. Another example of the photocopy machine algorithm is given in Figs. 4.13 (a)–(l). This time the final image is an approximately straight line. In Fig. 4.14 we show several images produced in the course of carrying out the photocopy machine algorithm in an inaccurate manner, starting from an image of a real fern.

Figures 4.15 and 4.16 show the result of applying the photocopy machine algorithm using a Canon PC-11 photocopier, this time with a condensation set: in each case, the preceding image is left in place at each generation.

We conceptually generalize the photocopy machine algorithm in several

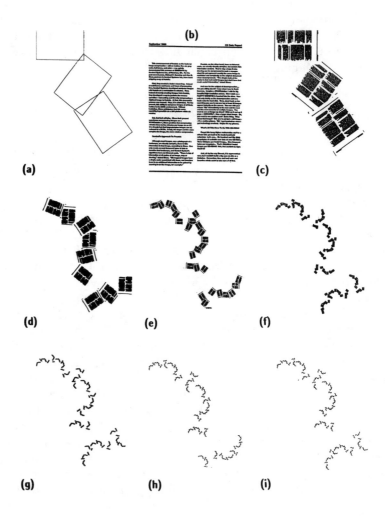

Figure 4.12. (a)–(i) The photocopy machine algorithm is applied to a page of text to make a fractal.

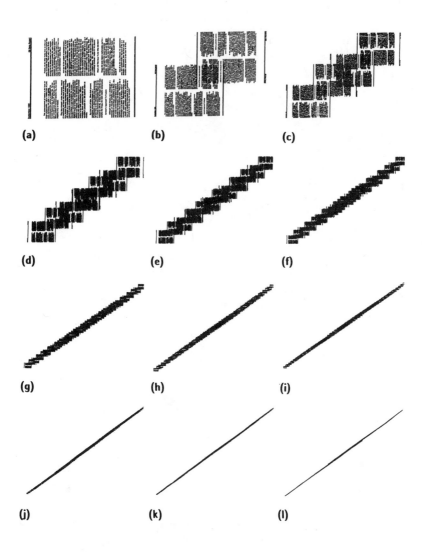

Figure 4.13. (a)–(l) Another example of the photocopy machine algorithm. This time the *final image* is an approximately straight line.

Figure 4.14. Several images produced in the course of carrying out the photocopy machine algorithm in an inaccurate manner, starting from an image of a real fern.

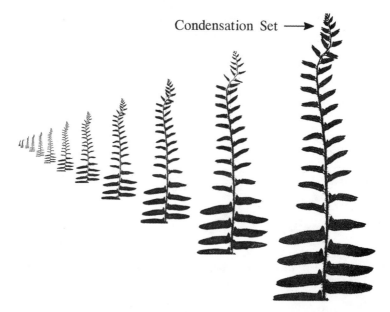

Figure 4.15. The result of applying the photocopy machine algorithm using a Canon PC-11 photocopier, with a condensation set: the preceding image is left in place during each iteration.

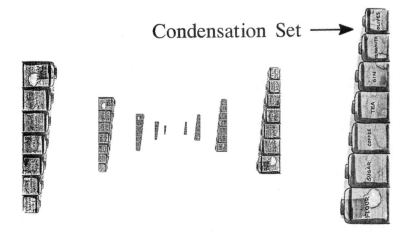

Figure 4.16. Another example of the photocopy machine algorithm with a condensation set.

ways. First, we imagine that all of the transformations are applied by the copier simultaneously: that is, one does not have to go through the laborious process, in the course of a single iteration, of making a number of shrunken copies, then pasting them into a single image. Second, we allow arbitrary transformations, in particular, arbitrary affine transformations, to be performed by the copier. Third, as is discussed in Section 4.10, we allow the copier to act upon grayscale images rather than simply black-and-white images.

4.7.   C Source Code for Computing the Attractor of an IFS

We illustrate the implementation of the photocopy machine algorithm on a personal computer. The following program computes and plots successive sets A_{n+1} starting from an initial set A_0 , in this case a square, using the IFS code in Table 4.1. The program is written for compilation using the Turbo C compiler by Borland; for other standard C compilers, the graphics output portion of the code would have to be modified. The program is designed to run under DOS on an IBM PC with an Intel 80286, 80386, or 80486 processor and VGA graphics. The uncompiled program consists of two files: IFS.H, which is a header file, and IFS.C, which is the main program.

```
-------------------------------------------------
FILE NAME: IFS.H
-------------------------------------------------
#include<stdio.h>
#define WIDTH 148
#define ITERATES 8
#define MAPS 3

typedef unsigned char Pixel;
typedef struct rectangle {Pixel **pixels;} Rectangle;
void show_rectangle(Rectangle *screen),
  apply_affine_maps(Rectangle *screen1, Rectangle *screen2),
  clear_rectangle(Rectangle *screen);

static float a[MAPS] = {0.5, 0.5, 0.5},
     b[MAPS] = {0,0,0},
     c[MAPS] = {0,0,0},
     d[MAPS] = {.5,.5,.5},
     e[MAPS] = {1,WIDTH/2,WIDTH/2},
     f[MAPS] = {1,1,WIDTH/2};


-------------------------------------------------
FILE NAME: IFS.C
-------------------------------------------------
#include <stdio.h>
#include <graphics.h>
#include <alloc.h>
#include "ifs.h"

main()
{
  Rectangle screen1, screen2;
  int i,j,iterate;

/* Turbo C Graphics Routines (modify as necessary) */

  int gdriver = DETECT, gmode, errorcode;
  initgraph(&gdriver,&gmode,"");
  errorcode=graphresult();
  if (errorcode != grOk)
  {
  fprintf(stderr,"Graphics error: %s\n",
```

```
      grapherrormsg(errorcode));
    exit(1);
    }

/* Initialize screen1 and screen2 */

  screen1.pixels=(Pixel **) calloc(WIDTH,sizeof(Pixel *));
  screen2.pixels=(Pixel **) calloc(WIDTH,sizeof(Pixel *));
  for (i=0;i<WIDTH;i++)
    {
      screen1.pixels[i]=(Pixel *)
        calloc(WIDTH,sizeof(Pixel));
      screen2.pixels[i]=(Pixel *)
        calloc(WIDTH,sizeof(Pixel));
    }

  for (i=0;i<WIDTH;i++)
    for (j=0;j<WIDTH;j++)
        screen1.pixels[i][j] = BLACK;

  for (i=0;i<WIDTH;i++)
    screen1.pixels[0][i]=
    screen1.pixels[WIDTH-1][i]=
    screen1.pixels[i][0]=
    screen1.pixels[i][WIDTH-1]=WHITE;

/* Loop */

  for (iterate=0;iterate<ITERATES/2;iterate++)
    {
      /* omit for condensation set */
      clear_rectangle(&screen2);
      apply_affine_maps(&screen1,&screen2);
      show_rectangle(&screen2);

      /* omit for condensation set */
      clear_rectangle(&screen1);
      apply_affine_maps(&screen2,&screen1);
      show_rectangle(&screen1);
    }

/* pause */
```

```
  getch();

/* close graphics screen */

  closegraph();
  return(0);
}

void show_rectangle(Rectangle *screen)
  {
    int x,y;
    for (x=0;x<WIDTH;x++)
      for (y=0;y<WIDTH;y++)
 putpixel(x,y,screen->pixels[x][y]);
  }

void clear_rectangle(Rectangle *screen)
  {
    int x,y;
    for (x=0;x<WIDTH;x++)
      for (y=0;y<WIDTH;y++)
 screen->pixels[x][y]=BLACK;
  }

void apply_affine_maps(Rectangle *screen1,
  Rectangle *screen2)
{
  int x,y,map;
  for (x=0;x<WIDTH;x++)
    for (y=0;y<WIDTH;y++)
      {
        if (screen1->pixels[x][y]==WHITE)
          {
            for (map=0;map<MAPS;map++)
              screen2->pixels[a[map]*x+b[map]*y+
                e[map]][c[map]*x+d[map]*y+f[map]]=WHITE;
          }
      }
}
```

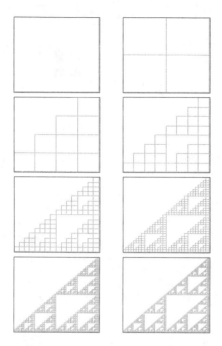

Figure 4.17. A printout of screens captured when IFS.EXE is run.

Compile Instruction:
To compile the object module, enter the DOS command line:
```
tcc -ms -c -v IFS.C
```
To link the object module IFS.C with Turbo C graphics library, and produce the executable function IFS.EXE, enter the Turbo C command line:
```
tcc -ms -v IFS.OBJ graphics.lib
```
Running Instructions:
To run IFS.EXE, enter the DOS command line:
```
IFS
```
Sample Output:
   A printout of screen capture as a result of running the program is shown in Fig. 4.17.

   The reader can modify the program to use, for example, the data in Tables 4.2, 4.3, or 4.4 instead of that from Table 4.1, by editing the file IFS.H.

   In Fig. 4.18, we show several generations resulting from applying the photocopy machine algorithm on a PC, with general affine transformations. The starting image in this case is a black square.

Figure 4.18. A number of generations resulting from applying the photocopy machine algorithm digitally, with general affine transformations. The starting image in this case is a filled square.

Table 4.2. IFS code for a Square.

w	a	b	c	d	e	f	p
1	0.5	0	0	0.5	1	1	0.25
2	0.5	0	0	0.5	50	1	0.25
3	0.5	0	0	0.5	1	50	0.25
4	0.5	0	0	0.5	50	50	0.25

Table 4.3. IFS code for a fern.

w	a	b	c	d	e	f	p
1	0	0	0	0.16	0	0	0.01
2	0.85	0.04	-0.04	0.85	0	1.6	0.85
3	0.2	-0.26	0.23	0.22	0	1.6	0.07
4	-0.15	0.28	0.26	0.24	0	0.44	0.07

Table 4.4. IFS code for a fractal tree.

w	a	b	c	d	e	f	p
1	0	0	0	0.5	0	0	0.05
2	0.42	-0.42	0.42	0.42	0	0.2	0.4
3	0.42	0.42	-0.42	0.42	0	0.2	0.4
4	0.1	0	0	0.1	0	0.2	0.15

4.8.   The Collage Theorem

The following theorem is central to the design of IFS's whose attractors are close to given sets. It is a prototype for many variants of the same basic principle, which is used in diverse fractal image compressions systems. The general principle is discussed further in Section 6.2.

Theorem (The Collage Theorem)   *Let* $(\mathbf{X}, d)$ *be a complete metric space. Let* $T \in \mathcal{H}(\mathbf{X})$ *be given, and let* $\epsilon \geq 0$ *be given. Choose an IFS (or IFS with condensation)* $\{\mathbf{X}; (w_0), w_1, w_2, \ldots, w_N\}$ *with contractivity factor* $0 \leq s < 1$ *so that*

$$h\left(T, \bigcup_{n=1_{(n=0)}}^{N} w_n(T)\right) \leq \epsilon,$$

where $h(d)$ *is the Hausdorff metric. Then*

$$h(T, A) \leq \frac{\epsilon}{1} - s,$$

where A *is the attractor of the IFS. Equivalently,*

$$h(T, A) \leq (1 - s)^{-1} h\left(T, \bigcup_{n=1_{(n=0)}}^{N} w_n(T)\right) \quad \text{for all } T \in \mathcal{H}(\mathbf{X}).$$

Proof.   See [FE].

4.9.   Fractal Image Compression Using IFS Fractals

The collage theorem tells us that to find an IFS whose attractor is *close to* or *looks like* a given set, one must try to find a set of transformations, contraction mappings on a suitable space within which the given set lies, such that the union, or *collage*, of the images of the given set under the transformations is close to or looks like the given set. The degree to which two images *look alike* is measured using the Hausdorff metric.

The central goal of fractal image compression is to find resolution independent models, defined by finite length (and hopefully short) strings of zeros and ones, for real world images. If our real world image is one of many basic shapes, such as a leaf or a letter of the alphabet, or a black-and-white silhouette of a fern, or a black cat sitting in a field of snow, or a rook's feather on a white starched sheet, or a black crack in a white teacup, or a snowflake lying on a frozen lump of coal, or a circle or a square, or a Julia set, or the outline of a pine tree or many pine trees against the skyline at dusk, or a component of an image received, or to be sent, via a fax machine, or the graph of a complicated function, or one of a multitude of familiar shapes and forms, such that a model is appropriately made in black-and-white alone, as described in (i) of Section 2.3; in such cases, one can achieve fractal image compression via the *IFS compression algorithm*, which is an interactive image modeling method based on the collage theorem [Patent 1], [BJMRS].

The IFS compression algorithm starts from a target image T, which lies in $\square$. T may be either a digitized image (for example, a white leaf on a black background) or a polygonalized approximation (for example, a polygonalized leaf boundary). T is rendered on a computer graphics monitor. An affine transformation,

$$w_1(x) = w_1 \begin{bmatrix} x \\ y \end{bmatrix} = \begin{bmatrix} a_1 & b_1 \\ c_1 & d_1 \end{bmatrix} \begin{bmatrix} x \\ y \end{bmatrix} + \begin{bmatrix} e_1 \\ f_1 \end{bmatrix} = A_1 x + t_1,$$

is introduced, with coefficients initialized at $a_1 = d_1 = 0.25, b_1 = c_1 = 0.25$. The image $w_1(T)$ is displayed on the monitor in a different color from T. The image $w_1(T)$ is a quarter-sized copy of T, centered closer to the point (0,0). The user now interactively adjusts the coefficients by specifying changes with a mouse or some other interaction technique, so that the image $w_1(T)$ is variously translated, rotated, and sheared on the screen. The goal of the user is to transform $w_1(T)$ so that it lies over a part of T. It is important that the dimensions of $w_1(T)$ are smaller than those of T, to ensure that w_1 is a contraction. Once $w_1(T)$ is suitably positioned, it is fixed, its coefficients are recorded, and a new affine transformation $w_2(x)$ and a new subcopy $w_2(T)$ are introduced. The image w_2 is adjusted interactively until $w_2(T)$ covers a subset of those pixels (assuming we are working with a pixel-based representation) in T that are not in $w_1(T)$. Overlaps between $w_1(T)$ and $w_2(T)$ are allowed, but in general should be made as small as possible.

In this manner, the user determines a set of contractive affine transformations $\{w_1, w_2, w_3, \ldots, w_N\}$ with this property: the original target T, and the set

$$\tilde{T} = \bigcup_{n=1}^{N} w_n(T)$$

are visually close, while N is as small as possible. The mathematical indicator of the closeness of T and $\tilde{T}$ is the Hausdorff distance between them,

Figure 4.19. Illustration of good and bad collages of a polygonal leaf target and the corresponding attractors.

$h(T, \tilde{T})$. By "visually close", we mean that "$h(T, \tilde{T})$ is small." The coefficients of the transformations $\{w_1, w_2, w_3, \ldots, w_N\}$ thus determined are stored. The collage theorem assures us that the attractor A of this IFS will also be visually close to T. Moreover, if $T = \tilde{T}$, then $A = T$.

Not only does A approximate T, but also it provides a resolution independent model for it, while using only a finite string of zeros and ones. The IFS compression algorithm is illustrated in Fig. 4.19, which shows a polygonal leaf target T at the upper left and the lower left. In each case, T has been approximately covered by four affine transformations of itself. The task has been poorly carried out in the lower image and well-done in the upper image. The corresponding attractors are shown on the right-hand side: the upper one is much closer to the target because the collage is better.

A collage associated with the IFS that generates the *Black Spleenwort* fern, shown in Fig. 4.20, consists of four affine maps in the form

$$w_i \begin{pmatrix} x \\ y \end{pmatrix} = \begin{pmatrix} r\cos\theta & -s\sin\phi \\ r\sin\theta & s\cos\phi \end{pmatrix} \begin{pmatrix} x \\ y \end{pmatrix} + \begin{pmatrix} h \\ k \end{pmatrix} (i = 1, 2, 3, 4).$$

The IFS code for a similar set of transformations is given in Table 4.5.

The collage theorem also tells us that if we make only small changes in transformations w_n, while keeping the contractivity factor constant, such that the change in $w_n(T)$ is small, then we make only a small change in the attractor — that is, if each transformation w_n, viewed as a mapping from $\mathcal{H}(\Box)$ (for example) to itself, depends uniformly continuously on a parameter in w_n, with fixed contractivity, then the attractor of the corresponding IFS also depends continuously on the parameter. In other words,

Table 4.5. The IFS code for the *Black Spleenwort*, expressed in scale and angle format.

	Translations		Rotations		Scalings	
Map	h	k	θ	ϕ	r	s
1	0.0	0.0	0	0	0.0	0.16
2	0.0	1.6	-2.5	-2.5	0.85	0.85
3	0.0	1.6	49	49	0.3	0.34
4	0.0	0.44	120	-50	0.3	0.37

in general, small changes in the parameters will lead to small changes in the attractor, provided that the system remains hyperbolic. This tells us that we can continuously control the attractor of an IFS, by adjusting parameters in the transformations. This is precisely what is done in image compression applications.

The continuous dependence of attractors of IFS on embedded parameters is illustrated in Fig. 4.21, which shows smooth deformations of a fractal fern obtained by continuous changes in the coefficients in the corresponding IFS code.

More complex images can be built up using many segments, with each segment represented by an IFS. In addition, there are more elaborate methodologies, all variants on the basic IFS idea, and all making fundamental use of affine transformations and the continuous dependence theme,

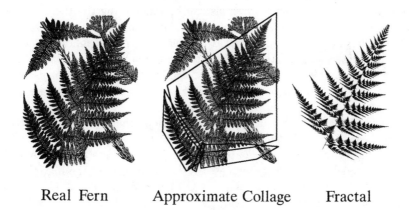

Real Fern   Approximate Collage   Fractal

Figure 4.20. A collage and the associated attractor, obtained when the collage theorem is exploited interactively to achieve fractal image compression of a Black Spleenwort fern image.

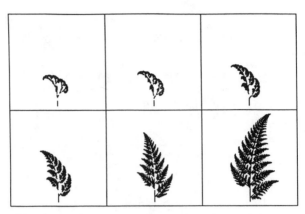

Figure 4.21. This figure illustrates continuous dependence of attractors of IFS on embedded parameters.

to achieve fractal image compression. For example, the IFS compression algorithm also works in the case of IFS with condensation. Not only that, but the condensation set itself may be an attractor of an IFS, which allows for the hierarchical build up of more elaborate resolution independent models for real world images. Examples can be seen in Figs. 4.8 to 4.11. The theory and application is discussed in [BJMRS]. It is applied in [DFDS2].

Even more elaborate constructions can be made using the theory of recurrent iterated function systems (RIFS), for which an extended version of the collage theorem applies [BEH]. A sequence of magnifications on a fern constructed with a RIFS is illustrated in Fig. 4.22. This variant of the IFS compression algorithm is applied in [VRIFS] (vector recurrent iterated function system), an interactive fractal image system that runs on a Sun workstation.

If each coefficient in the affine transformations that describe an IFS is represented using one byte, then an IFS of four transformations requires 16 bytes of data to represent it. As the number of coefficients used to provide a fractal model for an image increases, so does the size of the digital files used to store the coefficients. One is then led to consider lossless data compression methods for storing these coefficients. This is dealt with in the next chapter. A suprising and exciting unification is obtained when we discover that IFS theory itself, applied to the IFS codes, achieves the desired lossless data compression in an optimal manner.

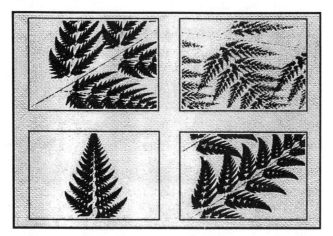

Figure 4.22. A sequence of magnifications on a fern constructed with a RIFS.

4.10. Measures and IFS's with Probabilities for Grayscale Images

The material in this section is included for reference, as it is needed at various points in the subsequent text. It is summarized from [FE], and assumes some familiarity with measure theory, which is not covered in this book. Relevant introductory material and references can be found in [FE]. A more intuitive description of what is going on here can be found at the start of the next section, where we rephrase the ideas, as they relate to fractal image compression, in terms of the grayscale photocopy algorithm.

Definition *An iterated function system* with probabilities *consists of an IFS $\{\mathbf{X}; w_1, w_2, \ldots, w_N\}$ together with an ordered set of numbers $\{p_1, p_2, \ldots, p_N\}$, such that*

$$p_1 + p_2 + \ldots + p_N = 1 \text{ and } p_i > 0 \text{ for } i = 1, 2, 3, \ldots N.$$

The probability p_i is associated with the transformation w_i.

Throughout this section, we restrict attention to the case where $\mathbf{X}$ is $\square \subset \mathbb{R}^2$.

Definition *Let μ be a Borel measure on $\square \subset \mathbb{R}^2$. If $\mu(\square) = 1$, then μ is said to be* normalized.

Definition *Let $\mathcal{P}$ denote the set of normalized Borel measures on $\square$. The*

Hutchinson metric d_H on $\mathcal{P}$ is defined by

$$d_H(\mu, \nu) = \sup\{\int_\square f\, d\mu - \int_\square f\, d\nu : \quad f : \square \to \mathbb{R} \text{ is continuous}$$

$$\text{and obeys } |f(x) - f(y)| \le d(x,y) \quad \forall x, y \in \square\},$$

for all $\mu, \nu \in \mathcal{P}$.

Theorem *Let $\mathcal{P}$ denote the set of normalized Borel measures on $\square$ and let d_H denote the Hutchinson metric. Then $(\mathcal{P}, d_H)$ is a compact metric space.*

Proof. See [FE].

Let $\mathcal{B}$ denote the Borel subsets of $\square$. Let $w : \square \to \square$ be continuous. Then one can prove that $w^{-1} : \mathcal{B} \to \mathcal{B}$. It follows that if ν is a normalized Borel measure on $\square$, then so is $\nu \circ w^{-1}$. In turn, this implies that the operator defined next indeed takes $\mathcal{P}$ into itself.

Definition *Let $\{\square; w_1, w_2, \ldots, w_N; p_1, p_2, \ldots, p_N\}$ be a hyperbolic IFS with probabilities. The* Markov operator *associated with the IFS is the function $M : \mathcal{P} \to \mathcal{P}$ defined by*

$$M(\nu) = p_1\nu \circ w_1^{-1} + p_2\nu \circ w_2^{-1} + \ldots + p_N\nu \circ w_N^{-1}$$

for all $\nu \in \mathcal{P}$.

Lemma *Let M denote the Markov operator associated with a hyperbolic IFS. Let $f : \square \to \mathbb{R}$ be either a simple function or a continuous function. Let $\nu \in \mathcal{P}(\square)$. Then*

$$\int_\square f\, d(M(\nu)) = \sum_{i=1}^{N} p_i \int_\square f \circ w_i\, d\nu.$$

Proof. See [FE].

Theorem (Hutchinson's Theorem) *Let $M : \mathcal{P} \to \mathcal{P}$ be the Markov operator associated with an IFS with probabilities, where each transformation has contractivity factor $0 \le s < 1$. Then M is a contraction mapping, with contractivity factor s, with respect to the Hutchinson metric on $\mathcal{P}$; that is,*

$$d_H(M(\nu), M(\mu)) \le s\, d_H(\nu, \mu) \text{ for all } \nu, \mu \in \mathcal{P}.$$

In particular, there is a unique measure $\mu \in \mathcal{P}$ such that $M\mu = \mu$. Also, if $\nu \in \mathcal{P}$, then

$$\lim_{n \to \infty} M^{\circ n}(\nu) = \mu,$$

where the convergence is with respect to the Hutchinson metric on $\mathcal{P}$.

Definition *Let μ denote the fixed point of the Markov operator, promised by Hutchinson's theorem. μ is called the* invariant measure *of the IFS with probabilities.*

Theorem *Let $\{\square; w_1, w_2, \ldots w_N; p_1, p_2, \ldots, p_N\}$ be a hyperbolic IFS with probabilities. Let μ be the associated invariant measure. Then the support of μ is the attractor of the IFS $\{\square; w_1, w_2, \ldots, w_N\}$.*

Proof. See [FE].

Theorem (The Collage Theorem for Measures)
Let $\{\square; w_1, w_2, \ldots, w_N; p_1, p_2, \ldots, p_N\}$ be a hyperbolic IFS with probabilities. Let μ be the associated invariant measure. Let $s \in (0, 1)$ be a contractivity factor for the IFS. Let $M : \mathcal{P}(\square) \to \mathcal{P}(\square)$ be the associated Markov operator. Let $\nu \in \mathcal{P}(\square)$. Then

$$d_H(\nu, \mu) \leq \frac{d_H(\nu, M(\nu))}{(1 - s)}.$$

Proof. See [FE].

Theorem (Elton's Theorem) *Let $\{\square; w_1, w_2, \ldots, w_N; p_1, p_2, \ldots, p_N\}$ be a hyperbolic IFS with probabilities. Let $\{x_n\}_{n=0}^{\infty}$ denote an orbit of the IFS produced by the random iteration algorithm, starting at x_0; that is,*

$$x_n = w_{\sigma_n} \circ w_{\sigma_{n-1}} \circ \ldots \circ w_{\sigma_1}(x_0),$$

where the maps are chosen independently according to the probabilities $p_1, p_2, \ldots, p_N$, for $n = 1, 2, 3, \ldots$. Let μ be the unique invariant measure for the IFS. Then with probability one (that is, for all code sequences $\sigma_1, \sigma_2, \ldots$ except for a set of sequences having probability zero),

$$\lim_{n \to \infty} \frac{1}{n+1} \sum_{k=0}^{n} f(x_k) = \int_{\square} f(x) \, d\mu(x)$$

for all continuous functions $f : \square \to \mathbb{R}$ and all x_0.

Proof. See [FE].

The theory of IFS with probabilities can be extended to include a *condensation measure*. A condensation measure is a Borel measure μ_0 supported on $\Box$ with

$$|\mu_0| = \int_\Box d\,\mu_0(x) < 1.$$

An IFS with probabilities and condensation measure takes the form

$$\{\Box; \mu_0, w_1, w_2, \ldots, w_N; p_1, p_2, \ldots, p_N\},$$

with

$$|\mu_0| + p_1 + p_2 + \ldots + p_N = 1 \text{ and } p_i > 0 \text{ for } i = 1, 2, 3, \ldots, N.$$

The associated Markov operator is now defined by

$$M(\nu) = \mu_0 + p_1\nu \circ w_1^{-1} + p_2\nu \circ w_2^{-1} + \ldots + p_N\nu \circ w_N^{-1}.$$

One can show that M is contractive with respect to the Hutchinson metric, with contractivity factor s, where $0 < s < 1$, provided that the w_i are contractive with the same contractivity factor. This means that both Hutchinson's theorem and the collage theorem for measures are true when a condensation measure is included in the Markov operator.

4.11. Grayscale Photocopy Algorithm

We begin here with an intuitive description, in terms of images, of what Borel measures on $\Box$ are. Our goal in this section is to explain the grayscale photocopy algorithm. This is a procedure for calculating the invariant measure μ, the unique solution of $M\mu = \mu$, $\mu \in \mathcal{P}$. The procedure works with the aid of a fascinating photocopy machine, which is used in much the same way as we used a standard photocopy machine in connnection with the standard photocopy machine algorithm, but this time working with *grayscale* images in place of black-and-white images.

Consider a grayscale photograph supported on $\Box$. In one second of time, the picture reflects a certain total amount of light. We can imagine that the source of illumination of the image is adjusted so that it reflects a unit number of photons per second. Photons are reflected from different parts of the picture at different rates which depend on the lightness or darkness of the place of reflection. Dark regions reflect relatively few photons per second, while bright white regions reflect relatively large numbers of photons per second.

White pigment in the surface of the photograph causes it to reflect more or less light. To describe the photograph, we introduce a function μ, which describes the amount of white pigment in different regions of the photograph. What is special about μ, and the reason why we introduce measures, is that μ assigns values to subsets of the image, rather than simply to points. If S is a subset of $\square$, then $\mu(S)$ is the total *amount* of white pigment in S, or equivalently, the total number of photons reflected by S per second.

Notice that one can modify the *density* of pigment at a single point, without altering the amount of light reflected by any small region (but of finite area) surrounding the point. Thus, measures assign values to sets. For logical reasons, the kinds of sets to which they assign values are restricted, for example, to Borel subsets — not just any subset of $\square$ will do. Any closed subset of $\square$ is a Borel subset. Any open subset of $\square$ is a Borel subset.

Our photograph is represented by $\mu \in \mathcal{P}$, where $\mathcal{P}$ is the set of all normalized Borel measures on $\square$. The measure is normalized to unity because we have insisted that the total number of photons reflected by $\square$ per second is one unit number of photons; that is, $\mu(\square) = 1$. Normalized Borel measures provide models for real world images, as described in Section 2.3. A normalized Borel measure can also be described as a probability density: loosely, we can say that if a photon emitted by the picture is picked at random, then $\mu(S)$ is the probability that the photon was emitted by the subset S of $\square$. The statement that $\mu(\square) = 1$ tells us that the photon came from somewhere in the image.

Some illustrations of measures $\mu \in \mathcal{P}$ are shown in Figs. 4.23 to 4.26. Figures 4.23 and 4.24 illustrate the brightness concept, while Figs. 4.25 and 4.26 represent measures that are fixed points of the Markov operator M associated with IFS's of affine maps. The latter were computed using the random iteration algorithm, as described in [BJMRS] and [FE]. They could instead have been computed by a digital implementation of the grayscale photocopy algorithm, which follows.

Figure 4.27 illustrates a grayscale photocopy machine, with four lenses and four filters. It corresponds to an iterated function system with probabilities

$$\{\square; w_1, w_2, w_3, w_4; p_1, p_2, p_3, p_4\}.$$

A grayscale image is input and illuminated; this image corresponds to a measure $\nu \in \mathcal{P}$. The brightness b of the illumination can be controlled. Light is emitted by different parts of the grayscale image in proportion to their whiteness. This emitted light is collected by four lens systems, which apply the four affine transformations w_i, for $i = 1, 2, 3, 4$; these four affine transformations of the input image are focused on the sheet of special photographic paper that will be output. The affine transformations are adjusted by means of four affine map control knobs. As the light passes from the lens system to the photographic output, it travels through a filter

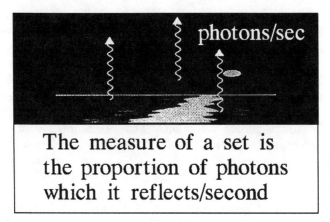

Figure 4.23. This figure illustrates the brightness concept for a measure $\mu \in \mathcal{P}$. Photons bounce off of the moontrail on the water's surface.

that attenuates its brightness. Each lens system has its own filter p_i, for $i = 1, 2, 3, 4$. The filter p_i attenuates the light that passes through it by a factor proportional to the number p_i. The images falling on the photographic paper are recorded (*photographed*) in such a way that in regions where copies overlap, their brightnesses are added. The overall brightness b is adjusted to ensure that the total number of photons/sec emitted by the output image is the same as that for the input image. The resulting output image is $M(\nu)$.

In this manner, we have a physical implementation of the Markov operator M, described in the previous section. We are restricted to four affine transformations in the present implementation. The grayscale photocopy algorithm proceeds as follows: once the photocopy machine has been appropriately adjusted, according to the specifications of the given IFS with probabilities, apply the machine to an arbitrary input image $\nu \in \mathcal{P}$ to produce $M(\nu)$. Take the resulting output image and make a grayscale photocopy of it, to produce a new grayscale image $M^{\circ 2}(\nu)$. Take this output image and make a photocopy of it, $M^{\circ 3}(\nu)$. Continue in this manner. Because M is a contraction mapping on the complete metric space $\mathcal{P}$, the sequence of images

$$M^{\circ 1}(\nu), M^{\circ 2}(\nu), M^{\circ 3}(\nu), \ldots$$

converges to the unique grayscale image or measure μ such that $M(\mu) = \mu$, the fixed point of the Markov operator, the invariant measure of the IFS with probabilities.

In practice, one would obtain a sequence of images that change less and less as successive iterations are made; the sequence of images approach

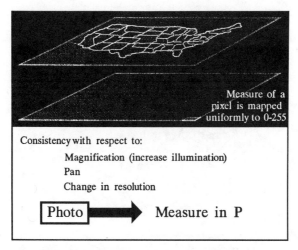

Figure 4.24. This figure illustrates the idea that a measure $\mu \in \mathcal{P}$ is a model for a grayscale photograph.

Figure 4.25. This figure illustrates a measure $\mu \in \mathcal{P}$, which is a fixed point of the Markov operator M associated with an IFS of affine maps. See also color Plate 6.

Figure 4.26. This figure illustrates a measure $\mu \in \mathcal{P}$, which is a fixed point of the Markov operator M associated with an IFS of affine maps. See also color Plate 7.

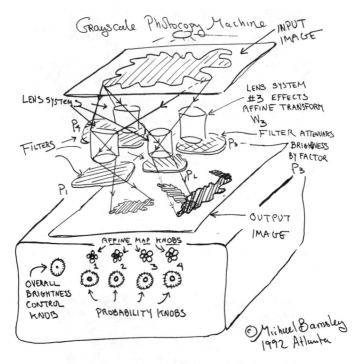

Figure 4.27. This figure illustrates a grayscale photocopy machine, with four lenses and four filters. Would you like to buy one of these?

more and more closely an image that would not change; that is, one which is essentially the same before and after a photocopy of it is made. This grayscale image is invariant under the photocopy machine (i.e., under the Markov operator M). Notice that the invariant grayscale image μ does not depend on the starting image ν. The invariant measure μ is indeed the attractor for the Markov operator M.

The photocopy machine algorithm can be extended to include the case of a condensation measure μ_0. To do this, a "picture" of μ_0 must be projected onto each output image, in addition to the pictures of the affine transformed originals, attenuated by their probability factors.

The photocopy machine algorithm can be applied in a digital computing environment; computer algorithms can be designed both to mimic the steps involved in applying the Markov operator M, and also to produce sequences of digital grayscale images that approximate the sequence of measures $M^{\circ 1}(\nu), M^{\circ 2}(\nu), M^{\circ 3}(\nu), \ldots$. For practical reasons, it is necessary to restrict the resolution of the digital measures $M^{\circ n}(\nu)$; as a consequence, the result of the computation process is a finite resolution approximation to the invariant measure of the IFS with probabilities. The collage theorem for measures assures us that the errors induced by discretization tend to zero as the resolution tends to infinity; that is, discretization errors are under control.

4.12. Fractal Image Compression Using the Collage Theorem for Measures

The collage theorem for measures tells us that to find an IFS with probabilities whose attractor is *close to* or *looks like* a given measure $\tau \in \mathcal{P}$ (for now, grayscale images and normalized Borel measures are considered to be interchangeable), one must find a set of contractive affine transformations and probabilities, such that $M(\tau)$ is close to or looks like the target image $\tau \in \mathcal{P}$. The degree to which two images *look alike* is measured using the Hutchinson metric, for example. With care to maintain contractivity, one can continuously control the attractor of an IFS with probabilities, by adjusting parameters in the transformations and the probabilities. A systematic process for seeking M is documented in [Patent 1].

The basic idea is as follows. Imagine that one has a grayscale photocopy machine with as many lens systems and filters as are needed. All probabilities are set to zero except p_1. The transformation w_1 and the probability p_1 are adjusted to make the output image be an as-good-as-possible approximation to part of the target image τ. This should be done *from below*, that is, so that $p_1 \tau \circ w_1^{-1}(B) < \tau(B)$ for all Borel subsets B of $\Box$. The latter condition is to ensure that $\tau - p_1 \tau \circ w_1^{-1}(B)$ is itself a Borel measure, which in turn invites the use of condensation measures; see the following. The next step is to allow $p_2 > 0$, and to adjust both p_2 and the coefficients of w_2 so that $p_1 \tau \circ w_1^{-1} + p_2 \tau w_2^{-1}$ is an as-good-as possible approximation to a larger part of τ. Again, it is desirable to maintain that the approximation be from below. New probabilities and transformations, activated by setting their probabilities nonzero, added successively to the IFS with probabilities to improve the approximation of τ by $M(\tau)$. At all stages, the contractivity of the Markov operator is maintained to be s by insisting that each affine map have a contractivity factor less than s, where $0 < s < 1$. When the output image looks sufficiently like the input image, either the probabilities are all multiplied by the factor $(p_1 + p_2 + \ldots + p_N)^{-1}$, to ensure that $M(\tau) \in \mathcal{P}$, or in the case that one wishes to use a condensation set μ_0, and one has constrained the parameters so that $p_1 \tau \circ w_1^{-1} + p_2 \tau \circ w_2^{-1} + \ldots + p_N \tau w_N^{-1} < \tau$, we set $\mu_0 = \tau - (p_1 \tau \circ w_1^{-1} + p_2 \tau \circ w_2^{-1} + \ldots + p_N \tau w_N^{-1})$. In either case, the result is a sufficiently accurate *collage* $M(\tau)$ of τ. The output image from

Figure 4.28. This figure shows a root image, the fixed point of a Markov operator with condensation. The image was constructed using the collage theorem for measures. The software used was [VRIFS]. See also color Plate 8.

the grayscale photocopy machine looks sufficiently like the input image.

In the case where there is no condensation set, the final compressed representation of the input image τ consists of the coefficients of the affine transformations that constitute the IFS, together with their probabilities. Using only this information, we can construct $\mathcal{A}$, the attractor of the IFS with probabilities. $\mathcal{A}$ is our approximation for τ. By the collage theorem, we know that the error $d_H(\mathcal{A}, \tau)$ is less than $(1-s)^{-1} d_H(M(\tau), \tau)$.

In the case where condensation is used, the measure μ_0 is itself represented using an IFS with probabilities. Again, the error must be controlled. An illustration is shown in Fig. 4.28, which shows a picture of a plant root; it is the invariant measure of an IFS with probabilities with a condensation measure. Figure 4.29 shows the structure of the IFS used to make the image. Small changes in any of the affine transformations involved here have only a small effect on the visual appearance of the image.

More complicated constructions can be made using the theory of recurrent iterated function systems (RIFS) with probabilities, for which an extended version of the collage theorem applies [BEH]. This variant of IFS compression is used in [VRIFS]. An example of an image computed using VRIFS is shown in color Plate 8. It is made of a number of segments, each of which is constructed using a recurrent IFS with probabilities. The grayscale values, for each segment, are mapped into color values using a lookup table, which is adjusted interactively at the end of the process to yield a final image that looks most like the original.

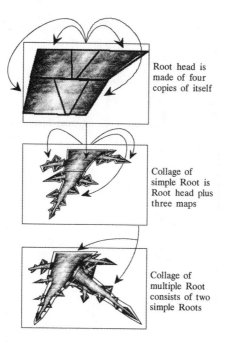

Root head is made of four copies of itself

Collage of simple Root is Root head plus three maps

Collage of multiple Root consists of two simple Roots

Figure 4.29. This figure shows the structure of the two IFS's used to make the image in Fig. 4.28.

4.13. Dudbridge's Fractal Image Compression Method

D. M. Monroe and F. Dudbridge [D1], [D2], [D3] have implemented a simple and effective method for image compression based on IFS's with probabilities. The method focuses on the representation of small image blocks, treating each block as an image in its own right. Thus, for example, a 256×256 grayscale digital image is divided into 256 square blocks, each of which is eight pixels wide and eight pixels tall. The grayscale value of each pixel is represented by a single byte; that is, 256 shades of gray are represented. Each 8×8 block is represented by an IFS with probabilities. In this case, $\square$ denotes a single image block, and the corresponding small image is represented by the IFS

$$\{\square; w_1, w_2, w_3, w_4; p_1, p_2, p_3, p_4\}.$$

The ranges of the affine transformations w_1, w_2, w_3, w_4 tile the block $\square$ as shown in Fig. 4.30.

Let the grayscale values over the image block be represented by a mea-

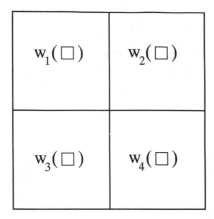

Figure 4.30. The tiling of $\square$ by the ranges of four transformations $W_i : \square \to \square$, used in Dudbridge's scheme for fractal image compression.

sure μ. Then, with the aid of the original image data, one can calculate the moments

$$\mathcal{M}(m,n) = \int_{\square} x^m y^n \, d\mu(x,y)$$

for any integer $m, n \in \{0, 1, 2, 3, \ldots\}$. Let $\tilde{\mu}$ denote the invariant measure of the IFS. Then one can write down explicit formulas for the moments of $\tilde{\mu}$ in terms of the coefficients and probabilities in the IFS. In fact, each of the numbers

$$\tilde{\mathcal{M}}(m,n) = \int_{\square} x^m y^n \, d\tilde{\mu}(x,y)$$

is linear in the probabilities. It turns out that one can solve the set of equations

$$\frac{\mathcal{M}(m,n)}{\mathcal{M}(0,0)} = \tilde{\mathcal{M}}(m,n),$$

with an appropriately chosen set of indices m and n, to yield explicit values for the coefficients of w_1, w_2, w_3, w_4, and the four probabilities p_1, p_2, p_3, p_4. This yields an explicit fractal approximant for each image block. Extensions to the method are also described by Dudbridge. See also [Be].

4.14. References

[B] M. Barnsley, (1) *Fractals* and (2) *Chaos*, BCS Conference Documentation Displays Group, State of the Art Seminar, Fractals and Chaos, 6th–7th December 1989, London (The British Computer Society, 13 Mansfield Street, London W1M 0BP). Lectures by the author on the photocopy machine algorithm were presented at the Max Planck Institute in the Spring of 1988, an account of which can be found in H.O. Peitgen et al., *Scientific American*, 60–70 (August 1990).

[Be] J. M. Beaumont, "Image Data Compression Using Fractal Techniques," *B.T. Journal*, Volume 9, Number 4, 93–108 (1991).

[BD] M. Barnsley and S. Demko, "Iterated Function Systems and the Global Construction of Fractals", *Proceedings of the Royal Society of London*, A399, 243–275 (1985).

[BEH] M. Barnsley, J. Elton, and D. Hardin, "Recurrent Iterated Function Systems," *Constructive Approximation* 5: 3–31 (1989).

[BJMRS] M. Barnsley, A. Jacquin, F. Malassenet, L. Reuter, and A.D. Sloan, "Harnessing Chaos for Image Synthesis," *Siggraph Proceedings* 1988.

[BAS] M. Barnsley and A. Sloan, "A Better Way to Compress Images", *Byte*, January 1988.

[BEHL] M. Barnsley, V. Ervin, D. Hardin, and J. Lancaster, "Solution of an Inverse Problem for Fractals and other Sets," *Proceedings of the National Academy of Science* 83, 1975–1977, (1986).

[BS] P.C. Bressloff and J. Stark, "Neural Networks, Learning Automata, and Iterated Function Systems," in [CEJ].

[CEJ] A.J. Crilly, R.A. Earnshaw, and H. Jones, *Fractals and Chaos*, Springer-Verlag, London (1991).

[D1] D. M. Monroe and F. Dudbridge, "Fractal Block Coding of Images," *Electronics Letters*, Volume 28, No. 11, 1053 (1992).

[D2] F. Dudbridge, *Image Approximation by Self Affine Fractals*, Ph.D. Thesis, Department of Computing, Imperial College of Science, Technology, and Medicine, London.

[D3] D. M. Monroe, and F. Dudbridge, "Fractal Approximation of Image Blocks," ICASSP-92, Volume 3, *Multidimensional Signal Processing* (1992).

[DFDS1] M. Barnsley, *Desktop Fractal Design System*, Academic Press, Boston (1989).

[DFDS2] M. Barnsley, *Desktop Fractal Design System Version 2.0*, Academic Press, Boston (1992).

[DS] P. M. Diaconis, M. Shashahani, "Products of Random Matrices and Computer Image Generation", *Contemporary Mathematics*, 50:173–182 (1986).

[FE] M. Barnsley, *Fractals Everywhere*, Academic Press, Boston (1988).

[GE] Gerald A. Edgar, *Measure, Topology, and Fractal Geometry*, Springer-Verlag, Berlin (1990).

[GH] J. S. Geronimo, and D. Hardin, "Fractal Interpolation Surfaces and a Related 2-D Multiresolution Analysis," Preprint, School of Mathematics, Georgia Institute of Technology, Atlanta (1990).

[HD] John C. Hart, and Thomas A. DeFanti, "Efficient Antialiased Rendering of 3-D Linear Fractals," *Computer Graphics*, 25, 91–100 (1991).

[AH] A. Horn, "IFSs and the Interactive Design of Tiling Structures," in [CEJ].

[H] J. Hutchinson, "Fractals and Self-Similarity", *Indiana University of Journal of Mathematics*, 30, 713–747 (1981).

[K1] T. Kaijser, "On a New Contraction Condition for Random Systems with Complete Connections, *Rev Roum Math Pure Appl*, Volume 24, 383–412 (1981).

[K2] T. Kaijser, "A Limit Theorem for Markov Chains in Compact Metric Spaces with Applications to Products of Random Matrices," *Duke Math Journal*, Volume 45, 311–349, (1978).

[McG] R. McGehee, "Attractors for Closed Relations on Compact Hausdorff Spaces," Preprint, School of Mathematics, University of Minnesota, Minneapolis (1991).

[M1] B. B. Mandelbrot, *Fractal Geometry of Nature*, W.H. Freeman and Co., New York (1982).

[M2] B.B. Mandelbrot, *Form, Chance, and Dimension*, W.H. Freeman and Co., New York (1982).

[MW], R. D. Maudlin, and S. C. Williams, "Hausdorff Dimension in Graph Directed Constructions," *Trans. Amer. Math. Soc.* 309, 811-829 (1988).

[MMC] Manuel Moran Cabre, "Fractal Series and Infinite Products," Preprint, Documento de Trabajo 9021, Facultad de Ciencias Economicas Y Empresariales, Universidad Complutense Campus de Somosaguas, Madrid.

[Patent 1] M. Barnsley, and A. Sloan, United States Patent # 5065447, "Method and Apparatus for Image Compression." (1991)

[PJS] H.-0. Peitgen, H. Jurgens, and D.Saupe, *Fractals and Chaos*, Springer Verlag, Berlin (1992).

[VR] E. R. Vrscay, C. J. Roehrig, "Iterated Function Systems and the Inverse Problem of Fractal Construction Using Moments," *Computers and Mathematics* (Editors: E. Kaltofen and S.M. Watt), 250–259, Springer-Verlag, New York (1989).

[VRIFS] M. Barnsley and A. Sloan, "Vector Recurrent Iterated Function System, Interactive Fractal Image Compression on a Sun Workstation,"Iterated Systems, Inc., Norcross, Georgia (1988).

5

Mathematical Foundations for Fractal Image Compression II

5.1. Goals of This Chapter

We have already seen how it is that a fractal model for a real world image can be expressed by a finite string of zeros and ones. Is this string the most efficient representation for the fractal model? Clearly not. Something more is needed.

So far, we have understood one way of going from an infinitely extensible image to a finite discrete set of data, as expressed in this diagram:

INFINITE EXTENSIBLE IMAGE	IFS THEORY $\longrightarrow$	FINITE DISCRETE DATA

In this chapter, we learn about the connnection between finite discrete data and compressed finite discrete data. The link is provided by information theory; thus:

FINITE DISCRETE DATA	INFORMATION THEORY $\longrightarrow$	COMPRESSED FINITE DISCRETE DATA

We discover that if the finite discrete data is random, then arithmetic compression achieves the goal of optimal compression. We conclude this chapter with the exciting observation that arithmetic compression can be efficiently understood and implemented using IFS theory. Thus:

FINITE DISCRETE DATA	IFS THEORY $\longrightarrow$	OPTIMAL COMPRESSED FINITE DISCRETE DATA

5.2.   Information Sources and Zero-Order Markov Sources

Throughout this chapter, our focus is data compression. We want to encode long, finite digital files losslessly, in as few bits as possible. What is the fewest number of bits required to describe a particular file?

Consider the collection of all digital files N bits long, where N is a positive integer. There are 2^N such files, and each file must be represented by a compressed file. By the pigeonhole principle, if some compressed files are shorter than their originals, then other compressed files will be longer than their originals. Hence, no compression scheme can guarantee that all compressed files are shorter than their originals. Any scheme that shortens some files must lengthen others.

However, we do not want to compress an arbitrary file, but a subclass, consisting of files of interest. For example, we may be interested only in files that represent binary images, or comic book pictures, or line drawings, or pictures of clouds, or files that represent speech, or bank balances. We would like to be able to specify for a given file how likely it is that we would want to compress it; we aim to trade compression of probable files for expansion of unlikely ones. A basic approach to compression consists of exploiting the asymmetries in the input stream to effect compression of the average file.

Information theory was originally conceived to deal with a time-varying signal. A branch of information theory concerns itself with continuously varying signals. However, we shall concentrate on digital signals in which

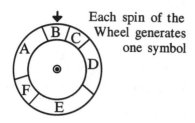

Each spin of the
Wheel generates
one symbol

Figure 5.1. A zero-order Markov source is illustrated using a wheel of fortune.

time is divided into discrete steps and function values are quantized. Informally, a *digital information source* is a black box that outputs symbols from a fixed finite alphabet at the rate of one symbol per unit of time. At each time step, the source puts out one definite symbol. The source is often assumed to be random, in one way or another.

An example of an information source involves a loaded die. To get the next symbol, you roll the die; different symbols appear with different probabilities. An alternate way of constructing such a source is by dividing a wheel of fortune into uneven sections, as illustrated in Fig. 5.1. Such models are called zero-order Markov sources.

Definition *A* zero-order Markov source *(or Markov chain)* consists of a symbol alphabet, $S = s_1, s_2, \ldots, s_n$ and a probability p_i for each symbol, with $p_1 + p_2 + \cdots + p_n = 1$ and $0 \leq p_i \leq 1$ for all i.

The probabilities in a zero-order Markov source are fixed. They do not depend either on the position of the symbol in the string or upon the symbols previously encountered. A source with these properties is said to be independent and identically distributed (i.i.d.). For realistic sources, neither of these assumptions is true. However, we can ask what compression is possible considering just the symbol probabilities.

Zero-order Markov sources are important, and we consider them in some detail. The more skewed the probabilities, the more compressible the data stream. A number called the *entropy* will be associated with the stream; it provides the average number of bits per symbol required when the stream is compressed as efficiently as possible.

Exercises

1. Which of the following can be modeled as a zero-order Markov source:

(a) successive flips of a coin?

(b) rolls of a fair die?

(c) rolls of a loaded die?

(d) the position of a particle undergoing Brownian motion?

(e) the intensity values of points chosen at random from a picture?

(f) the intensity value of points chosen sequentially in a fixed scanning pattern from a picture ?

5.3. Codes

We introduce concepts of *information* and *entropy*, from the point of view of data compression, by addressing the problem of how to construct efficient compressed codes for zero-order Markov sources. We attempt to write the symbols emanating from a source as compactly as possible, to eliminate redundancy. The absolute minimum size achievable is a measure of the information content of the source. The techniques used yield insight into the underlying theory.

Definition *By a code, we shall mean any translator of strings from an input alphabet S_I to an output alphabet S_O. A code takes in a stream of symbols and outputs another stream of symbols.*

The simplest form of code is a *block code*. A block code takes a fixed-length block of symbols from one alphabet to a fixed-length block of symbols of another alphabet. This is what occurs when an 8-bit binary number is written as a two-digit hexadecimal number, or vice versa. A useful feature of block codes is that the division of the output into codewords is trivial. The disadvantage of block codes is that since strings are sent to strings of a fixed length, it is not possible to achieve compression.

Definition *A (one-to-many) code from an input alphabet S_I to an output alphabet S_O consists of a function C that assigns to each symbol s_i in S_I a codeword from S_O . A codeword from an alphabet is a nonempty finite string of symbols chosen from that alphabet. We write a one-to-many code explicitly as*

$$C = \{s_1 \rightarrow \text{codeword}_1, s_2 \rightarrow \text{codeword}_2, \ldots s_n \rightarrow \text{codeword}_n\},$$

where n is the number of symbols in S_I.

What is the efficiency of such a code? Given a symbol from S_I , what is the average number of symbols from S_O required to encode it? The justification for variable length codes occurs when some symbols are more probable than others. It is advantageous to shorten the length of codewords corresponding to frequently used symbols at the expense of lengthening codewords corresponding to rare ones.

Definition *The* average code length *of a code C is obtained by summing the lengths of its codewords weighted by their probabilities,*

$$l_{av} = \sum_{i=1}^{n} p_i l_i,$$

where l_i is the length of the codeword $C(s_i)$, p_i is its probability, and n is the number of codewords.

If codewords have different lengths, we need to be able to tell when one codeword ends and the next begins. We assume that the codewords come out in a continuous stream. There is no pause between codewords as there is, for example, in a Morse code transmission, which was one of the first examples of a variable length code. Because codewords have no official end, we must insist that output strings have at most one interpretation as a concatenation of codewords.

Definition *A code $\{s_1 \rightarrow \text{codeword}_1, s_2 \rightarrow \text{codeword}_2, \ldots s_n \rightarrow \text{codeword}_n\}$, is uniquely decipherable if*

$$s = \text{codeword}_{v_1} \text{codeword}_{v_2} \ldots \text{codeword}_{v_k}$$

and

$$s = \text{codeword}_{w_1} \text{codeword}_{w_2} \ldots \text{codeword}_{w_m}$$

implies that $k = m$ and $v_i = w_i$ for $1 \leq i \leq k$. Here, the v_i and w_i are between 1 and n, where n is the number of possible codewords.

Examples:

(i) The code $\{A \rightarrow 00, B \rightarrow 000\}$ is not uniquely decipherable. The string "000000" could arise both from the string "AAA" and from the string "BB."

(ii) All block codes are uniquely decipherable.

(iii) The code $\{A \rightarrow 0, B \rightarrow 11\}$ is uniquely decipherable.

(iv) The code $\{A \rightarrow 01, B \rightarrow 011\}$ is uniquely decipherable. However, if one is handed symbols one at a time, and one receives the substring 01, one has to wait for the next symbol to decide whether it is the entire codeword for "A" or the beginning of the codeword for "B."

(v) The code $\{A \rightarrow 0, B \rightarrow 01, C \rightarrow 11\}$ is uniquely decipherable. However, if one receives the symbol 0, one has to wait to see if the subsequent string of 1's has even or odd length. There is no finite bound on the length of time required to unambiguously decide on the symbol. In applications, an arbitrarily large number of symbols may have to be buffered.

To avoid this kind of indeterminate delay in example (v), we restrict attention to a more specialized kind of code.

Definition *An* instantaneous code *is one in which no codeword occurs as the prefix to another.*

In an instantaneous code, codewords can be recognized as soon as they are received. An instantaneous code can be visualized as a walk through a logical tree. To find the codeword associated with a given input symbol, first find the input symbol among the leaves of the tree. The output codeword for that input symbol is described by the labels lying on the path from the root to the input symbol.

Instantaneous codes have obvious advantages. Is there any possible performance gain by using codes that are uniquely decipherable but not instantaneous? No, because it can be shown that any set of codeword lengths achievable by uniquely decipherable codes is also achievable with instantaneous codes. The justification for this statement will be provided when we discuss the Kraft–McMillan inequality in the next section.

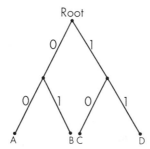

Figure 5.2. This is Code Tree 1. An instantaneous code is visualized as a walk through this tree. The leaf labels are the input symbols and the branch labels from root to leaf list the symbols in the corresponding output codeword.

Examples:

(i) Consider a source with four symbols, $\{A, B, C, D\}$ and probabilities p_A, p_B, p_C, p_D. Assume that $p_A = p_B = p_C = p_D = 1/4$. Code Tree 1 in Fig. 5.2 shows one possible code. Each input symbol corresponds to a two-bit codeword as shown in Table 5.1.

The average codeword length for this code is

$$
\begin{aligned}
l_{\mathrm{av}} &= p_A l_A + p_B l_B + p_C l_C + p_D l_D \\
&= (0.25)^2 + (0.25)^2 + (0.25)^2 + (0.25)^2 \\
&= 2 \text{ bits per codeword,}
\end{aligned}
$$

where l_A, l_B, l_C, l_D are the lengths of the four possible codewords.

(ii) An alternate code for the source used in example (i) is shown in Fig. 5.3. The respective codewords are shown in Table 5.2. Although the codewords have different lengths, the code is still instantaneous, and all codewords are decipherable as soon as they are received.

Table 5.1. Codewords for Code Tree 1.

A	$\rightarrow$	00
B	$\rightarrow$	01
C	$\rightarrow$	10
D	$\rightarrow$	11

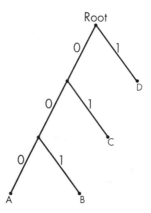

Figure 5.3. This illustrates Code Tree 2. Although this tree assumes the same input symbols as those in Fig. 5.2, it yields a different code.

This new code gives an average codeword length of

$$
\begin{aligned}
l_{\text{av}} &= p_A l_A + p_B l_B + p_C l_C + p_D l_D \\
&= (0.25)^3 + (0.25)^3 + (0.25)^2 + (0.25)^1 \\
&= 2.25 \text{ bits per codeword,}
\end{aligned}
$$

where l_A, l_B, l_C, l_D are the lengths of the four possible codewords.

(iii) Let $p_A = p_B = 0.125, p_C = 0.25, p_D = 0.5$. With these probabilities, the average codeword length for Code Tree 1 shown in Fig. 5.2 is

$$
\begin{aligned}
l_{\text{av}} &= p_A l_A + p_B l_B + p_C l_C + p_D l_D \\
&= (0.125)^2 + (0.125)^2 + (0.25)^2 + (0.5)^2 \\
&= 2 \text{ bits per codeword,}
\end{aligned}
$$

where l_A, l_B, l_C, l_D are the lengths of the four possible codewords.

Table 5.2. Codewords for Code Tree 2.

A	$\rightarrow$	000
B	$\rightarrow$	001
C	$\rightarrow$	01
D	$\rightarrow$	1

It appears that every set of probabilities gives an average codeword length of two for this code. Can you do better?

(iv) If the probabilities are those in example (iii) and the code is Code Tree 2 shown in Fig. 5.3, then the average codeword length is

$$
\begin{aligned}
l_{\text{av}} &= p_A l_A + p_B l_B + p_C l_C + p_D l_D \\
&= (0.125)^3 + (0.125)^3 + (0.25)^2 + (0.5)^1 \\
&= 1.75 \text{ bits per codeword,}
\end{aligned}
$$

where l_A, l_B, l_C, l_D are the lengths of the four possible codewords.

Clearly, we are onto something! Intuitively, it is easy to see what is happening. If some input symbols are rare, it makes sense to give them longer codewords, thereby allowing one to use shorter codewords for the more frequent symbols.

No code is ideal for all situations; the average codeword length depends on the specific probabilities. These examples lead to the following questions:

(a) Given an input alphabet $S = \{s_1, s_2 \ldots s_n\}$ with corresponding probabilities $(p_1, p_2, \ldots p_n)$ and an output alphabet $A = \{a_1, a_2, \ldots a_n\}$, what is the smallest average codeword length achievable?

(b) How does one go about achieving this smallest average length?

The following sections will answer both these questions and generalize the answer to a larger class of sources.

Exercises

1. Which of the following codes is uniquely decipherable and/or instantaneous?

(a) $\{A \rightarrow 0, B \rightarrow 10, C \rightarrow 110\}$.

(b) $\{A \rightarrow 00, B \rightarrow 01, C \rightarrow 010\}$.

2. Prove that any set of codewords can be extended to an instantaneous code by appending a delimiter symbol to the end of each codeword.

5.4.   Kraft–McMillan Inequality

To make the average codeword length small, all the codeword lengths should be made as small as possible. On the other hand, assuming we wish to use an instantaneous code, every short codeword deprives us of any codeword containing it as a prefix. To solve for the smallest average codeword length requires that we balance these two factors. If the input alphabet has n symbols and the output alphabet has r symbols, when can we write a code that uses a specified set of lengths $l_1, l_2, \ldots l_n$?

For instantaneous codes, the answer is provided by the following theorem [RH].

Theorem (Kraft's Theorem)   *An input alphabet of n symbols can be described by an instantaneous code with codewords of length $l_1, l_2, \ldots l_n$, built from an output alphabet of r symbols if and only if*

$$\sum_{i=1}^{n} \frac{1}{r^{l_i}} \leq 1.$$

Examples:

(i) If the codewords all have the same length l, then a code exists provided $n \leq r^l$. This can be written as

$$\sum_{i=1}^{n} \frac{1}{r^l} \leq 1.$$

(ii) By pruning the code in example (i), we can add a codeword of length $(l - 1)$ by subtracting r codewords of length l. In the sum in the inequality in example (i), this means adding $1/r^{l-1}$ and subtracting r/r^l. The codeword lengths have changed, but the inequality still holds; that is,

$$\sum_{i=1}^{n} \frac{1}{r^{l_i}} \leq 1.$$

(iii) Discarding codewords from any code satisfying this inequality still leaves the inequality true. Every code can be formed through a combination of the two procedures just described.

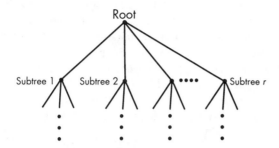

Figure 5.4. The proof of the Kraft inequality follows by induction on the possible subtrees for which the inequality is assumed to hold.

Proof. (**Kraft's Theorem**) First, we show that any instantaneous code must satisfy the inequality. The proof of this proceeds by induction on the maximum codeword length. If the maximum codeword length is 1, then the greatest number of branches is r. It follows that $n \leq r$ and

$$\sum_{i=1}^{n} \frac{1}{r} = \frac{n}{r} \leq 1.$$

This establishes the base of our induction.

Now suppose that the inequality holds for all codewords of length at most n. Then we prove that it holds for instantaneous codes of length $n + 1$ as follows. First, observe that the trees generated from the children of the root form instantaneous codes of their own with (a) depth at most n, which is our inductive hypothesis, and (b) codeword lengths one less than the length of the original code. Hence, for any branch,

$$\sum_{i=1}^{m} \frac{1}{r^{l_i - 1}} \leq 1,$$

where m is the number of codewords in the branch. Therefore,

$$\sum_{i=1}^{m} \frac{1}{r^{l_i}} \leq \frac{1}{r}.$$

Since the original code is made up of at most r of these branches, the inequality holds for it as well. This completes the induction, and the proof in the foward direction. See Fig. 5.4.

The proof of "only if" consists of showing that given an input alphabet, output alphabet, and a set of codeword lengths satisfying the inequality, one can construct an instantaneous code having these lengths. This is demonstrated constructively by the program listing KRAFT.C. The algorithm consists of the following steps. First, the codeword lengths are sorted into ascending order. Then the codewords are chosen successively by picking the first codeword in lexicographic order that does not contain a previous codeword as a prefix. If this ceases to be possible, the program halts, executing the statement marked /*ESCAPE*/. The remainder of the proof consists of showing that this statement is executed only if the codeword lengths fail to satisfy the Kraft inequality. This part of the proof is left as an exercise.

McMillan showed that the Kraft inequality holds true for the larger class of uniquely decipherable codes. McMillan's theorem implies that any uniquely decipherable code can be replaced by an instantaneous code having the same codeword lengths. For a proof, see [RH].

Theorem (McMillan's Theorem)   *An input alphabet of n symbols can be described by a uniquely decipherable code with codewords of length $l_1, l_2, \ldots l_n$, built from an output alphabet of r symbols if and only if*

$$\sum_{i=1}^{n} \frac{1}{r^{l_i}} \leq 1. \qquad \textit{[The Kraft--McMillan inequality]}$$

Exercises

1. Show that the Kraft inequality holds for the codes constructed in Section 5.3.

2. Prove that equality holds in the Kraft inequality if and only if the code tree has no empty branches.

3. Prove that the /* ESCAPE */ statement in KRAFT.C, in the next section, will be reached only when the specified codeword lengths fail to satisfy the Kraft inequality. *Hint: use induction on the maximum codeword length.*

5.5.   C Source Code for Illustrating Kraft's Theorem

One can illustrate Kraft's theorem on a personal computer. The following program is written for compilation using the Turbo C Version 1.0 compiler by Borland and is designed to run under DOS on an IBM PC with an Intel

80286, 80386, or 80486 processor. The uncompiled program consists of a single file, KRAFT.C.

This program takes as input an alphabet size n = number of codewords, $n \leq 80$, an output alphabet size $r \leq 16$, and a sequence of n codeword lengths in ascending order. It outputs one possible instantaneous code with these constraints. The algorithm is described earlier in the proof of the Kraft inequality.

```
-------------------------------------------------
FILE NAME: KRAFT.C
-------------------------------------------------
#include <stdio.h>

#define MAXLENGTH    80
#define MAXCODEWORDS 80
#define MAXR         16

char output_alphabet[MAXR] = "0123456789ABCDEF";

main()
{
    short n,r,i,j,l[MAXCODEWORDS],last_symbol=0;
    char codeword[MAXLENGTH];

    printf("           Size of input alphabet? ");
    fflush(stdout);
    scanf("%d",&n);
    printf("Size of output alphabet (max 16)? ");
    fflush(stdout);
    scanf("%d",&r);
    printf("Input codeword l in ascending order (max 80).\n");

    for (i=0;i<n;i++)
      {
        printf("Length? ");
        fflush(stdout);
        scanf("%d",l+i);
      }

    printf("\nA possible instantaneous code is:\n\n");
```

```
/* The first codeword is all zeros */

   for (i=0;i<l[0];i++) codeword[i]=output_alphabet[0];
   codeword[l[0]]='\0';
   puts(codeword);

   for (i=1;i<n;i++)
     {
/* check whether last symbol in previous codeword is r-1 */

     while (last_symbol==r-1)
{

   /* otherwise back up until a symbol is not r-1 */
   /* if this is impossible, the tree is full */

        if (l[i-1]==1)
          {
            fprintf(stderr,
              "Lengths do not satisy Kraft inequality.\n");
  /* ESCAPE */
            exit(1);
          }
        else
          {
   /* back up until symbol can be incremented */
            l[i-1]--;
            last_symbol=index(codeword[l[i-1]-1]);
          }
}
     /* if the last symbol is not r-1, increment it */

     codeword[l[i-1]-1] = output_alphabet[++last_symbol];
     if (l[i]<l[i-1])
{
  fprintf(stderr,"Lengths not in ascending order.\n");
        exit(1);
}
     else if (l[i]>l[i-1])   /* pad with zeros */
       {
         last_symbol=0;
        for (j=l[i-1];j<l[i];j++)
          codeword[j]=output_alphabet[0];
```

```
            codeword[l[i]]='\0';
          }
        puts(codeword);
      }
    return(0);
}
/* This just converts from the character to its place */
/*  in the alphabet     */


index(char symbol)
{
  int i=0;
  while (symbol!=output_alphabet[i++]);
  return(i-1);
}
```

Compile Instructions:
To compile the object module, enter the DOS command line:
```
tcc -ms -c -v KRAFT.C
```

To produce the executable function KRAFT.EXE, enter the Turbo C command line:
```
tcc -ms -v KRAFT.OBJ
```

Running Instructions:

To run KRAFT.EXE, enter the DOS command line:
```
KRAFT
```

Sample Output:

```
Size of input alphabet? 4
Size of output alphabet (max 16)? 2
Input codeword 1 in ascending order (max 80).
Length?1
Length?2
Length?3
Length?4
A possible instantaneous code is:
0
10
110
1110
```

5.6. Entropy

We want to find the best possible average codeword length for an instantaneous code associated with a zero-order Markov source; of necessity, we are subject to the constraint imposed by the Kraft–McMillan inequality. In general, discrete optimization problems are difficult to solve. One technique is to treat the variables as continuous rather than discrete and bring calculus to bear on the problem.

First, we will consider the special case where all the probabilities are equal; this situation gives an upper bound on the average codeword length for any probabilities. Then we will exhibit a lower bound on codeword lengths for an arbitrary set of probabilities. We are then able to define the entropy of a source.

Theorem *Given a zero-order Markov source $S = \{s_1, s_2, \ldots s_n\}$ with probabilities $(p_1, p_2, \ldots p_n)$ with $p_i = 1/n$ for $1 \le i \le n$ and an output alphabet $A = \{a_1, a_2, \ldots a_r\}$, any instantaneous code satisfies*

$$l_{\mathrm{av}} = \frac{1}{n} \sum_{i=1}^{n} l_i \ge \log_r n.$$

Proof.   Since all codewords are equally likely, the most efficient code is obtained by minimizing the total length of the codewords

$$L(l_1, l_2, \ldots l_n) = \frac{1}{n} \sum_{i=1}^{n} l_i,$$

subject to the Kraft–McMillan inequality. The most efficient code would satisfy the equality, so our constraint equation is

$$K(l_1, l_2, \ldots l_n) = \sum_{i=1}^{n} \frac{1}{r^{l_i}} = 1.$$

This kind of constrained minimization problem can be solved by Lagrange multipliers. The gradient of the function to be minimized, L, must be parallel to the gradient of the constraint, K.

Solving, we find

$$\nabla L = \left(\frac{1}{n}, \frac{1}{n}, \ldots \frac{1}{n} \right)$$

and

$$\nabla K = \left(\frac{\log_e r}{r^{l_1}}, \frac{\log_e r}{r^{l_2}}, \ldots, \frac{\log_e r}{r^{l_n}} \right).$$

Setting $\nabla L = \lambda \nabla K$ yields $l_1 = l_2 = \cdots = l_n$ and substituting into the constraint equation provides

$$l_i = \log_e n, \text{ for } i = 1, 2, \ldots n.$$

It is straightforward to check that this critical point is a minimum.

If the probabilities are not all equal, the question becomes a little different because now one is interested in a weighted sum of codeword lengths; each codeword is weighted by its probability. The preceding proof goes through almost without change. The following theorem gives a lower bound for the average codeword length of any instantaneous (or uniquely decipherable) code.

Theorem *Any instantaneous code for a zero-order Markov source $S = \{s_1, s_2, \ldots s_n\}$ with probabilities $(p_1, p_2, \ldots p_n)$ and an output alphabet $A = \{a_1, a_2, \ldots a_r\}$, satisfies*

$$l_{\text{av}} = \sum_{i=1}^{n} p_i l_i \geq \sum_{i=1}^{n} p_i \log_r \frac{1}{p_i}.$$

Proof. In this case,

$$L(l_1, l_2, \ldots l_n) = \sum_{i=1}^{n} p_i l_i;$$

therefore,

$$\nabla L = (p_1, p_2, \ldots, p_n)$$

and

$$\nabla K = \left(\frac{\log_e r}{r^{l_1}}, \frac{\log_e r}{r^{l_2}}, \ldots, \frac{\log_e r}{r^{l_n}} \right).$$

Setting $\nabla L = \lambda \nabla K$ yields

$$l_i = \log_r \left[\frac{\lambda \log_e r}{p_i} \right], \text{ for } i = 1, 2, \ldots n.$$

Substituting into the equation for ∇K and solving for λ yields $\lambda = 1 / \log_e r$. Hence, the minimum average codeword length is achieved by

$$l_i = \log_r \frac{1}{p_i}, \text{ for } i = 1, 2, \ldots n.$$

The latter equation provides a quantity that we call the *information content* of the symbol s_i. This definition of information has the following properties.

Property 1. The information conveyed by a symbol is inversely proportional to its probability. Rare symbols contain more surprise and therefore more information. In the extreme, if a symbol occurs with probability one, it conveys no information at all.

Property 2. If two symbols occur independently, the probability of seeing one followed by the other is $p_i \cdot p_j$. The information conveyed by seeing this pair is $\log_r(1/(p_i \cdot p_j))$, which is the sum of $\log_r(1/p_i)$ and $\log_r(1/p_j)$. Probabilities multiply; information adds.

Definition *The* (base r) entropy *of a zero-order Markov source S with probabilities* $(p_1, p_2, \ldots p_n)$ *is defined by*

$$H_r(S) = \sum_{i=1}^{n} p_i \log_r \frac{1}{p_i} = -\sum_{i=1}^{n} p_i \log_r p_i.$$

The most common base is 2 and $H_2(S)$ is denoted simply as $H(S)$.

If any p_i is zero, this expression is undefined, but the singularity is removable in the sense that there is only one way of filling it in continuously. Thus, one defines

$$0 \log \frac{1}{0} = 0.$$

Examples:

(i) Consider a fair n-sided die with equal probabilities $p_i = 1/n$. The formula for the entropy yields $H_r(S) = \log_r n$.

(ii) A loaded coin shows heads with probability p and tails with probability $1 - p$. The entropy of this source is

$$H_r(S) = -p \log_r p - (1 - p) \log_r (1 - p).$$

Taking the derivative with respect to p reveals that the function has a single critical point that occurs at $p = \frac{1}{2}$. It is a maximum, as illustrated in Fig. 5.5. Therefore, the entropy of the coin must satisfy

$$H_r(S) \le \log_r 2.$$

It can be shown that for any zero-order Markov source with n symbols,

$$H_r(S) \le \log_r n.$$

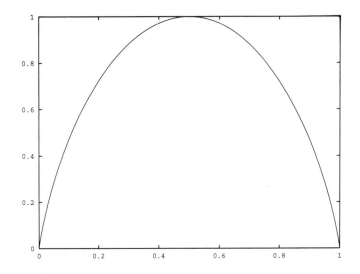

Figure 5.5. The graph of the function $H_r(S) = -p \log_r p - (1-p) \log_r (1-p)$.

This formula tells us that to be incompressible, a source must use every symbol with equal probability.

(iii) Suppose that a binary digital image has roughly nine times as many white pixels as black pixels. The entropy is given by

$$H_2(S) = -(0.9) \log_2(0.9) - (0.1) \log_2(0.1) \simeq 0.47,$$

which means that the file can be compressed by 53 %, simply treating it as a zero-order Markov source.

Exercises

1. Figure 5.6 shows the graph of $-p \log_2 p$. Prove that the graph has a vertical tangent at $p = 0$ and achieves its maximum value at $p = 1/e$.

2. Prove that the entropy of any zero-order Markov source with n symbols and probability vector $(p_1, p_2, \ldots p_n)$ satisfies $H_r(S) \leq \log_r n$. One possible approach is showing that if $p_i \neq p_j$, the entropy of a new source obtained by replacing p_i and p_j by their average must be strictly higher than the original entropy.

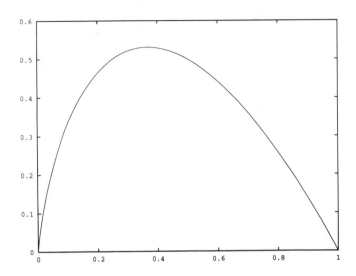

Figure 5.6. This figure shows the graph of $-p\log_2 p$. It has a vertical tangent at $p = 0$ and achieves its maximum at $p = 1/e$.

5.7. Shannon–Fano Codes

Shannon–Fano codes were discovered independently by Shannon and Weaver [CS1], [CS2], and Fano [RF]. These codes provide a way to construct instantaneous codes from a set of probabilities. Although Shannon–Fano codes have been overshadowed by Huffman codes [MN], [JS], their performance can be proved to be not far from optimal. They provide a convenient way of showing that the entropy of a source can be approached arbitrarily closely, at the expense of increasingly complex codes. We will describe the situation where $r = 2$; the results can be generalized to the case of an arbitrary output alphabet. An instantaneous code is represented by a tree whose leaves are assigned symbols. In a Shannon–Fano code, we start with a tree with one leaf labeled with the entire input alphabet. We split leaves to form new leaves. When every leaf corresponds to a single symbol, the algorithm halts.

Step 1. Partition the symbols in S into two subsets S_0 and S_1. These subsets are chosen so that the sum of the probabilities in each subset is as close as possible to $\frac{1}{2}$.

Step 2. Construct two new nodes, one connected via a branch labeled zero, corresponding to the set S_0, and the other labeled with a one corresponding to S_1.

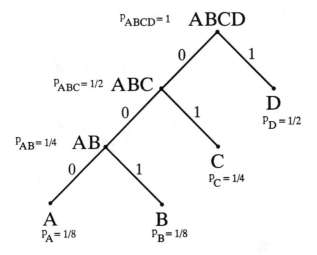

Figure 5.7. This figure illustrates a Shannon–Fano code.

Step 3. If the subset at a branch has only one element, it is a called a *leaf* or *terminal node* and is left unchanged. Otherwise, apply the preceding procedure to the symbols in the subset.

It can be proved that the resultant codeword lengths satisfy

$$\log_2 \frac{1}{p_i} \le l_i \le \log_2 \frac{1}{p_i} + 1.$$

The codeword lengths never depart by more than one from the theoretical optimum. Taking averages, one obtains

$$\sum_{i=1}^{n} p_i \log_2 \frac{1}{p_i} \le \sum_{i=1}^{n} p_i l_i \le \sum_{i=1}^{n} p_i \log_2 \frac{1}{p_i} + 1.$$

Therefore, the average codeword lengths for a Shannon–Fano code obey

$$H(S) \le l_{\text{av}} \le H(S) + 1. \tag{5.1}$$

Example:

(i) Let an input alphabet S have four symbols with probabilities $p_A = 1/8, p_B = 1/8, p_C = 1/4$, and $p_D = 1/2$. The steps taken in forming the corresponding Shannon–Fano code are:

Step 1. Form the root node with all four symbols.

Step 2. Divide the symbols into two sets, $S_0 = \{A, B, C\}$, $S_1 = \{D\}$, to form two new nodes connected to the root. The node containing S_1 has a single symbol and will not be touched further.

Step 3. Divide the node containing $\{A, B, C\}$, into sets $S_0 = \{A, B\}$ and $S_1 = \{C\}$. The node containing the symbol C is completed.

Step 4. Divide the remaining node into sets $S_0 = \{A\}$ and $S_1 = \{B\}$. The code is now complete.

The codewords are $A \to 000, B \to 001, C \to 01$ and $D \to 1$ as shown in Fig. 5.7. The average codeword length is 1.5 bits/codeword.

Exercises

1. Construct the Shannon–Fano code for a source with four symbols and probabilities $p_A = 2/5, p_B = 2/5, p_C = 1/10, p_D = 1/10$. Can you find another code tree not using the Shannon–Fano algorithm with a lower average codeword length?

2. Prove that for Shannon–Fano codes,

$$\log_2 \frac{1}{p_i} \le l_i \le \log_2 \frac{1}{p_i} + 1.$$

While elegant from a theoretical standpoint, the Shannon–Fano algorithm is cumbersome to implement. The process of partitioning a set into near-equal halves is computationally cumbersome. An alternate scheme for producing instantaneous codes known as Huffman codes has the advantage of being faster to implement while producing codes that are provably at least as good and often better. A discussion of Huffman codes follows in Section 5.11.

5.8.   Extensions of Sources

The assignment of a codeword to each symbol imposes a granularity on the code. While the previous entropy calculation gives a real number as the optimal codeword length, any particular code has codewords of a fixed size. One way to increase efficiency is to allow a stream of output symbols to represent a sequence of input symbols, as is done in arithmetic coding considered later in this chapter.

To achieve the entropy of a source, it is necessary to use complicated codes.

Definition *The "k"th extension of a source S of n symbols is a new source, S^k, obtained by sending symbols in blocks of k symbols. The new source has n^k symbols. New probabilities are obtained by multiplying the probabilities of the composite symbols.*

For example, if the original source has input alphabet $\{0,1\}$ with probability vector (p_0, p_1), its third extension has alphabet

$$\{000, 001, 010, 011, 100, 101, 110, 111\}$$

with probability vector

$$(p_0^3, p_0^2 p_1, p_0^2 p_1, p_0 p_1^2, p_0^2 p_1, p_0 p_1^2, p_0 p_1^2, p_1^3).$$

The extension is a zero-order Markov source; one can show as an exercise that the entropy of the source S^k satisfies

$$H_r(S^k) = k H_r(S). \tag{5.2}$$

From Eq. (5.1), we deduce that the Shannon–Fano code for the the kth extension of a source obeys

$$H(S^k) \le l_{\text{av}} \le H(S^k) + 1,$$

and, using Eq. (5.2), we find

$$H(S) \le l_{\text{av}}/k \le H(S) + 1/k.$$

Hence, we have the following theorem.

Theorem (Shannon) *If S is a zero-order Markov source, any instantaneous code to an output alphabet with r symbols has an average length that satisfies*

$$H_r(S) \le l_{\text{av}}.$$

By passing to the kth extension, one can find an instantaneous code whose average length per input symbol satisfies

$$l_{\text{av}} \le H_r(S) + 1/k.$$

This theorem tells us that by passing to high enough extensions, Shannon–Fano codes can be made to approach the theoretical optimal entropy of a zero-order Markov source as closely as desired.

Exercises

1. Let S have three symbols with equal probabilities $p_A = p_B = p_C = 1/3$.

(a) What is the (base 2) entropy of this source?

(b) Construct a Shannon–Fano code for this source and compute its average codeword length.

(c) Construct a Shannon–Fano code for the source S^2, which has nine symbols, and compute its average codeword length.

2. Prove Eq. (5.2).

3. Why would passing to an extension help in compressing a black-and-white image of text?

5.9.   Higher–Order Markov Sources

Zero-order Markov sources are inadequate for describing most information sources encountered in real life. Text files do not look random and neither do image files. What is needed is a generalization of the zero-order source. Often, the probability of encountering a symbol depends on the context in which we find it. In a zero-order Markov source, the probability of occurrence of a particular symbol is fixed and independent of previous symbols; in higher-order models, this probability may depend on previous symbols.

An example of a zero-order Markov source is a biased roulette wheel. Different symbols come up with different probabilities, but one spin has no effect on the next.

An example of a first-order Markov source is a sticky roulette wheel. Imagine a wheel with the property that half the time you spin it, the ball stays in the same symbol; it sticks. The other half of the time, it gives a random choice among the possible symbols. The wheel has memory. Another example is provided by a collection of wheels of fortune, each of which yields symbols of the input alphabet with probabilities that are associated with that particular wheel. One wheel is associated with each

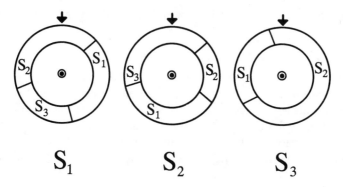

$$S_1 \qquad S_2 \qquad S_3$$

Figure 5.8. This figure illustrates a first-order Markov source.

symbol of the input alphabet. The wheel corresponding to the latest symbol produced by the source is used to generate the next symbol.

Definition *A* first-order Markov source *is defined as an alphabet* $S = \{s_1, s_2, \ldots, s_n\}$, *probability vector* $p = (p_1, p_2, \ldots, p_n)$, *and a transition probability matrix* $M = (p_{ij})$, *where for* $1 \le i, j \le n$, p_{ij} *is the probability of occurrence of symbol* s_j *given that the previous symbol is* s_i, *and* p_i *is the probability of occurrence of symbol* s_i. *The matrix* M *is also called a* Markov matrix.

Figure 5.8 illustrates a first-order Markov source, and Fig. 5.9 illustrates a second-order Markov source. The construction of a code for a first-order Markov source involves assigning a code to each state; if the source is in state s_i and the next symbol is s_j, the output symbol is obtained by inputting the s_j symbol to the s_i code. This means that, to determine an optimal code, we need to know all of the transition probabilities p_{ij} .

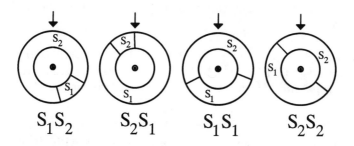

$$S_1 S_2 \qquad S_2 S_1 \qquad S_1 S_1 \qquad S_2 S_2$$

Figure 5.9. This figure illustrates a second-order Markov source.

The average codeword length achievable for code i is given by

$$\left[-\sum_{j=1}^{n} p_{ij} \log_r p_{ij}\right].$$

Given the transition probabilities p_{ij} , this equation allows us to compute the average codeword length associated with each code; the overall average codeword length for the source requires that we sum over the different codes. The contribution from code i must be weighted by the probability p_i of being in the corresponding state s_i. It follows that the optimal average output code length for a first-order Markov source is

$$H_r(S) = \sum_{i=1}^{n} p_i \left[-\sum_{j=1}^{n} p_{ij} \log_r p_{ij}\right].$$

Our previous definition includes the probabilities p_i and the transition probabilities p_{ij}, and treats them as though they have nothing to do with one another. In general, this is not the case; if we initialize a large number of such systems by choosing in each case the first symbol to be s_i with probability $p_i^{(0)}$, then we find that the probability $p_j^{(1)}$ of the subsequent symbol s_j is

$$p_j^{(1)} = \sum_{i=1}^{n} p_i^{(0)} \cdot p_{ij},$$

for $j = 1, 2, \ldots, n$. This can be written as $p^{(1)} = M^T p^{(0)}$, where M^T is the transpose of the Markov matrix

$$M = \begin{bmatrix} p_{11} & p_{12} & \cdots & p_{1n} \\ p_{21} & p_{22} & \cdots & p_{2n} \\ \vdots & \vdots & \vdots & \vdots \\ p_{n1} & p_{n2} & \cdots & p_{nn} \end{bmatrix},$$

and $p^{(i)}$ is the column vector whose ith element is $p_i^{(i)}$. This suggests the following definition, which concerns the situation where the probabilities remain fixed in time.

Definition *A Markov source is* stationary *if its probabilities are invariant over time; that is, $p = M^T p$, where p is the column vector whose "i"th element is p_i, and M^T denotes the transpose of the matrix M.*

Exercises

1. Write down the transition matrix for a source with three symbols, $\{A, B, C\}$, and the following constraints:

(a) The symbol "A" never follows "B."

(b) The symbol "C" is always followed by an "A."

(c) All legal transitions from a state occur with equal probabilities.

In each case, find probabilities p so that the corresponding Markov source is stationary.

2. Construct an example of a transition matrix for two symbols, for which there are two distinct sets of probabilities, each of which provides a stationary Markov source.

Theorems about finding efficient codes for high-order Markov sources often require that they are *ergodic*. An ergodic source has the property that *most* very long strings produced by the source have the same type of behavior. This means that in order to take an average over all possible initial conditions, it suffices to observe a single string produced by the source, albeit a very long one: the behavior of the sytem cannot be subdivided into different behaviors associated with different types of initial probability distributions $p^{(0)}$.

We explain the concept of an ergodic source with the aid of a special roulette wheel with a ball that is so sticky that whatever symbol (number) it starts with, it produces that number from then on. The only possible strings that can be produced by this source are:

$$s_1 s_1 s_1 s_1 s_1 s_1 s_1 s_1 s_1 s_1 s_1 s_1 s_1 s_1 s_1 s_1 s_1 s_1 s_1 s_1 s_1 s_1 s_1 s_1 s_1 \ldots$$
$$s_2 s_2 s_2 s_2 s_2 s_2 s_2 s_2 s_2 s_2 s_2 s_2 s_2 s_2 s_2 s_2 s_2 s_2 s_2 s_2 s_2 s_2 s_2 s_2 \ldots$$
$$.$$
$$.$$
$$.$$
$$s_n s_n s_n s_n s_n s_n s_n s_n s_n s_n s_n s_n s_n s_n s_n s_n s_n s_n s_n s_n s_n s_n \ldots$$

Each behavior is entirely different, and the source is not ergodic. However, if we weaken the statement that the ball is 100% sticky to merely 99.999% sticky, and allow a tiny probability that the ball becomes unstuck at any spin and transfers to any other symbol, the situation changes radically. The probability that the system remains locked into any one of the described behaviors approaches zero as the length of the source string increases. The behavior of *most* strings produced by the source is essentially the same, and might be described as typical. The source becomes ergodic. See Fig. 5.10.

Another example of a non-ergodic Markov source is illustrated in Fig. 5.11. Here, a source is constructed using six wheels of fortune. It is such that it

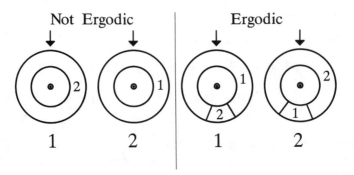

Figure 5.10. This figure illustrates two first-order Markov sources, each constructed using two wheels of fortune. One is ergodic and the other is not.

can output the numbers one, two, and three only if it has never produced a six. There exist pairs of states not reachable from one another.

We would like a unique answer for the probability of being in a given state. If the source is not ergodic, the different populations would give different numbers. Some regions would be more compressible than others.

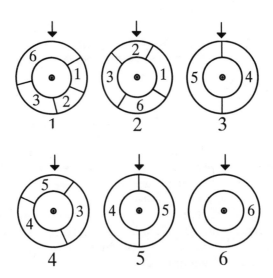

Figure 5.11. This figure illustrates a non-ergodic first-order Markov source, constructed using six wheels of fortune. Can you find two fundamentally different behaviors of the system?

The probability of going from state s_i to state s_j in two steps is a sum over all possible intermediate nodes,

$$\sum_{k=1}^{n} p_{ik} \cdot p_{kj}.$$

This expression is precisely the (i, j) entry of the matrix M^2. A similar argument holds for the probability of getting from state s_i to state s_j in r time steps. The probabilities are the corresponding elements in M^r. In order for a first-order Markov source never to be prohibited from transitioning to any state, and not to become trapped in a nontypical behavior, we require that for some integer r, all of these probabilities are positive. We want to rule out behaviors such as the following: consider a system with two states A and B, with the transition probability between them equal to unity; then there are transitions from every state to every other, yet there are only two possible orbits, $ABABABABA\ldots$ and $BABABABAB\ldots$, which continue like two white bishops on a chess board, never meeting. To rule out such behaviors, we can ask that the matrix M has the following property.

Definition *The Markov matrix M, defined earlier, is* irreducible *if there is an integer $r \geq 1$ such that $M^r = (a_{ij})$, where $a_{ij} > 0$.*

Theorem *If the matrix M is irreducible, then there is a unique probability vector p such that $M^T p = p$.*

Proof. See [WF], for example.

In other words, if a first-order Markov source is irreducible, then there is a unique p such that it is a stationary source.

Definition *A first-order Markov source is said to be* ergodic *if it is irreducible and stationary.*

Putting together the preceding definitions, and the computation of the entropy made before, we have the following theorem.

Theorem *If a first-order Markov source is ergodic, then the optimal achievable average binary output code length is given by the formula*

$$H(S) = \sum_{i=1}^{n} p_i \left[-\sum_{j=1}^{n} p_{ij} \log_2 p_{ij} \right]. \tag{5.3}$$

Examples:

(i) For the first-order Markov source with transition matrix

$$M = \begin{bmatrix} 0 & 1 \\ 1 & 0 \end{bmatrix},$$

one checks that $M^r = M$ if r is odd and

$$M^r = \begin{bmatrix} 1 & 0 \\ 0 & 1 \end{bmatrix}$$

if r is even. The entries of M are never all positive; the matrix is not irreducible and the source cannot be ergodic.

(ii) For the first-order Markov source whose transition matrix is

$$M = \begin{bmatrix} 1/2 & 1/2 \\ 0 & 1 \end{bmatrix},$$

one finds that

$$M^r = \begin{bmatrix} 1/2^r & 1 - 1/2^r \\ 0 & 1 \end{bmatrix}.$$

Since the lower left corner is never positive, it follows that this source is not ergodic.

(iii) The first-order Markov source with transition matrix

$$M = \begin{bmatrix} 1/2 & 1/2 \\ 1/3 & 2/3 \end{bmatrix}$$

is ergodic because all transition probabilities are positive. The probabilities p_1 and p_2 can be computed by solving the eigenvalue equation $M^T p = p$ subject to the constraint $p_1 + p_2 = 1$. We find that $p_1 = 2/5$, $p_2 = 3/5$. Substituting into Eq. (5.3) gives the entropy

$$
\begin{aligned}
H(S) &= \sum_{i=1}^{n} p_i \left[-\sum_{j=1}^{n} p_{ij} \log_2 p_{ij} \right] \\
&= \frac{2}{5} \left(\frac{1}{2} \log_2 2 + \frac{1}{2} \log_2 2 \right) \\
&+ \frac{3}{5} \left(\frac{1}{3} \log_2 3 + \frac{2}{3} \log_2 \frac{3}{2} \right) \simeq 0.95 \text{ bits}.
\end{aligned}
$$

Unlike the formal models we define here, real world information does not necessarily have correlations limited to a single symbol. However, we can approximate a real information source by a suitable choice of model. As an example, we can try to model a first-order source as a zero-order source by ignoring the transition probabilities.

What happens if we try to model this example as a zero-order source? The best approximation would be given by choosing $p_1 = 2/5$, $p_2 = 3/5$ and ignoring the higher-order terms. The entropy calculated this way is

$$H(S) = \frac{2}{5} \log_2 \frac{5}{2} + \frac{3}{5} \log_2 \frac{5}{3} \simeq 0.97 \text{ bits.}$$

The entropy has gone up; the compressibility has gone down.

Practically speaking, we may not be able to prove that an observed source is ergodic. Luckily, however, our code for a Markov model does not require ergodicity. The condition of being ergodic arises when we want to predict the efficiency of the code.

A general Markov source also has a corresponding notion of an extension. Higher-order Markov sources base the probability of a symbol's occurrence on a number of predecessors. For example, the probability of an "e" in English text is much greater given that the preceding two letters are "th" than would be predicted from the fact that the previous letter is an "h." Happily, by a process of recoding, higher-order sources can be reduced to a previously solved case; they correspond to first-order sources with larger alphabets.

The trick is to recode a sequence $s_1 s_2 s_3 s_4 \ldots$ as a new sequence from the alphabet S^2 of the form $(s_1 s_2)(s_2 s_3)(s_3 s_4) \ldots$. The transition probability from a pair $(s_i s_j)$ to $(s_k s_l)$ is zero unless $s_j = s_k$, in which case it is the probability of encountering s_l given that the preceding symbols were s_i and s_j. The generalization to longer correlations is immediate. By passing to extensions, one can approach the optimal rate as closely as desired. The conclusions are summarized in the following theorem.

Theorem (Shannon's Noiseless Coding Theorem) *If S is an ergodic Markov source, any instantaneous code with output alphabet with r symbols has an average length satisfying $H_r(S) \leq l_{av}$. By passing to the "k"th extension, one can find an instantaneous code whose average length per input symbol satisfies $l_{av} \leq H_r(S) + 1/k$.*

Proof. See [RH]

Exercises

1. Show that if there is a positive integer r such that $M^r = (a_{ij})$ with $a_{ij} > 0$, then this is true for some $r < n$.

2. Increasing the order of a Markov source improves asymptotic compression at the expense of complicating the model. Assume that an image is stored as an 8-bit (256 gray level) stream of pixel values. Estimate the storage necessary to express the image probabilities as a first-order Markov source.

5.10.   Huffman Codes for Compression

One possible way of constructing codes for an ergodic Markov source is to define a Shannon–Fano code for each state. A better way is by assigning to each state a *Huffman code* as described in this section. The same construction applies if the Markov source is not ergodic; however, the performance is no longer guaranteed by the theorem.

While Shannon–Fano codes use a splitting algorithm, Huffman codes use a merging algorithm. In a Shannon–Fano code, we start with a single node and add branches. In a Huffman code, many small trees are progressively glued together until they form a big tree. As we did with Shannon–Fano codes, we will restrict our attention to a binary output alphabet. The steps of the algorithm are:

Step 1. List the symbols in order of probability.

Step 2. Make a tree whose branches, labeled zero and one, are the two symbols with lowest weight.

Step 3. Remove the two symbols just used from the list and add to the list a new symbol representing the newly formed tree with probability equal to the total weight of the branches.

Step 4. Make a tree whose branches, labeled zero and one, are the two symbols with lowest weight in the new list. This tree may consist of two other symbols, or it could consist of a symbol and the tree just constructed.

Step 5. Repeat this procedure until one large tree is formed.

At each stage in the merging, we decide which newly formed branch to label zero and which to label one. This choice is made arbitrarily; the Huffman tree is not unique. A more important source of non-uniqueness arises when two nodes have the same weight. This leads not only to ties between symbol probabilities, but also to ties between partially formed trees that get manipulated by the algorithm in the same way as individual

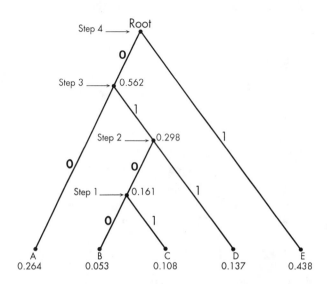

Figure 5.12. Construction of a Huffman tree.

symbols. A good heuristic to use for ties is to use the shorter of two possible subtrees first. One puts the new trees formed at the end of the list and always takes pairs to be combined from the beginning. The rationale for this heuristic is explored further in the exercises.

Examples:

(i) Consider five symbols $\{A, B, C, D, E\}$ with probabilities

$$p_A = 0.264, \quad p_B = 0.053, \quad p_C = 0.108, \quad p_D = 0.137, \quad p_E = 0.438.$$

These are the probabilities of the first five letters of the alphabet in English text according to [RL]. The steps taken in constructing a Huffman tree are illustrated in Fig. 5.12 for the indicated set of probabilities.

Step 1. Merge $\{B, C\}$ to form a tree with weight $p_{BC} = 0.161$. Here, we use the notation p_{BC} to mean the probability of seeing either symbol B or symbol C.

Step 2. Merge BC and D to form a tree with weight $p_{BCD} = 0.298$.

Step 3. Merge A and BCD to form a tree with weight $p_{ABCD} = 0.562$.

Step 4. Merge $ABCD$ and E, completing the tree.

The codewords are:

$$A \to 10, \quad B \to 1111, \quad C \to 1110, \quad D \to 110, \quad E \to 0.$$

(ii) What advantages does a Huffman code have over a Shannon–Fano code?

    (a) The merging process is simple and fast. The determination of the smallest two nodes can be done in linear time. A Shannon–Fano code requires selecting a partition of the set into probabilities as near as possible to one-half.

    (b) Huffman codes have a better performance for a given set of probabilities than do Shannon–Fano codes.

Figure 5.13 shows two different code trees for the code whose symbols have probabilities $(p_A = 2/5, p_B = 2/5, p_C = 1/10, p_D = 1/10)$. The first part of the figure represents the code that results from applying the Shannon–Fano algorithm. The average codeword length for this code is

$$l_{av} = 2\left(\frac{2}{5}\right) + 2\left(\frac{2}{5}\right) + 2\left(\frac{1}{10}\right) + 2\left(\frac{1}{10}\right) = 2 \text{ bits} .$$

Take the following steps to apply the Huffman algorithm to the same tree:

Step 1. Merge C and D to form a subtree with weight $p_{CD} = 1/5$.

Step 2. Merge CD and B to form a subtree with weight $p_{BCD} = 3/5$.

Step 3. Merge BCD and A to complete the tree.

The Huffman code tree yields an average codeword length of only 1.8 bits,

$$l_{av} = \frac{2}{5} + 2\left(\frac{2}{5}\right) + 3\left(\frac{1}{10}\right) + 3\left(\frac{1}{10}\right) = 1.8 \text{ bits.}$$

Exercises

1. The Huffman algorithm stated previously leaves unresolved the question of ties. Different choices can lead to different codes. The following example serves to motivate the heuristic mentioned earlier. Figure 5.14 illustrates two valid Huffman codes for the probabilities $p_A = p_B = 1/3, p_C = p_D = 1/6$.

(a) Compute the average length of a codeword with each possible code.

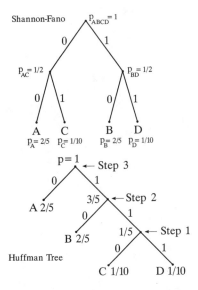

Figure 5.13. Two different code trees for the code whose symbols have probabilities $(p_A = 2/5, p_B = 2/5, p_C = 1/10, p_D = 1/10)$.

(b) Compute the variance of the codeword lengths for each code. The variance of a sequence of numbers $x_1, x_2, \ldots, x_n$ is the average square deviation from their mean,

$$\frac{1}{n} \sum_{i=1}^{n} (x_i - \bar{x})^2.$$

(c) What do you observe?

2. Use Table 5.3 to define a Huffman code for written English.

(a) What is the average code length of the code you constructed?

(b) What is the entropy of written English modeled as a zero-order Markov source?

(c) What does this result say about the compressibility of English text?

3. Figure 5.15 shows the Morse code. An exact equation for Morse code symbol length and bits is difficult, but we can compare relative lengths. Using the formula given in the caption for the duration of a Morse code symbol, compare the lengths of symbols in the Morse code to their length in an ideal code.

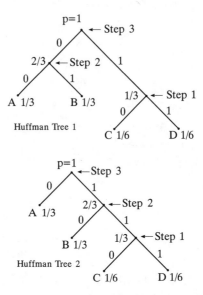

Figure 5.14. This figure illustrates two valid Huffman codes for the probabilities $p_A = p_B = 1/3, p_C = p_D = 1/6$.

Table 5.3. The probabilities of occurrence of the 26 letters in English text. How would this table change for Spanish?

A	0.0761	N	0.0711
B	0.0154	O	0.0765
C	0.0311	P	0.0203
D	0.0395	Q	0.0010
E	0.1262	R	0.0615
F	0.0234	S	0.0650
G	0.0195	T	0.0933
H	0.0551	U	0.0272
I	0.0734	V	0.0099
J	0.0015	W	0.0189
K	0.0065	X	0.0019
L	0.0411	Y	0.0172
M	0.0254	Z	0.0009

A → • −		N → − •
B → − • • •		O → − − −
C → − • − •		P → • − − •
D → − • •		Q → − − • −
E → •		R → • − •
F → • • − •		S → • • •
G → − − •		T → −
H → • • • •		U → • • −
I → • •		V → • • • −
J → • − − −		W → • − −
K → − • −		X → − • • −
L → • − • •		Y → − • − −
M → − −		Z → − − • •

Figure 5.15. The Morse code is one of the first examples of a code adjusted to compensate for frequencies. Warning: the pause between letters is part of the code! The length of a codeword is $4\times$ (duration of $-$) $= 2\times$ (duration of •) $= 2$, assuming standard timing. A dash has three times the duration of a dot, a dot's length separates symbols, and three dots' length separates letters [ARRL].

5.11. C Source Code Illustration of a Huffman Code

One can illustrate Huffman codes on a personal computer. The following program is written for compilation using the Turbo C compiler Version 1.0 by Borland and is designed to run under DOS on an IBM PC with an Intel 80286, 80386, or 80486 processor. The uncompiled program consists of a single file, HUFFMAN.C.

This program demonstrates the Huffman code algorithm. Its input is a set of probabilities and its output is a binary instantaneous code. Since the algorithm is concerned only with relative frequencies, the probabilities need not add to one.

A limit of 26 input symbols is imposed artificially. As an exercise, this constraint can be weakened. Also, each node carries a label of maximal possible length. This avoids memory allocation problems.

There are two constructs used. The Node structure forms a binary tree using the fields node —> zero and node —> one. In addition, the nodes are grouped into a linked list to keep track of the merging procedure. This is done via the field node —> next. Once the Huffman code is constructed, node —> next is irrelevant.

```
-------------------------------------------------
FILE NAME: HUFFMAN.C
-------------------------------------------------
#include <stdio.h>
#include <string.h>
#include <alloc.h>

#define MAXSYMBOLS 26

char symbols[] = "ABCDEFGHIJKLMNOPQRSTUVWXYZ";

typedef struct node {
  double weight;
  struct node *zero,*one;
  /* these pointers make up the tree structure */

  struct node *next;
  /* this pointer keeps track of list */

  char label[MAXSYMBOLS];
} Node;

extern void print_code(long n, Node *nodes),
       label_nodes(Node *root);
extern Node *insert_node(Node *node,Node *node_list);

main()
{
  long i,n=0,count=0;
  Node *new_node,*node_list=NULL,*auxilliary_nodes,*nodes;
  double p;
  nodes = (Node *) calloc(2*MAXSYMBOLS+1,sizeof(Node));
  auxilliary_nodes = nodes+MAXSYMBOLS;
  printf("\nInput probabilities (end with 0).\n\n");
  node_list=NULL;

  /* the symbols correspond to the leaves */
  /* in the tree and are stored in */
  /* the array nodes.  The weights do not have to */
  /* be normalized (add to 1) */
  /* so relative frequency information will do as well. */

  for (i=0;i<MAXSYMBOLS;i++)
```

```
     {
       printf("p(%c) = ",symbols[i]);
       fflush(stdout);
       scanf("%lf",&p);
       if(p==0.) break;
       nodes[i].weight=p;
       node_list=insert_node(&nodes[i],node_list);
       n++;
     }

   /* node_list maintains a list of nodes  */
   /* which have yet to be merged */
   /* the algorithm terminates  */
   /* when it has only one element */

   while (NULL!=node_list->next)
     {
       new_node = auxilliary_nodes+(count++);
       new_node->zero=node_list;
       new_node->one=node_list->next;
       new_node->weight=node_list->weight+
     node_list->next->weight; /* combine weight of children */
       node_list=(node_list->next)->next;
       node_list=insert_node(new_node,node_list);
     }
   label_nodes(node_list);
   print_code(n,nodes);
   free(nodes);
   return(0);
}

/* insert node into node_list; list is sorted by weight */
/* in the first loop, this function effects
   an insertion sort */

Node *insert_node(Node *node,Node *node_list)
{
  if (node_list==NULL)
    return(node);
  else if (node_list->weight>node->weight)
    {
      node->next=node_list;
      return(node);
```

```c
      }
  else
    {
      node_list->next=insert_node(node,node_list->next);
      return(node_list);
    }
}


/* recursively assign labels to the nodes */

void label_nodes(Node *root)
{
  if (root->zero)
    {
      strcpy(root->zero->label,root->label);
      strcat(root->zero->label,"0");
      label_nodes(root->zero);
    }
  if (root->zero)
    {
      strcpy(root->one->label,root->label);
      strcat(root->one->label,"1");
      label_nodes(root->one);
    }
}


/* print symbols and their codewords */

void print_code(long n,Node *nodes)
{
  short i;
  putchar('\n');
  for (i=0;i<n;i++)
    printf("%c --> %s\n",symbols[i],nodes[i].label);
}
```

Compile Instructions:

To compile the object module enter the DOS command line:
```
  tcc -ms -c -v HUFFMAN.C
```

To produce the executable function `HUFFMAN.EXE` enter the Turbo C command line:

```
tcc -ms -v HUFFMAN.OBJ
```

Running Instructions:
To run `HUFFMAN.EXE` enter the DOS command line:

```
HUFFMAN
```

Sample Output:

```
Input probabilities (end with 0).

p(A) = 3
p(B) = 9
p(C) = 1
p(D) = 1
p(E) = 1
p(F) = 5
p(G) = 0

A --> 110
B --> 0
C --> 11110
D --> 11111
E --> 1110
F --> 10
```

5.12.   Addresses on Fractals

This section may be omitted on a first reading; it is included because it is relevant to the arithmetic compression method approached from the point of view of IFS. Our goal here is to recall the definition and structure of *code space* Σ on N symbols, and to describe its relationship to addresses on fractals. The symbols in code space are the integers $\{1, 2, ..., N\}$. A typical point in Σ is a semi-infinite word such as

$$x = 2\ \ 17\ \ 0\ \ 0\ \ 1\ \ 21\ \ 15\ \ N\ \ 30\dots$$

There are infinitely many symbols in this sequence. In general, for a given element $\sigma \in \Sigma$, we can write

$$\sigma = \sigma_1\sigma_2\sigma_3\sigma_4\sigma_5\sigma_6\sigma_7\sigma_8\dots,$$

where each $\sigma_i \in \{1, 2, \dots, N\}$.

Definition *Let* $\{\mathbf{X}; w_1, w_2, \ldots, w_N\}$ *be a hyperbolic IFS. The* code space *associated with the IFS,* (Σ, d_C), *is defined to be the code space on* N *symbols* $\{1, 2, \ldots, N\}$, *with the metric* d_C *given by*

$$d_C(\omega, \sigma) = \sum_{n=1}^{\infty} \frac{|\omega_n - \sigma_n|}{(N+1)^n} \text{ for all } \omega, \sigma \in \Sigma.$$

One can verify that (Σ, d_C) is indeed a metric space. One can also show that d_C is equivalent to the metric d_E on Σ defined by

$$d_E(\omega, \sigma) = \left| \sum_{n=1}^{\infty} \frac{\omega_n - \sigma_n}{(N+1)^n} \right| \text{ for all } \omega, \sigma \in \Sigma.$$

Consider a hyperbolic IFS $\{\mathbf{X}; w_1, w_2\}$. Let A denote its attractor. Then $A = w_1(A) \cup w_2(A)$, from which we deduce that:

$$w_1(A) = w_1(w_1(A)) \cup w_1(w_2(A)), \text{ and } w_2(A) = w_2(w_1(A)) \cup w_2(w_2(A)).$$

Hence,

$$A = w_1(w_1(A)) \cup w_1(w_2(A)) \cup w_2(w_1(A)) \cup w_2(w_2(A)).$$

By induction, we deduce that for any positive integer M,

$$A = \bigcup_{\sigma_1 \sigma_2 \ldots \sigma_M = 1}^{2} w_{\sigma_1}(w_{\sigma_2}(\ldots(w_{\sigma_M}(A)))). \tag{5.4}$$

(The union here is taken over all finite sequences $\sigma_1 \sigma_2 \ldots \sigma_M$, where $\sigma_i \in \{1, 2\}$.) This tells us that, for any positive integer M, each point in the attractor A also belongs to at least one of the sets $w_{\sigma_1}(w_{\sigma_2}(\ldots w_{\sigma_M}(A)))$. By using the fact that both of the transformations w_1 and w_2 are contractive, with a contractivity factor smaller than one, one can show that the size of the set $w_{\sigma_1}(w_{\sigma_2}(\ldots w_{\sigma_M}(A)))$ tends to zero as M tends to infinity; that is,

$$\lim_{M \to \infty} \max_{x, y \in A} d(w_{\sigma_1}(w_{\sigma_2}(\ldots w_{\sigma_M}(x))), w_{\sigma_1}(w_{\sigma_2}(\ldots w_{\sigma_M}(y)))) = 0$$

for any point σ in code space Σ, of the two symbols $\{1, 2\}$,

$$\sigma = \sigma_1 \sigma_2 \sigma_3 \ldots \sigma_M \sigma_{M+1} \ldots$$

Hence, we have

$$\lim_{M \to \infty} w_{\sigma_1}(w_{\sigma_2}(\ldots w_{\sigma_M}(A))) = \text{ a single point } a \in A.$$

Notice that here the limit is taken over a decreasing sequence of sets. Each set is contained in the one that precedes it. Convergence to a single point, the only point which belongs to all of the sets, $a \in A$ is assured because each set is compact. This being the case, we say that the sequence of symbols $\sigma_1 \sigma_2 \sigma_3 \ldots \sigma_M \ldots$ is an *address* of the point $a \in A$. Eq. (5.4) tells us that every point of A has at least one address. If furthermore $w_1(A) \cap w_2(A) = \emptyset$, then one can show that every point of A has exactly one address [FE].

This discussion is readily generalized to the case of a hyperbolic IFS $\{\mathbf{X}; w_1, w_2, \ldots w_N\}$ consisting of more than two transformations. In fact, quite generally, one can construct a continuous transformation ϕ from the code space associated with an IFS onto the attractor of the IFS, as the following theorem tells us.

Theorem (Address Theorem) *Let $(\mathbf{X}, d)$ be a complete metric space. Let $\{\mathbf{X}; w_n : n = 1, 2, \ldots, N\}$ be a hyperbolic IFS. Let A denote the attractor of the IFS. Let (Σ, d_C) denote the code space associated with the IFS. For each $\sigma \in \Sigma, n \in \mathbf{N}$, and $x \in \mathbf{X}$, let*

$$\phi(\sigma, n, x) = w_{\sigma_1} \circ w_{\sigma_2} \circ \cdots w_{\sigma_n}(x).$$

Then

$$\phi(\sigma) = \lim_{n \to \infty} \phi(\sigma, n, x)$$

exists, belongs to A, and is independent of $x \in \mathbf{X}$. If K is a compact subset of $\mathbf{X}$, then the convergence is uniform over $x \in K$. The function $\phi : \Sigma \to A$ thus provided is continuous and onto.

Proof. See [JH], [FE].

The Address theorem allows us to formalize our definition of the address of a point in the attractor of an IFS, as follows.

Definition *Let $\{\mathbf{X}; w_n, n = 1, 2, 3, \ldots, N\}$ be a hyperbolic IFS with associated code space Σ. Let $\phi : \Sigma \to A$ be the continuous function from code space onto the attractor of the IFS constructed in the address theorem. An address of a point $a \in A$ is any member of the set*

$$\phi^{-1}(a) = \{\omega \in \Sigma : \phi(\omega) = a\}.$$

This set is called the set of addresses of $a \in A$.

The subject of addresses on fractals is considered in more detail in [FE].

An important case is where each point on the attractor has exactly one address. In this case A is totally disconnected. Another case is where the set of points that have more than one address is relatively small or unimportant; this is stated using measure theory. For example, we may have a Borel measure μ on the attractor, and we may be able to say that the measure of the points $a \in A$ that have more than one address is zero. Precisely this latter situation occurs in the following section.

5.13. Arithmetic Compression and IFS Fractals

In this section, we show how optimal lossless compression is achieved using fractal geometry. Specifically, we construct an IFS fractal and locate a point on the fractal whose address is specified by the source file. To compress the file, we convert the address of the point to its Euclidean specification. Furthermore, to generate the point, we use the chaos game algorithm. What could be more lovely than to use this wild theory, central to the understanding of chaos, to achieve optimal compression. We seem to be looking at the heart of the matter.

Before beginning, we note that a drawback of Huffman codes is the fact that codewords have an integral number of symbols. Instead of the theoretically optimal code length $-p \log p$, the length is rounded to an integer. In the extreme case of a data stream with two symbols, no compression is possible without passing to a more complicated model, such as an extension. Arithmetic codes provide an elegant way around this problem, which achieves a rate as close as desired to the entropy, while coding one symbol at a time. See [MN] and [WNC]. This optimal method of compression turns out to be deeply related to IFS and the chaos game algorithm.

We consider a zero-order Markov source, which generates the symbols $1, 2, \ldots n$ with independent probabilities $p_1, p_2, \ldots, p_n$. In order to compress strings of symbols produced by this source, we introduce the IFS

$$\{[0,1] \subset \mathbb{R} : w_1, w_2, \ldots, w_n\},$$

where the transformation $w_i : [0,1] \to [0,1]$ is a contractive affine map, given by

$$w_i(x) = p_i x + t_i, \quad \text{for } i = 1, 2, \ldots, n,$$

with

$$t_i = p_{i-1} + p_{i-2} + \cdots + p_1, \quad \text{and } t_1 = 0.$$

This IFS is such that

$$[0,1] = \cup \, w_i([0,1]),$$

so that its attractor is $[0,1]$. In fact, this IFS is *just-touching*, (see [FE]) because

$$[0,1) = \cup\, w_i([0,1)),$$

and

$$w_i([0,1)) \cap w_j([0,1)) = \emptyset, \text{ for } i \neq j.$$

Now let

$$\sigma = \sigma_1 \sigma_2 \sigma_3 \sigma_4 \sigma_5 \sigma_6 \sigma_7 \sigma_8 \ldots \sigma_k \ldots$$

denote a string of symbols produced by the source. Then the arithmetic encoding process involves the generation of a sequence of points

$$\{\ldots x_0, x_1, \ldots, x_k, \ldots\} \subset \mathbb{R}$$

as follows:

Step 1. Choose x_0 in the interval $[0,1)$.

Step 2. Apply the transformation w_{σ_1}, corresponding to the first symbol σ_1, to the point x_0 to produce a new point $x_1(x_0)$ in the interval $[0,1]$,

$$x_1(x_0) = w_{\sigma_1}(x_0).$$

Step 3. Apply the transformation w_{σ_2}, corresponding to the second symbol σ_2, to the point x_1 to produce

$$x_2(x_0) = w_{\sigma_2}(x_1) = w_{\sigma_2}(w_{\sigma_1}(x_0)).$$

Step 4. Continue in this manner, to produce a sequence of points

$$\{x_0, x_1, \ldots, x_k, \ldots\} \subset [0,1], \text{ with}$$

$$x_k(x_0) w_{\sigma_k} \circ w_{\sigma_{k-1}} \circ \cdots w_{\sigma_1}(x_0).$$

The process is illustrated in Fig. 5.16.

We say that the Markov source has been used to *drive* the IFS. The IFS $\{[0,1] \subset \mathbb{R} : w_1, w_2, \ldots, w_n\}$ is *driven* by the string

$$\ldots \sigma_1 \sigma_2 \sigma_3 \sigma_4 \sigma_5 \sigma_6 \sigma_7 \sigma_8 \ldots \sigma_k \ldots,$$

starting from the point x_0. The output at the end of k steps is the value of x_k in, e.g., binary decimal units.

From only the information consisting of the approximate value of the last point x_k, together with the IFS maps, we can reconstruct the string

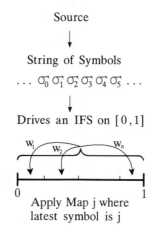

Source

↓

String of Symbols

... σ_0^- σ_1^- σ_2^- σ_3^- σ_4^- σ_5^- ...

↓

Drives an IFS on $[0,1]$

Apply Map j where
latest symbol is j

Figure 5.16. This figure illustrates the use of a zero-order Markov source to drive an IFS. The process yields a wild orbit on the interval $[0, 1]$, ending up at the point x_k. The forward orbit of x_k regenerates the original string emitted by the source: the input string is encoded as x_k.

$\sigma_1\sigma_2\sigma_3\sigma_4\sigma_5\sigma_6\sigma_7\sigma_8 \ldots \sigma_k$. To do this, we need the piecewise affine map $f : [0, 1] \to [0, 1]$, which we call the *foward map*, defined by

$$f(x) = w_i^{-1}(x) \quad \text{for } x \in w_i([0,1)), \quad \text{for } i = 1, 2, \ldots, n,$$
$$\text{and}$$
$$f(1) = w_n^{-1}(1).$$

This function is illustrated in Fig. 5.17.

It is readily verified that, since f is a kind of inverse of the collection of IFS transformations, the orbit of the point x_k under f commences with the sequence of points $x_{k-1}, x_{k-2}, \ldots x_1$; that is,

$$f^{\circ j}(x_k) = x_{k-j}, \text{ for } j = 1, 2, 3, \ldots, k.$$

From this sequence of points, one can reconstruct the sequence of symbols σ_j as follows:

$$\sigma_{k-j} = m, \text{ where } m \in \{1, 2, ..., n\} \text{ is such that } f^{\circ j}(x_k) \in w_m([0,1));$$

that is, one simply tracks the orbit of x_k under the foward map f, and determines in what subinterval $w_m([0,1))$ lies for each point on this orbit. Thus, we are able to decode the string $\sigma_1, \sigma_2, \ldots \sigma_k$ from the knowledge of x_k alone. An example of a decompression orbit is illustrated in Fig. 5.18.

Compression is achieved because it is only necessary to provide a limited number of digits of accuracy for x_k; it only needs to be sufficiently accurate

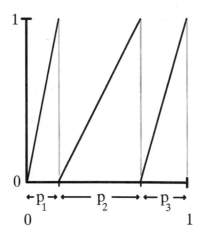

Figure 5.17. This figure illustrates the forward map f, associated with an IFS, which is used in the decompression of arithmetic codes.

for the points on the orbit of x_k to lie in the appropriate subinterval of $[0, 1]$ at each step. Let us consider a typical input string σ in which the symbol i occurs n_i times, for $i = 1, 2, \ldots, n$. Then $n_1 + n_2 + \cdots + n_n = k$, where k

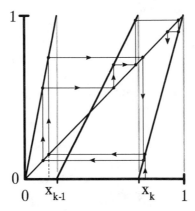

Figure 5.18. This figure illustrates the decompression of an arithmetic code using the forward map associated with an IFS. In arithmetic compression, the compressed string is simply the location of the point on a fractal whose address is given by the input string!

is the length of the string. We find that if x_0 lies in $[0, 1)$, then

$$x_k(x_0) \in I_k = [x_k(0), x_k(1)) = [x_k(0), x_k(0) + \prod_{i=1}^{n} p_i^{n_i}),$$

because each time the transformation w_i is applied, distances between points are shrunk by the factor p_i. Clearly, the orbit of any point in I_k leads to the same output string $\sigma_1, \sigma_2, \ldots, \sigma_k$. The output code can be represented by any point in I_k. One can readily show that there lies a point $\tilde{x}_k \in I_k$, which in base 2 is accurately represented by its decimal expansion truncated after the first

$$-\log_2 \prod_{i=1}^{n} p_i^{n_i}$$

binary decimal places. If we use this point, then the compression ratio is

$$\frac{\text{length of output string}}{\text{length of input string}} = \frac{-\log_2 \prod_{i=1}^{n} p_i^{n_i}}{n_1 + n_2 + \cdots + n_n}$$

$$= \sum_{i=1}^{n} \frac{-n_i}{n_1 + n_2 + \cdots + n_n} \log_2 p_i.$$

Clearly, if the input string is a *typical* input string, generated by the source, then when the length of the string is large,

$$\frac{n_i}{n_1 + n_2 + \cdots + n_n} \simeq p_i$$

and the compression ratio approaches the entropy.

The preceding process can also be understood in terms of the chaos game algorithm [FE]. The *random source* is used to drive a just-touching IFS whose attractor is the interval $[0, 1]$. The IFS is *tuned* so that its invariant measure, when driven by the source, is a uniform Lebesgue measure on $[0, 1]$. This means that almost all orbits generated by the system will distribute themselves uniformly over the interval; in turn, this implies that *typical* points on the orbit are most efficiently represented using standard base r decimal representation because then the digits in the expansion will be uniformly distributed and the entropy will be maximal.

5.14. C Source Code Illustration for Arithmetic Encoding and Decoding

One can illustrate arithmetic encoding and decoding on a personal computer. The following program is written for compilation using the Turbo

C Version 1.0 compiler by Borland, and is designed to run under DOS on an IBM PC with an Intel 80286, 80386, or 80486 processor. The uncompiled encoding and decoding programs are called A_ENC.C and A_DEC.C, respectively.

A_ENC.EXE demonstrates arithmetic encoding. The input alphabet is A, B, C and the output is a real number. If the string is long enough, the program will underflow. Exactly when this occurs depends on the probabilities assigned to the symbols; however, some strings will never underflow. The program gets the length of the string from the input data.

It should be stressed that a finite string corresponds to an interval. In this program, the midpoint of the interval is sent. For compression, one would instead send the cheapest (in terms of number of bits in numerator and denominator) rational number in the interval.

A_DEC.EXE demonstrates arithmetic decoding. The input is a real number and the length of the desired string. The output is a string of A's, B's, and C's. Note that any real number can be decoded to as long a string as desired, even though symbols beyond the point at which one stopped encoding are nonsense. As an exercise, one can let the number of symbols get big and explain the patterns that emerge. Decoding the value 0.25 is especially interesting.

The probabilities can be changed by editing the source code and recompiling the program.

```
------------------------------------------------
FILE NAME: A_ENC.C
------------------------------------------------
#include <stdio.h>
#include <string.h>

double probs[] = {0.2, 0.2, 0.4},
   lower_limit[]={0.,0.2,0.4};
        /* cumulative sum of the probabilities */
main()
{
   short i,n;
   char string[80];
   /* maximum number of characters to prevent
      underflow */
   double x,offset,length;
   printf("Input string (symbols are A, B, or C) : ");
   fflush(stdout);
   scanf("%s",string);
   n = strlen(string);
```

```
    /* bottom of interval of possible real numbers */
    offset=0.;
    /* length of interval of possible real numbers */
    length=1.;
    for (i=0;i<n;i++)
      {
        if (string[i]=='A')
          {
            offset+=length*lower_limit[0];
            length*=probs[0];
          }
        else if (string[i]=='B')
          {
            offset+=length*lower_limit[1];
            length*=probs[1];
          }
        else if (string[i]=='C')
          {
            offset+=length*lower_limit[2];
            length*=probs[2];
          }
        else
          {
            fprintf(stderr,"Illegal symbol %c.\n",string[i]);
            exit(1);
          }
      }
  x=offset+length/2;   /* pick midpoint of interval */
   /* actually any point in interval will do */
  printf("%lf\n",x);
  return(0);
}
```

Compile Instructions:
To compile the object module, enter the DOS command line:

```
tcc -ms -c -v A_ENC.C
```

To produce the executable function A_ENC.EXE, enter the Turbo C command line:

```
tcc -ms -v A_ENC.OBJ
```

Running Instructions:
To run A_ENC.EXE, enter the DOS command line:

```
A_ENC
```

Sample Output:

```
Input string (symbols are A, B, or C) :    ABCABCAABC
0.056899
```

FILE NAME: A_DEC.C

```c
#include <stdio.h>

double probs[] = {0.2, 0.2, 0.4},
       lower_limit[]={0.,0.2,0.4};
       /* cumulative sum of the probabilities */

main()
{
  short i,n;
  double x;
  printf("     Input number of symbols n: ");
  fflush(stdout);
  scanf("%d",&n);
  printf("Input real number x (0<=x<=1) : ");
  fflush(stdout);
  scanf("%lf",&x);
  for (i=0;i<n;i++)
    {
      if (x<lower_limit[1])
        {
          putchar('A');
          x/=probs[0];
        }
      /* one can store reciprocals and multiply */
      /* in practical applications one has to guard */
      /* against underflow */
      else if (x<lower_limit[2])
        {
          putchar('B');
          x-=lower_limit[1];
          x/=probs[1];
```

```
        }
    else
        {
            putchar('C');
            x-=lower_limit[2];
            x/=probs[2];
        }
    }
 putchar('\n');
 return(0);
}
```

Compile Instructions:
To compile the object module enter the DOS command line:

`tcc -ms -c -v A_DEC.C`

To produce the executable function A_DEC.EXE enter the Turbo C command line:

`tcc -ms -v A_DEC.OBJ`

Running Instructions:
To run A_DEC.EXE, enter the DOS command line:

`A_DEC`

Sample Output:

Input number of symbols n: 7
Input real number $x(0 \leq x \leq 1)$: 0.056899
ABCABCA

5.15. References

[ARRL] Charles L. Hutchinson and Joel P. Kleinman (editors), *The ARRL Handbook for Radio Amateurs* (6th edition) American Radio Relay League, Newington, CT (1992)

[CS1] C. E. Shannon, and W. Weaver, *The Mathematical Theory of Communication*, University of Illinois Press, Urbana, IL (1949).

[CS2] C. E. Shannon, "Coding Theorems for a Discrete Source with a Fidelity Criterion," *IRE Nat'l Conv. Rec., Part 4*, 142–163 (1959).

[FE] M. Barnsley, *Fractals Everywhere*, Academic Press, Boston (1988).

[JS] J. R. Storer, *Data Compression: Methods and Theory*, Computer Science Press, Rockville, MD (1988).

[JH] J. Hutchinson, "Fractals and Self-Similarity," *Indiana University Mathematics Journal*, 30, 731–747.

[RH] R.W. Hamming, *Coding and Information Theory*, Prentice Hall, Englewood, N J (1980).

[MN] Mark Nelson, *The Data Compression Book*, M&T Books, Redwood City, CA (1991).

[RF] R. Fano, Ph.D. Thesis, Massachusetts Institute of Technology, Cambridge, MA (1949).

[WF] William Feller, *An Introduction to Probability Theory and Its Applications*, (second Edition) Wiley & Sons, New York (1957).

[RL] Robert W. Lucky, *Silicon Dreams: Information, Man and Machine*, St. Martin's Press, New York (1989).

[WNC] Ian H. Witten, Radford M. Neal, and John Cleary, "Arithmetic Coding for Data Compression," *Commun. ACM*, Volume 30, Number 6 (1987).

6

Fractal Image Compression II : The Fractal Transform

6.1. Goals of This Chapter

In this chapter, we introduce fractal transform theory and its application to image compression. Fractal transform theory is the theory of *local* iterated function systems, abbreviated as *local IFS*. A local IFS is an IFS wherein the constraint on the transformations that their domains be the whole space is relaxed to allow domains that are subsets of the space. A fractal transform of an image is essentially an IFS code that includes specification of the domains of the transformations. The use of local domains complicates the theory but simplifies the process of automatic fractal image compression. We say "automatic", because our previous approaches, in Chapter 4, have all been manual — involving some form of interactive geometrical modelling.

A local transformation on a space **X** is one whose domain is a subset of the space **X**; the transformation need not act on all points in the space. A global transformation is defined on all points of the space. By extending IFS theory from global to local, and restricting attention to affine symmetry transformations, we are able to develop computationally practical schemes to automate a generalized collage theorem.

This chapter includes C source code for implementation of elementary fractal transforms; this is included to show how discretized applications of the theory can be developed. Digital computer implementation of the image compression procedures described in this chapter is covered by U.S. Patent #5,065,447 and by corresponding patents in other countries worldwide. If you wish to set up an image compression system on a digital computer using the fractal transform, you should apply for a license to:

>Licensing Department
>Iterated Systems, Inc.
>5550-A Peachtree Parkway, Suite 650
>Norcross, GA 30092

Iterated Systems, Inc., can also provide you with the latest commerical implementations of fractal transform technology.

Fractal image compression using techniques described in this chapter are referred to in [JB], [AJ], [FBJ], [BS], [PJS] and [JW]. Examples of commercial products that use fractal transform technology are [ME] and [II].

6.2. General Description of Fractal Image Compression Methodology

The fractal image compression methods discussed in this book involve the same three basic ingredients:

1. *A model* **Y** *for the space* ℜ *of real world images, as described in Chapter 2.* Each "point" in **Y** represents a real world image, has a support □, chromatic attributes, and so on. Examples of **Y** include spaces of sets, function spaces, and measure spaces.

2. *A metric d on the space* **Y**, *such that* (**Y**, d) *is a complete metric space.*

3. *A contractive operator O, which acts upon the space* (**Y**, d). That is, the operator O is such that there exists a real number s with $0 \le s < 1$, and

$$d(O(\phi), O(\psi)) \le s \cdot d(\phi, \psi) \text{ for all } \phi, \psi \in \mathbf{Y}.$$

The operator O is built up from a finite set of elementary contractive functions that act upon the underlying space □ and upon the chromatic attributes.

An example of O is W, the Hutchinson operator

$$W = \bigcup w_i,$$

which is used in the case of binary images, where $\mathbf{Y}$ is the space $\Re_i$ defined in Chapter 2, and d is the Hausdorff distance [FE], as discussed in Chapter 4. Another example is the Markov operator

$$M(\nu) = p_1\nu \circ w_1^{-1} + p_2\nu \circ w_2^{-1} + \cdots + p_N\nu \circ w_N^{-1},$$

which is used in the case of grayscale images modelled by Borel measures supported on $\square$, where $\mathbf{Y}$ is the space $\Re_{iii}$ defined in Chapter 2, and d is the Hutchinson metric, discussed in Chapter 4. In each example the operator is constructed with succintly expressible functions w_i. In practice, the latter are contractive affine transformations of one form or another; and as such they can be described by finite sets of coefficients, the full set of which represents the "code" for the operator O. In this chapter, the operator O will be constructed using local affine transformations.

The consequences of having the ingredients 1, 2, and 3 can be summarized in the following theorems and expectations:

(1) **Theorem (Existence of Attractors)** *Since O is contractive, and the metric space $\mathbf{Y}$ is complete, there exists an unique image $\phi \in \mathbf{Y}$ such that*

$$O(\phi) = \phi.$$

Proof. See [FE] or any text on metric spaces.

(2) **Expectation (Fractal Character of Attractors)** *We anticipate that ϕ has a resolution independent character because of the contractivity of the functions from which O is constructed: the whole invariant image is the same as a sum or union of contractions applied to it, and thus it is made of shrunken copies of (parts of) itself. Depending on the way in which the contractions act, the focus may be on spatial contractivity, intensity contractivity, or measure theoretic contractivity, and we expect that the attractor ϕ will inherit corresponding fractal characteristics.*

(3) **Theorem (Computation of Attractors)** *To compute ϕ, we can use the fact that if $\psi \in \mathbf{Y}$ then the result of repeatedly applying O to ψ converges to the attractor ϕ; that is*

$$\lim_{n \to \infty} O^{\circ n} = \phi.$$

Moreover, if there exists a real constant C such that $d(\phi_1, \phi_2) < C$ for all $\phi_1, \phi_2 \in \mathbf{Y}$, then we have the error estimate $d(O^{\circ n}(\psi), \phi) \leq s^n C$.

Proof. See [FE].

The latter equation tells us that invariant images can be computed by algorithms similar to the photocopy machine algorithm and the greyscale photocopy algorithm. The error estimate allows one to predict the number of iterations required to achieve a given accuracy.

(4) Theorem (General Collage Theorem Estimate) *The distance between $\psi \in \mathbf{Y}$ and the attractor ϕ of O is bounded by the estimate*

$$d(\phi, \psi) \leq \frac{d(\psi, O(\psi))}{(1 - s)}.$$

Proof. See [FE].

The set $O(\psi)$ is called a *collage*, while the distance $d(\psi, O(\psi))$ is called a *collage error.* The theorem says that if we wish to find an operator O whose attractor is approximately ψ, then we have only to solve the problem of choosing O such that application of O to ψ does not change ψ very much. For example, if a grayscale photocopy machine is adjusted so that its output "looks like" its input, then the associated invariant image "looks like" the input, too.

Thus, whenever we have the ingredients 1, 2, and 3, we are able to develop some sort of fractal image compression system. For example, in Chapter 4 we show that there are diverse ways in which collections of *globally* defined transformations can be put together to form operators O so that the structure described previously comes into play. In each case, the result is an interactively controllable system for fractal image compression, appropriate to fractal image modelling; attractors of these systems can be defined as sets, and as measures corresponding to different models for real world images.

In fractal transform theory the basic ingredients 1, 2, and 3 are provided by collections of *local* transformations. These are assembled in various ways to produce an operator O and a corresponding system for generating resolution-independent, fractal attractors. Each variant leads to a different procedure for automatic fractal image compression; the local character of the transformations enables automatic rather than interactive selection of the transformations.

6.3. Local Iterated Function Systems

In order to introduce fractal transform theory, and to show how fractals defined using local transformations lead to automatic image compression methods, we consider here what happens when IFS theory is applied using local transformations to the case of binary images. A simple scheme for automatic fractal compression of binary images is described.

Definition *Let* $(\mathbf{X}, d)$ *be a compact metric space. Let R be a nonempty subset of* $\mathbf{X}$. *Let $w : R \to \mathbf{X}$ and let s be a real number with $0 \le s < 1$. If*

$$d(w(x), w(y)) \le s \cdot d(x, y) \text{ for all } x, y \text{ in } R,$$

then w is called a local contraction mapping *on* $(\mathbf{X}, d)$. *The number s is a contractivity factor for w.*

Definition *Let* $(\mathbf{X}, d)$ *be a compact metric space, and let $w_i : R_i \to \mathbf{X}$ be a local contraction mapping on* $(\mathbf{X}, d)$, *with contractivity factor s_i, for $i = 1, 2, \ldots, N$, where N is a finite positive integer. Then*

$$\{w_i : R_i \to \mathbf{X} : i = 1, 2, \ldots, N\}$$

is called a local iterated function system (local IFS). *The number $s = \max\{s_i : i = 1, 2, \ldots, N\}$ is called the contractivity factor of the local IFS.*

Local IFS's can be used to define contractive operators on image spaces. Here, we consider examples of the following type. Let S denote the set of all subsets of $\mathbf{X}$. Then we can define an operator $W_{\text{local}} : S \to S$ according to

$$W_{\text{local}}(B) = \bigcup_{i=1}^{N} w_i(R_i \cap B), \text{ for all } B \in S.$$

With appropriate constraints, we can also treat W_{local} as an operator on the the Hausdorff space $\mathcal{H}(\mathbf{X})$ consisting of nonempty compact subsets of $\mathbf{X}$; then, very loosely speaking, we find that W_{local} is contractive on certain compact subsets of $\mathcal{H}(\mathbf{X})$, with contractivity factor s with respect to the Hausdorff metric. That is, very roughly, we have the ingredients for a fractal compression system as described in Section 6.2, when W_{local} is chosen to be the operator O acting on the space $\mathbf{Y} = \mathcal{H}(\mathbf{X})$.

We say that a nonempty subset A of $\mathbf{X}$ is an attractor or invariant set of the local IFS if

$$W_{\text{local}}(A) = A.$$

A local IFS may have no attractor, and it may have many fundamentally distinct ones. If A and B are attractors, then so is $A \cup B$, which tells us that, if there is an attractor, then there is a largest one, namely one which contains all of the others. This is obtained by taking the union of all of the attractors of W_{local}. In general, this is the one to which we refer when we talk of *the* attractor of W_{local}.

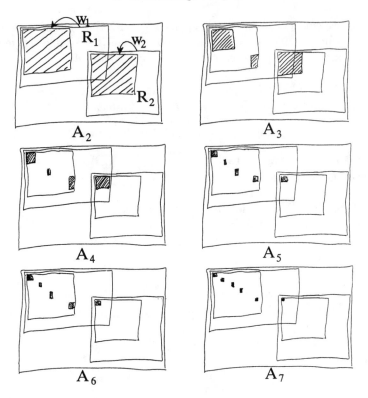

Figure 6.1. A decreasing sequence of sets converging to an attractor of a local iterated function system that consists of two local contractive affine transformations $w_1 : R_1 \rightarrow$ □ and $w_2 : R_2 \rightarrow$ □. How robust is this attractor? Can you find another nonempty attractor for the system?

Let $\{w_i : R_i \rightarrow \mathbf{X} : i = 1, 2, \ldots, N\}$ denote a local IFS, where we suppose that the sets R_i are compact. Then we can define a sequence of compact subsets of $\mathbf{X}, \{A_n : n = 0, 1, 2, 3, \ldots\}$, by

$$A_0 = \mathbf{X},$$

$$A_n = \bigcup_{i=1}^{N} w_i(R_i \cap A_{n-1}) \text{ for } n = 1, 2, 3, \ldots$$

It is straightfoward to verify that

$$A_0 \supset A_1 \supset A_2 \supset A_3 \supset \cdots$$

That is, $\{A_n : n = 0, 1, 2, 3, \ldots\}$ is a decreasing sequence of compact sets.

In particular, there exists a compact set $A \subset \mathbf{X}$ so that

$$\lim_{n \to \infty} A_n = A$$

and

$$A = \bigcup_{i=1}^{N} w_i(R_i \cap A) = W_{\text{local}}(A).$$

Then, if it is not empty, A is an attractor — in fact the maximal attractor — for the local IFS. The possibility that A is empty is ruled out if one can find a nonempty compact set B so that $W_{\text{local}}(B) \supset B$. This occurs, for example, if $w_i(R_i) \subset R_i$ for any i.

An example of the above construction is illustrated in Fig. 6.1.

6.4.   The Collage Theorem for a Local IFS

Despite the lack of a general clean contractive operator, we can cautiously treat a local IFS just as though it is a standard IFS. What happens when we apply the associated collage theorem?

Let a black-and-white binary target image be given, represented by a subset $G \subset \square$. In order to create a fractal model for G, we tile $\square$ with little squares, denoting those that intersect G by D_i for $i = 1, 2, \ldots, N$, as illustrated in Fig. 6.2. Then, for each $i = 1, 2, 3, \ldots, N$ we seek a local affine transformation $w_i : R_i \to \square$, with contractivity factor s, such that

$$w_i(R_i) = D_i$$

and

$$w_i(R_i \cap G) \simeq D_i \cap G.$$

Here, the criterion for approximate equality may be that the Hausdorff distance between $R_i \cap G$ and $D_i \cap G$ be small, say

$$h(w_i(R_i \cap G), D_i \cap G) < \epsilon, \text{ for } i = 1, 2, \ldots, N.$$

Other metrics can also be used.

In a practical application, the transformations may be chosen to be of the form

$$w(\,\cdot\,) = 0.5A \cdot + \, t$$

where $A : \square \to \square$ is one of the affine symmetries in Table 6.1. Then R_i is a little block, twice the size of D_i, as illustrated in Fig. 6.2.

If each block D_i is of the same size, for $i = 1, 2, \ldots, N$, then the local IFS is fully specified by providing for each i the x and y coordinates (D_x, D_y)

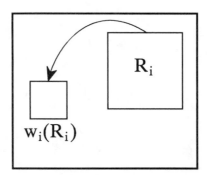

Figure 6.2. A region $R_i \subset \square$ and its image $w_i(R_i)$ in a local IFS.

of the lower left corner of D_i, the coordinates (R_x, R_y) of the lower left corner of R_i, and an integer that indicates the choice of affine symmetry A in Table 6.1. The result, which we call a *local IFS code* can be expressed as in Fig. 6.3, which also shows a target image, how it is encoded, and the attractor.

Table 6.1. The dihedral group of the square. Rotations are counter-clockwise.

Symmetry	Matrix	Description
0	$\begin{pmatrix} 1 & 0 \\ 0 & 1 \end{pmatrix}$	identity
1	$\begin{pmatrix} -1 & 0 \\ 0 & 1 \end{pmatrix}$	reflection in y-axis
2	$\begin{pmatrix} 1 & 0 \\ 0 & -1 \end{pmatrix}$	reflection in x-axis
3	$\begin{pmatrix} -1 & 0 \\ 0 & -1 \end{pmatrix}$	180° rotation
4	$\begin{pmatrix} 0 & 1 \\ 1 & 0 \end{pmatrix}$	reflection in line $y = x$
5	$\begin{pmatrix} 0 & 1 \\ -1 & 0 \end{pmatrix}$	90° rotation
6	$\begin{pmatrix} 0 & -1 \\ 1 & 0 \end{pmatrix}$	270° rotation
7	$\begin{pmatrix} 0 & -1 \\ -1 & 0 \end{pmatrix}$	reflection in line $y = -x$

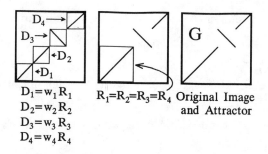

$$D_1 = w_1 R_1$$
$$D_2 = w_2 R_2$$
$$D_3 = w_3 R_3$$
$$D_4 = w_4 R_4$$

$R_1 = R_2 = R_3 = R_4$ Original Image and Attractor

Map#	D_x	D_y	R_x	R_y	Symmetry
1	0	0	0	0	0
2	4	4	0	0	0
3	8	8	0	0	2
4	12	12	0	0	0

Figure 6.3. A simple target image, an associated LIFS, showing the blocks D_i, R_i, and the attractor. The LIFS code is also shown.

6.5.   Calculation of Binary Attractors of Local IFS Using the Escape Time Algorithm

A simple technique for computation of the attractor A of a local IFS for a binary image, as just described, is the *escape time algorithm* described in [FE]. Let $D = \cup D_i$ and define

$$f : D \to \square$$

by

$$f(x) = w_i^{-1}(x) \text{ for } x \in D_i \quad \text{ for } i = 1, 2, 3, \ldots, N.$$

Notice that $f(D_i) = R_i$. It is for this reason that we use the notation R_i for the domain of w_i and D_i for its range, rather than the other way about. The piecewise affine function $f : D \subset \square \to \square$ provides us with a dynamical system whose repelling set is the attractor associated with the local IFS. The regions D_i are called *domain blocks* while the regions R_i are called *range blocks*.

The attractor A of the local IFS and a decreasing sequence of approximations A_n to A are computed as follows:

(0) Initialize a counter to zero, and specify a maximum number of iterations n.

(1) Input $x \in \square$.

(2) Does $x \in D$? If yes, replace x by $f(x)$. If no, output "$x \notin A$" and exit.

(3) Increment the counter; if counter $= n$, output "$x \in A_n$" and exit.

(4) Go to (1).

This algorithm enables one to answer the question "Does x belong to A?" In practice, it yields $A_n = W^{on}_{local}(D) \supset A$. If $n = \infty$, then inputs which cause the algorithm to run on endlessly belong to A.

6.6.   The Black and White Fractal Transform

A system for automatic fractal image compression of binary images based on the foregoing discussion is described in U.S. Patent #5,065,447. Here is an example of the main steps.

0. Input a binary image G, a subset of $\square \subset \mathbb{R}^2$.

1. Cover G with domain blocks, D_i, as illustrated in Fig. 6.4. The total set of domain blocks $\{D_i : i = 1, 2, \ldots, n\}$ taken together must cover G. Domain blocks do not overlap one another; there are some considerations regarding the edges of the blocks, but we ignore these to keep the exposition simple. Each range block is a square.

2. Introduce a collection of possible range blocks $R \subset \square$, each such that $R \cap G \neq \emptyset$. These are squares whose sides are twice as long as those of the domain blocks. The possible coordinates (R_x, R_y) of the lower left corner of each possible range block are restricted to lie in a finite set L. Correspondingly, we define a collection T of local contractive affine transformations, mapping from range block R to the domain block D_i. That is, for $i = 1, 2, \ldots, n$,

$$T_i = \{w(D_i, R_x, R_y, j) : (R_x, R_y) \in L; j = 0, 1, 2, \ldots 7\},$$

where $w(D_i, R_x, R_y, j)$ is the contractive affine tranformation with domain R, range D_i, of the form

$$0.5A(j) \cdot + t$$

and $A(j)$ denotes the jth symmetry in Table 6.1. Some members of T_i are illustrated in Fig. 6.5.

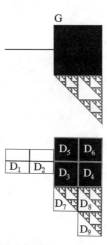

Figure 6.4. A binary image represented by a set G is covered with square domain blocks D_i.

3. Carry out the fractal transform process as follows. For each i, choose $w_i \in \mathcal{T}_i$ to minimize the Hausdorff distance

$$h(w_i(R \cap G), D_i \cap G).$$

That is, for each domain block, one chooses a corresponding range block and symmetry, so that the transformed part of the image in the range block looks most like the part of the image in the domain block. This is illustrated in Figs. 6.6 and 6.7.

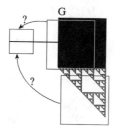

Figure 6.5. Some transformations and range blocks which might be used in representing the image G using a local IFS.

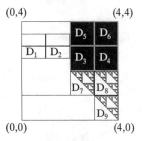

Figure 6.6. Choose a suitable set of x, y coordinates for the image G.

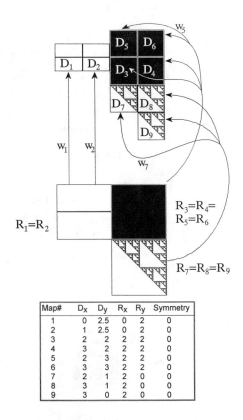

Map#	D_x	D_y	R_x	R_y	Symmetry
1	0	2.5	0	2	0
2	1	2.5	0	2	0
3	2	2	2	2	0
4	3	2	2	2	0
5	2	3	2	2	0
6	3	3	2	2	0
7	2	1	2	0	0
8	3	1	2	0	0
9	3	0	2	0	0

Figure 6.7. Corresponding to each domain block D_i an affine transformation w_i with domain R_i is chosen so that the Hausdorff distance $h(w_i(R_i \cap G), D_i \cap G)$ is minimized. A local IFS code is produced.

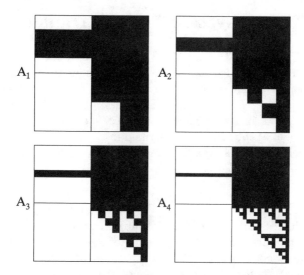

Figure 6.8. The local IFS code is decompressed using the escape time algorithm to produce a sequence of sets (binary images) A_n which converges to the fractal approximant A.

The set $W_{\text{local}}(G) = \cup w_i(R \cap G)$ is called the *collage* of the image G corresponding to the local IFS, while the number

$$h(w_i(R \cap G), D_i \cap G)$$

is called the corresponding *collage error*.

4. Write out the compressed data in the form of a local IFS code, as in the table in Fig. 6.3.

5. Apply a lossless data compression algorithm to the local IFS code, to obtain a compressed local IFS code.

In order to decompress the compressed image, one can apply the photocopy machine algorithm or the escape time algorithm. That is, one uses the compressed data to reconstruct the local IFS and the operator W_{local}; then one computes approximations to $\lim_{n \to \infty} W^{\circ n}(D)$. This is illustrated in Fig. 6.8.

In practice, these steps can be carried out on a digital image, and each step is expressed digitally. This involves standard quantization and discretization procedures, such as are customary in computer graphics. Since we include a model C source code implementation of the grayscale fractal transform, we do not give more details here.

6.7.   The Grayscale Fractal Transform

We now set up a local IFS structure appropriate to the automatic fractal compression of grayscale images. We use the model for the space of real world images $\Re$ that consists of the space $\mathbf{Y}$ of all real-valued functions $\phi : \square \to I$. Here, $I = [a, b] \subset \mathbb{R}$ is a real interval that represents the possible grayscale intensity values in images, such as the interval $[0, 255]$. This is a model of the type $\Re_{ii}$, described in Chapter 2.

We convert $\mathbf{Y}$ into a complete metric space by defining the distance between two functions $\phi_1, \phi_2 \in \mathbf{Y}$ as

$$d(\phi_1, \phi_2) = \sup\{|\phi_1(x, y) - \phi_2(x, y)| : (x, y) \in \square\}.$$

Here $|\cdot|$ denotes the absolute value of the real number $\cdot$, and sup denotes the supremum. Recall that the supremum of a set of real numbers S is the smallest number M with the property that $x \leq M$ for all $x \in S$. We refer to d as the ℓ^∞ *metric*. This metric is not the preferred one for distances between images — see, for example, the discussion of Hausdorff metrics in [FE] — but it enables us to establish a general convergence theorem. Experimentally, the fractal transform shows good convergence properties with respect to other more natural image metrics, but then the statements and proofs of convergence theorems become more complicated.

Let $\mathcal{D}$ denote a partition of $\square$ consisting of a finite collection of sets $D_i \subset \square, i = 1, 2, \ldots, M$; that is

$$\square = \bigcup_{i=1}^{M} D_i,$$

where $D_i \cap D_j = \emptyset$ for $i \neq j$. For each i, let $f_i : D_i \to \square$, with $f_i(D_i) = R_i$, and let $v_i : \mathbb{R} \to \mathbb{R}$ be a contractive transformation with contractivity factor s, with $0 \leq s < 1$. That is,

$$|v_i(z_1) - v_i(z_2)| < s \cdot |z_1 - z_2| \text{ for all } z_1, z_2 \in \mathbb{R},$$

for $i = 1, 2, \ldots, M$.

Then we define $F : \mathbf{Y} \to \mathbf{Y}$ by

$$(F\psi)(x, y) = v_i(\psi(f_i(x, y))) \text{ when } (x, y) \in D_i.$$

We say that s is the contractivity factor of F. We call F the *fractal transform operator*.

Theorem (Convergence of Fractal Transforms)   *Let the complete metric space* $(\mathbf{Y}, d)$ *and the operator* $F : \mathbf{Y} \to \mathbf{Y}$ *be defined as above. Then*

F is a contraction mapping on **Y***; that is, for all* $\phi_1, \phi_2 \in L^\infty(\square)$,

$$d(F(\phi_1), F(\phi_2)) \leq s \cdot d(\phi_1, \phi_2),$$

where s is the contractivity factor of F.

We have the ingredients 1, 2, and 3 in Section 6.2 for a fractal image compression system, using F for the operator O. In particular, there exists a unique function $\phi \in$ **Y** such that $F(\phi) = \phi$. The function ϕ is called the *attractor* of the fractal transform. To compute ϕ, we can use the fact that if $\psi \in$ **Y** then the result of repeatedly applying F to ψ converges uniformly to the attractor ϕ; that is

$$\lim_{n \to \infty} F^{\circ n}(\psi) = \phi;$$

moreover we have the error estimate

$$|F^{\circ n}(\psi)(x, y) - \phi(x, y)| \leq s^n |b - a| \text{ for all } (x, y) \in \square, \text{ where } I = [a, b].$$

The distance between $\psi \in$ **Y** and the attractor of the fractal transform operator F is bounded by the estimate

$$d(\phi, \psi) \leq \frac{d(\psi, F(\psi))}{(1 - s)}.$$

This is a collage theorem for the fractal transform operator F.

6.8. A Local IFS Associated with the Fractal Transform Operator

The fractal transform operator F is essentially the operator W_{local} for a local IFS that acts in three dimensions. To demonstrate this, we assume that the functions $f_i(x, y)$ are invertible on their domains. Then the above structure relates to the local IFS

$$\{\mathbf{w}_i : \mathbf{R}_i \to \mathbf{X} : i = 1, 2, \ldots, N\},$$

where $\mathbf{X} = \square \times [a, b]$, $\mathbf{R}_i = R_i \times [a, b]$, and $\mathbf{w}_i : \mathbf{R}_i \to \mathbf{X}$ is defined by

$$\mathbf{w}_i(x, y, z) = (w_i(x, y), v_i(z)) \text{ for all } (x, y, z) \in \mathbf{R}_i,$$

with $w_i(x, y) = f_i^{-1}(x, y)$, for $i = 1, 2, \ldots, N$. We associate the Euclidean metric d with $\mathbf{X}$ so that $(\mathbf{X}, d)$ is a compact metric space. If each of the functions w_i is contractive (which is not a condition required in the above theorem!) with contractivity factor s, then the local IFS is also contractive with the same contractivity factor. Let $\mathbf{Y} = \mathcal{H}(\mathbf{X})$ and define $\mathbf{W}_{\text{local}} : \mathbf{Y} \to \mathbf{Y}$ by

$$\mathbf{W}_{\text{local}} = \bigcup \mathbf{w}_i(\mathbf{R}_i \cup B).$$

It is easy to see that $\mathbf{W}_{\text{local}}$ maps those sets whose projection on the xy plane consists of all of $\square$, into itself, and in particular,

$$\mathbf{W}_{\text{local}}(\{(x, y, \psi(x, y) : (x, y) \in \square\}) = \{(x, y, F(\psi)(x, y)) : (x, y) \in \square\}.$$

That is, $\mathbf{W}_{\text{local}}$ maps the graph of $\psi \in \mathbf{Y}$ to the graph of $F(\psi)$. This means that the fixed point ϕ of F above is an attractor of $\mathbf{W}_{\text{local}}$; that is,

$$\mathbf{W}_{\text{local}}(\mathbf{A}) = \mathbf{A},$$

where

$$\mathbf{A} = \{(x, y, \phi(x, y)) : (x, y) \in \square\}.$$

6.9. Simple Examples of Grayscale Fractal Transforms

In order to obtain a simple image compression scheme for grayscale images we use affine transformations of the form

$$\mathbf{w}_i = \begin{bmatrix} x \\ y \\ z \end{bmatrix} = \begin{bmatrix} a_i & b_i & 0 \\ c_i & d_i & 0 \\ 0 & 0 & P \end{bmatrix} \begin{bmatrix} x \\ y \\ z \end{bmatrix} + \begin{bmatrix} R_x \\ R_y \\ Q_i \end{bmatrix},$$

where the coefficients $a_i, b_i, c_i,$ and d_i are such that the transformation acts in the xy plane according to the symmetries in Table 6.1, with a contractivity factor of 0.5. The coefficient P is a fixed positive number such that $0 < P \le s$; and

$$v_i(z) = Pz + Q_i.$$

To provide some simple examples of how this fractal transform system works, here we limit the collection of transformations to those corresponding to the range blocks illustrated in Fig. 6.9. We also limit the partition to sixteen domain blocks, labelled as in Fig. 6.10.

Then a local IFS and the corresponding fractal transform operator F are completely specified by providing the numbers R_x and R_y, a value for Q, and a symmetry corresponding to each of the domain blocks. This idea is illustrated in Fig. 6.11.

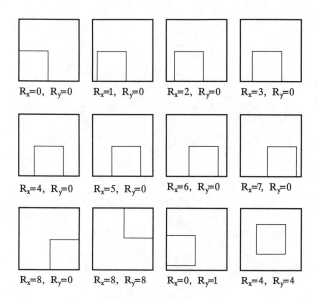

$R_x=0, R_y=0$ $R_x=1, R_y=0$ $R_x=2, R_y=0$ $R_x=3, R_y=0$

$R_x=4, R_y=0$ $R_x=5, R_y=0$ $R_x=6, R_y=0$ $R_x=7, R_y=0$

$R_x=8, R_y=0$ $R_x=8, R_y=8$ $R_x=0, R_y=1$ $R_x=4, R_y=4$

Figure 6.9. This illustrates the numbering convention for the set of range blocks associated with the fractal transform codes in Tables 6.2–6.8.

13	14	15	16
9	10	11	12
5	6	7	8
1	2	3	4

Figure 6.10. The numbering convention used for the domain blocks associated with Tables 6.2–6.8. Each domain block is associated with a map number.

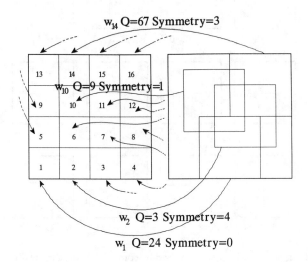

Figure 6.11. The association of some range blocks with some domain blocks in a fractal transform code.

Examples of corresponding fractal transform codes are presented in Tables 6.2–6.8. The corresponding attractors, as well as possible original images, are shown in Figs 6.12–6.18. In each case, the resolution is 32×32, with 8 bits of grayscale.

Table 6.2. An example of a fractal transform code. The corresponding attractor is shown in Fig. 6.12.

Map	R_x	R_y	Symmetry	Q
1	0	0	0	0
2	0	0	0	0
3	1	0	0	1
4	7	0	0	35
5	0	0	0	0
6	1	0	0	1
7	7	0	0	35
8	1	0	3	1
9	0	0	0	0
10	7	0	0	35
11	1	0	3	1
12	0	0	0	0
13	7	0	0	35
14	1	0	3	1
15	0	0	0	0
16	0	0	0	0

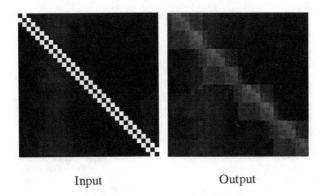

Input   Output

Figure 6.12. Input and output images corresponding to the fractal transform code in Table 6.2.

Table 6.3. Fractal transform code corresponding to Fig. 6.13.

Map	R_x	R_y	Symmetry	Q
1	8	0	0	0
2	1	0	0	16
3	8	0	0	0
4	8	0	0	0
5	8	0	0	0
6	1	1	0	20
7	8	0	0	0
8	8	0	0	0
9	8	0	0	0
10	1	1	0	20
11	8	0	0	0
12	8	0	0	0
13	8	0	0	0
14	1	0	2	16
15	8	0	0	0
16	8	0	0	0

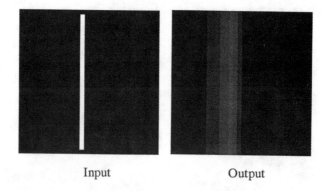

Input   Output

Figure 6.13. Input and output images corresponding to the fractal transform code in Table 6.3.

Table 6.4. Fractal transform code corresponding to Fig. 6.14.

Map	R_x	R_y	Symmetry	Q
1	3	0	0	-129
2	3	0	0	44
3	4	0	1	62
4	3	0	0	-129
5	3	0	0	-129
6	3	0	0	44
7	4	0	1	62
8	3	0	0	-129
9	3	0	0	-129
10	3	0	0	44
11	4	0	1	62
12	3	0	0	-129
13	3	0	0	-129
14	4	0	5	-119
15	4	0	5	-115
16	3	0	0	-129

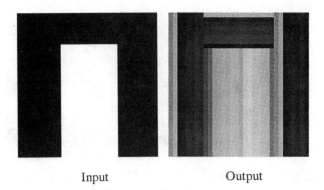

Input   Output

Figure 6.14. Input and output images corresponding to the fractal transform code in Table 6.4.

Table 6.5. Fractal transform code corresponding to Fig. 6.15.

Map	R_x	R_y	Symmetry	Q
1	0	8	0	-7
2	0	8	6	29
3	0	4	4	50
4	0	8	0	-4
5	0	8	0	-7
6	3	4	2	50
7	3	5	5	-16
8	0	6	3	50
9	0	8	0	-7
10	2	5	0	58
11	0	8	2	48
12	0	8	1	32
13	0	8	0	-7
14	0	5	5	-12
15	0	8	5	23
16	0	8	0	-7

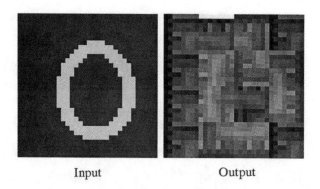

Input   Output

Figure 6.15. Input and output images corresponding to the fractal transform code in Table 6.5.

Table 6.6. Fractal transform code corresponding to Fig. 6.16.

Map	R_x	R_y	Symmetry	Q
1	0	8	8	-11
2	0	8	6	26
3	0	4	4	46
4	5	4	0	-74
5	0	8	0	-11
6	3	4	2	55
7	5	3	2	3
8	0	5	3	38
9	0	8	0	-11
10	2	5	0	57
11	5	4	4	30
12	0	8	1	28
13	0	8	0	-11
14	4	3	4	-61
15	0	8	5	19
16	0	8	0	-11

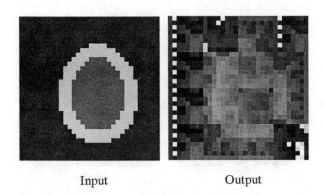

Input   Output

Figure 6.16. Input and output images corresponding to the fractal transform code in Table 6.6.

Table 6.7. Fractal transform code corresponding to Fig. 6.17.

Map	R_x	R_y	Symmetry	Q
1	0	0	0	-2
2	1	0	0	4
3	1	0	1	4
4	0	0	0	-2
5	0	0	0	-2
6	1	3	0	20
7	1	3	1	20
8	0	0	0	-2
9	0	0	0	-2
10	1	3	0	20
11	1	3	1	20
12	0	0	0	-2
13	4	0	4	23
14	5	5	5	70
15	4	5	7	65
16	0	0	3	14

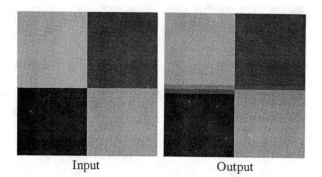

Input   Output

Figure 6.17. Input and output images corresponding to the fractal transform code in Table 6.7.

Table 6.8. Fractal transform code corresponding to Fig. 6.18.

Map	R_x	R_y	Symmetry	Q
1	0	8	0	-115
2	0	8	0	-115
3	0	8	0	39
4	0	8	0	39
5	0	1	0	6
6	0	1	0	6
7	1	8	4	37
8	1	8	4	37
9	0	8	0	50
10	0	8	0	50
11	0	8	0	-63
12	0	8	0	-63
13	0	8	0	50
14	0	8	0	50
15	0	8	0	-63
16	0	8	0	-63

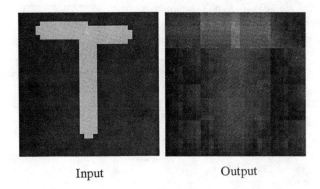

Input   Output

Figure 6.18. Input and output images corresponding to the fractal transform code in Table 6.8.

6.10.   C Source Code Implementation

This section provides C source code for implementation of an elementary fractal transform on a digital computer; this is included for precision of presentation and exposition purposes only. Computer implementation of the image compression procedures described here are covered by U.S. Patent #5,065,447, and by corresponding patents in other countries worldwide. If you wish to set up an image compression system on a digital computer using the fractal transform, you should apply for a license to:

> Licensing Department
> Iterated Systems, Inc.
> 5550-A Peachtree Parkway, Suite 650
> Norcross, GA 30092

Iterated Systems, Inc., can also provide you with the latest commerical implementations of fractal transform technology.

The following source code is written in Borland Turbo C Version 1.0. The programs consist of the files TGA.H, FRACTAL.H, UTIL.C, COMPRESS.C, and DECOMPRESS.C, and correspond to two executable functions: COMPRESS.EXE and DECOMPRESS.EXE.

The input to COMPRESS.EXE is a digital grayscale image file in Targa file format. Such files possess a header that gives information about the digital image, including the width and height of the image in pixels, followed by a list of bytes, representing the grayscale values of the pixels of the image in scanline order. The structure of the header of a Targa file is provided by the file TGA.H. The output from COMPRESS.EXE is a fractal transform code (FTC) file; this consists of the header from the Targa file from the uncompressed image, followed by a list of coefficients of affine transformations, as described below. The input to DECOMPRESS.EXE is an FTC file and the output is a Targa file, representing the decompressed image.

Flow charts showing how the two functions work are given in Figs. 6.19 and 6.20.

```
-------------------------------------------------------
FILE NAME: TGA.H
-------------------------------------------------------


#define TGA_GRAYSCALE 3

struct tga_hdr {
 unsigned char id,cmaptype,imtype,col1,col2,col3,col4,col5;
 short xorigin,yorigin,width,height;
 unsigned char depth,descriptor;
};



-------------------------------------------------------
FILE NAME: FRACTAL.H
-------------------------------------------------------


#include<stdio.h>
#include "tga.h"

#define DB_SIDE     8
#define MAX_PIXEL_VALUE 255
#define NSYMS       8
#define NUM_ITS    16
#define FLIP_X      1
#define FLIP_Y      2
#define FLIP_DIAG  4
#define ARBITRARY_PIXEL_VALUE 128

#define SWAPPED_RAS_MAGIC 0x956aa659

typedef unsigned char Pixel;
typedef unsigned char Symmetry;

typedef struct rectangle { unsigned short width,height;
  unsigned long length;
  Pixel *pixel;
} Rectangle;

typedef struct affinemap {
  unsigned short range_x,range_y;
  short shift;
  Symmetry symmetry;
```

```
} AffineMap;

typedef struct imageheader {
  unsigned short width,height;
} ImageHeader;

extern Pixel mean(Rectangle *rectangle);
extern long l2_distance(Rectangle *rect1,Rectangle *rect2);

extern void copy_rectangle(Rectangle *src_rect,short src_x,
 short src_y,Rectangle *dest_rect,short dest_x,
 short dest_y,short width,short height);

extern void reduce_image(Rectangle *src_rect,
 Rectangle *dest_rect);

extern void flip(Rectangle *range_block,
 Rectangle *transformed_range_block,
 Symmetry symmetry);

extern void
  intensity_shift(Rectangle *rectangle,short shift);

extern long swap_bytes(long qbyte);

extern void
  read_ras_header(FILE *image_file, ImageHeader *header);
extern void
  read_tga_header(FILE *image_file, ImageHeader *header);

extern void
  write_ras_header(FILE *image_file, ImageHeader *header);
extern void
  write_tga_header(FILE *image_file, ImageHeader *header);
```

```
----------------------------------------------------
FILE NAME: UTIL.C
----------------------------------------------------

#include "fractal.h"

Pixel mean(Rectangle *rectangle)
{
  int i;
  long sum=0;
  for (i=0;i<rectangle->length;i++)
    sum += rectangle->pixel[i];
  return(sum/rectangle->length);
}

void intensity_shift(Rectangle *rectangle,short shift)
{
  short i;
  for (i=0;i<rectangle->length;i++)
    rectangle->pixel[i]=rectangle->pixel[i]+shift;
}

long l2_distance(Rectangle *rect1,Rectangle *rect2)
  /* rect1 and rect2 must have the same length */
{
  long d,distance=0;
  int i;
  for (i=0;i<rect1->length;i++)
    {
      d=rect1->pixel[i]-rect2->pixel[i];
      distance += d*d;
    }
  return(distance);
}

void copy_rectangle
  (Rectangle *src_rect,short src_x,short src_y,
  Rectangle *dest_rect,short dest_x,short dest_y,
    short width,short height)
{
  int i,j;
  for (j=0;j<height;j++)
    for (i=0;i<width;i++)
```

```
        dest_rect->
          pixel[i+dest_x+(j+dest_y)*dest_rect->width] =
 src_rect->pixel[(src_x+i)+(src_y+j)*src_rect->width];
}

void reduce_image(Rectangle *src_rect,Rectangle *dest_rect)
{
  int i,j;
  for (j=0;j<dest_rect->height;j++)
    for (i=0;i<dest_rect->width;i++)
      {
          /* spatial rescale by 2 */

  dest_rect->pixel[i+j*dest_rect->width] =
    (src_rect->pixel[2*i+(2*j)*src_rect->width]+
    src_rect->pixel[2*i+1+(2*j)*src_rect->width]+
    src_rect->pixel[2*i+(2*j+1)*src_rect->width]+
    src_rect->pixel[2*i+1+(2*j+1)*src_rect->width])/4;

          /* intensity rescale by 3/4 */

          dest_rect->pixel[i+j*dest_rect->width] =
            (dest_rect->pixel[i+j*dest_rect->width]*3)/4;
      }
}

void flip
  (Rectangle *range_block,Rectangle *transformed_range_block,
  Symmetry symmetry)
{
  short i,j,x,y,t;

  for (j=0;j<range_block->height;j++)
    for (i=0;i<range_block->width;i++)
      {
 if (symmetry & FLIP_X) x=(range_block->width-1)-i;
 else x=i;
 if (symmetry & FLIP_Y) y=(range_block->height-1)-j;
 else y=j;
 /* not allowed unless width=height */
 if (symmetry & FLIP_DIAG)
   {
     t=y;
```

```
      y=x;
      x=t;
    }
  transformed_range_block->pixel[x+y*range_block->width] =
    range_block->pixel[i+j*range_block->width];
      }
}

void read_ras_header(FILE *image_file, ImageHeader *header)
{
  long int rheader[8];
  if (8 != fread(rheader,sizeof(long int),8,image_file))
    {
      fprintf(stderr,"Error reading raster header.\n");
      exit(1);
    }
  if (rheader[0] != SWAPPED_RAS_MAGIC)
    {
      fprintf(stderr,"Invalid raster file.\n");
      exit(1);
    }
  header->width=swap_bytes(rheader[1]);
  header->height=swap_bytes(rheader[2]);
}

void write_ras_header(FILE *image_file, ImageHeader *header)
{
  static long int rheader[]=
    {SWAPPED_RAS_MAGIC,0,0,0x8000000,0,0x1000000,0,0};
  rheader[1]=swap_bytes(header->width);
  rheader[2]=swap_bytes(header->height);
  rheader[4]=swap_bytes(header->width*header->height);
  if (8 != fwrite(rheader,sizeof(long int),8,image_file))
    {
      fprintf(stderr,"Error writing raster header.\n");
      exit(1);
    }
}

long swap_bytes(long qbyte)
{
  return(((qbyte&0xff000000)>>24) | ((qbyte&0xff0000)>>8) |
    ((qbyte&0xff00)<<8) | ((qbyte&0xff)<<24));
```

```
}

void read_tga_header(FILE *image_file, ImageHeader *header)
{
  struct tga_hdr tgaheader;
  if (1 !=
    fread(&tgaheader,sizeof(struct tga_hdr),1,image_file))
    {
      fprintf(stderr,"Error reading Targa header.\n");
      exit(1);
    }
  if ((tgaheader.imtype !=
    TGA_GRAYSCALE)||(tgaheader.depth!=8))
    {
      fprintf(stderr,"Invalid Targa file.\n");
      exit(1);
    }
  header->width=tgaheader.width;
  header->height=tgaheader.height;
}

void write_tga_header(FILE *image_file, ImageHeader *header)
{
  static struct tga_hdr tgaheader=
  {0,0,TGA_GRAYSCALE,0,0,0,0,0,0,0,0,0,8,0};
  tgaheader.width=header->width;
  tgaheader.height=header->height;
  if (1 !=
    fwrite(&tgaheader,sizeof(struct tga_hdr),1,image_file))
    {
      fprintf(stderr,"Error writing Targa header.\n");
      exit(1);
    }
}
```

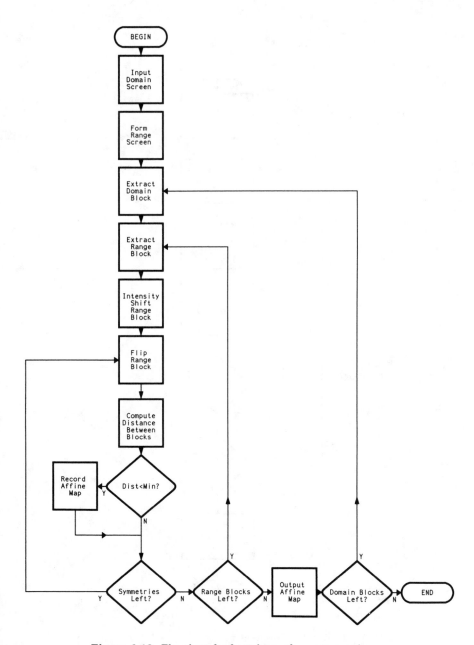

Figure 6.19. Flowchart for fractal transform compression.

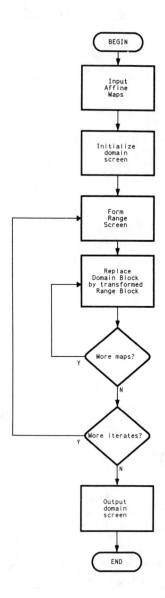

Figure 6.20. Flowchart for decompression of a fractal transform code.

```
-------------------------------------------------

FILE NAME: COMPRESS.C
-------------------------------------------------

#include <stdio.h>
#include <stdlib.h>
#include<alloc.h>

#include "fractal.h"

main(int argc,char **argv)
{
  FILE *image_file,*fractal_file;
  ImageHeader header;
  Rectangle image,domain_block,range_block,
    flipped_range_block,reduced_image;
  unsigned long current_distance,minimum_distance,infinity;
  Symmetry current_symmetry;
  short current_range_x,current_range_y,domain_x,
    domain_y,current_shift;
  Pixel domain_mean;
  AffineMap best_map;

  fprintf(stderr,
    "\nFractal Image Compression Demonstration
      - Version 1.0A\n");
  fprintf(stderr,
    "\nCopyright (c)1992 Lyman P. Hurd,
      Michael F. Barnsley\n");

  if (argc != 3)
    {
      fprintf(stderr,
        "\nUsage: compress image_file fractal_file.\n");
      exit(1);
    }
  /* Step 0: Allocate memory for blocks */

  domain_block.width=range_block.width=
  flipped_range_block.width=DB_SIDE;
  domain_block.height=range_block.height=
  flipped_range_block.height=DB_SIDE;
```

```
  domain_block.length=range_block.length=
flipped_range_block.length=DB_SIDE*DB_SIDE;

  domain_block.pixel =
  (Pixel *) calloc(DB_SIDE*DB_SIDE,sizeof(Pixel));
  range_block.pixel =
  (Pixel *) calloc(DB_SIDE*DB_SIDE,sizeof(Pixel));
  flipped_range_block.pixel =
  (Pixel *) calloc(DB_SIDE*DB_SIDE,sizeof(Pixel));

  infinity=255*255*DB_SIDE*DB_SIDE;

  /* Step 1: Input Image */

  if (NULL == (image_file=fopen(argv[1],"rb")))
    {
      fprintf(stderr,"Unable to open file %s.\n",
argv[1]);
      exit(1);
    }

  if (NULL == (fractal_file=fopen(argv[2],"wb")))
    {
      fprintf(stderr,"Unable to open file %s.\n",
argv[2]);
      exit(1);
    }

  read_tga_header(image_file,&header);

  fprintf(stderr,
    "Width %d Height %d\n",header.width,header.height);

  if (1!=fwrite(&header,sizeof(ImageHeader),1,fractal_file))
    {
      fprintf(stderr,
        "Error writing header to fractal file %s.\n",
argv[2]);
      exit(1);
    }

  image.width=header.width;
  image.height=header.height;
```

```
image.length=header.width*header.height;

image.pixel = (Pixel *) calloc(image.length,
  sizeof(Pixel));

reduced_image.width=header.width/2;
reduced_image.height=header.height/2;
reduced_image.length=header.width*header.height/4;

reduced_image.pixel =
  (Pixel *) calloc(reduced_image.length,sizeof(Pixel));

if (NULL == image.pixel)
  {
    fprintf(stderr,
      "Unable to allocate %ld bytes for image buffer.\n",
image.length);
    exit(2);
  }

if (image.length!=fread(image.pixel,
sizeof(Pixel),image.length,image_file))
  {
    fprintf(stderr,
      "Error reading header from image file %s.\n",
argv[1]);
    exit(1);
  }

fclose(image_file);

/* rescale(contract)image in spatial and */
/*    intensity directions */

reduce_image(&image,&reduced_image);

/* MAIN LOOP */

for (domain_y=0;domain_y<image.height;domain_y+=DB_SIDE)
  for (domain_x=0;domain_x<image.width;domain_x+=DB_SIDE)
    {

/* Step 2: Get Domain Block */
```

```
fprintf(stderr,"Dx %d Dy %d\n",domain_x,domain_y);

minimum_distance=infinity;

copy_rectangle(&image,domain_x,domain_y,&domain_block,0,0,
        DB_SIDE,DB_SIDE);
domain_mean=mean(&domain_block);

for (current_range_y=0;current_range_y<=
 reduced_image.height-DB_SIDE;
 current_range_y++)
  for (current_range_x=0;current_range_x<=
 reduced_image.width-DB_SIDE;
 current_range_x++)
 {

  /* Step 3: Get Range Block */

    copy_rectangle(&reduced_image,current_range_x,
       current_range_y,&range_block,0,0,DB_SIDE,DB_SIDE);


  /* best mean square fit is given by shifting */
  /* means to be equivalent */

    current_shift = ((short) domain_mean)
      -((short) mean(&range_block));

    intensity_shift(&range_block,current_shift);

  /* Step 3: Loop Over Symmetries */

    for (current_symmetry=0;current_symmetry<NSYMS;
      current_symmetry++)
      {
        flip(&range_block,&flipped_range_block,
 current_symmetry);
        current_distance = l2_distance(&domain_block,
 &flipped_range_block);

        if (current_distance<minimum_distance)
 {
```

```
        minimum_distance=current_distance;
        best_map.shift=current_shift;
        best_map.symmetry=current_symmetry;
        best_map.range_x=current_range_x;
        best_map.range_y=current_range_y;
      }
        }
    }
        fprintf(fractal_file,
           "%d %d %d %d \n",best_map.range_x,
           best_map.range_y,best_map.symmetry,best_map.shift);
        }
    fclose(fractal_file);
    free(image.pixel);
    return(0);
}



-------------------------------------------------
FILE NAME: DECOMPRESS.C
-------------------------------------------------

#include <stdio.h>
#include <stdlib.h>
#include <alloc.h>
#include "fractal.h"

#define DEFAULT_ITERATES 16

main(int argc,char **argv)
{
  AffineMap *affine_map_array,*map_ptr;
  FILE *image_file,*fractal_file,*initial_file;
  ImageHeader header,initial_header;
  short iterate,arg_offset=0,iterates=DEFAULT_ITERATES;
  long number_of_maps,i;
  short domain_x,domain_y;
  Rectangle image,reduced_image,range_block,
    transformed_range_block;

  fprintf(stderr,
 "\nFractal Image Decompression Demonstration -
   Version 1.0A\n");
```

```
    fprintf(stderr,
 "\nCopyright (c)1992 Lyman P. Hurd, Michael F. Barnsley\n");

    if ((argc < 3)||(argc>5))
      {
        fprintf(stderr,
 "\nUsage: decompress [num_iterates] [initial_image]
    fractal_file image_file.\n");
        exit(1);
      }

    if (argc==4)
      {
        iterates=atoi(argv[1]);
        arg_offset=1;
      }

    if (argc==5)
      {
        iterates=atoi(argv[1]);
        initial_file=fopen(argv[2],"rb");
        arg_offset=2;
      }

/* Read in affine maps and header information. */

    if (NULL == (fractal_file=fopen(argv[arg_offset+1],"rb")))
      {
        fprintf(stderr,"Unable to open fractal file %s.\n",
 argv[arg_offset+1]);
        exit(1);
      }

    if (NULL == (image_file=fopen(argv[arg_offset+2],"wb")))
      {
        fprintf(stderr,"Unable to open image file %s.\n",
 argv[arg_offset+2]);
        exit(1);
      }

    if (1!=fread(&header,sizeof(ImageHeader),1,fractal_file))
      {
        fprintf(stderr,
```

```
        "Error reading header from fractal file %s.\n",
argv[arg_offset+1]);
      exit(1);
    }

  write_tga_header(image_file,&header);

  number_of_maps =
    header.width*header.height/(DB_SIDE*DB_SIDE);
  affine_map_array = (AffineMap *)
    calloc(number_of_maps,sizeof(AffineMap));


  image.width = header.width;
  image.height = header.height;
  image.length = header.width*header.height;
  image.pixel = (Pixel *)
    calloc(image.length,sizeof(Pixel));

  reduced_image.width = header.width/2;
  reduced_image.height = header.height/2;
  reduced_image.length = header.width*header.height/4;
  reduced_image.pixel = (Pixel *)
    calloc(reduced_image.length,sizeof(Pixel));

  range_block.width = DB_SIDE;
  range_block.height = DB_SIDE;
  range_block.length = DB_SIDE*DB_SIDE;
  range_block.pixel =
    (Pixel *) calloc(range_block.length,sizeof(Pixel));

  transformed_range_block.width = DB_SIDE;
  transformed_range_block.height = DB_SIDE;
  transformed_range_block.length = DB_SIDE*DB_SIDE;
  transformed_range_block.pixel = (Pixel *)
    calloc(transformed_range_block.length,sizeof(Pixel));


  if (argc<5)
    {
      for (i=0;i<image.length;i++)
image.pixel[i]=ARBITRARY_PIXEL_VALUE;
    }
```

```
    else
      {
        read_tga_header(initial_file,&initial_header);
        fread(image.pixel,image.length,sizeof(Pixel),
          initial_file);
      }
/* Loop over domain blocks. */

      for (domain_y=0,map_ptr=affine_map_array;
    domain_y<image.height;domain_y+=DB_SIDE)
  for (domain_x=0;domain_x<image.width;
    domain_x+=DB_SIDE,map_ptr++)
      {


        fscanf(fractal_file,
        "%d %d %d %d \n",&map_ptr->range_x,&map_ptr->range_y,
        &map_ptr->symmetry,&map_ptr->shift);


      }

              fclose(fractal_file);

/* Loop for a prescribed number of iterations. */

  for (iterate=0;iterate<iterates;iterate++)
    {

      reduce_image(&image,&reduced_image);

/* Loop over domain blocks. */

      for (domain_y=0,map_ptr=affine_map_array;
    domain_y<image.height;domain_y+=DB_SIDE)
  for (domain_x=0;
    domain_x<image.width;domain_x+=DB_SIDE,map_ptr++)
      {

/* Extract range block. */

        copy_rectangle(&reduced_image,map_ptr->range_x,
        map_ptr->range_y,&range_block,0,0,
```

```
        DB_SIDE,DB_SIDE);

      intensity_shift(&range_block,map_ptr->shift);

/* Apply indicated symmetry. */

      flip(&range_block,&transformed_range_block,
        map_ptr->symmetry);

/* Insert transformed block into image. */

      copy_rectangle(&transformed_range_block,0,0,&image,
        domain_x,domain_y,DB_SIDE,DB_SIDE);
    }
     }

  if (image.length !=
    fwrite(image.pixel,
      sizeof(Pixel),image.length,image_file))
    {
      fprintf(stderr,"Error writing data to %s.\n",
        argv[arg_offset+2]);
      exit(1);
    }

  free(affine_map_array);
  free(image.pixel);
  free(reduced_image.pixel);
  fclose(image_file);
  return(0);
}
```

6.11. Illustrations of Fractal Transform Compression

Figures 6.21-6.24 show images compressed at various compression ratios, using a low-cost commercial software fractal transform system called *Images Incorporated*, from Iterated Systems.

Color plates 9–16 show color images and zooms, using fractal transform image compression.

Figure 6.21. An original color photograph was scanned at 150 dpi on an HP ScanJet IIc scanner to create an 8-bit grayscale Targa file with a resolution of 509 by 760 pixels, giving a file size of 386,858 bytes.

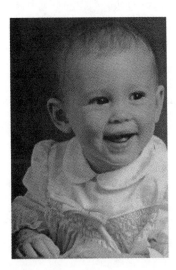

Figure 6.22. *Images Incorporated* is used (i) to compress the original file down to a 127,369 byte FIF file, (ii) decompress the FIF file back to the screen, and (iii) print the resulting image on an HP Laser Jet III at 300 dpi. At this compression ratio, the only perceptable difference is that some of the highlights are less obvious.

Figure 6.23. The compressed file size for this image was 12,392 bytes. Given the relatively limited resolution of the HP Laser Jet III, it is hard to see any difference from the image shown in Fig. 6.21

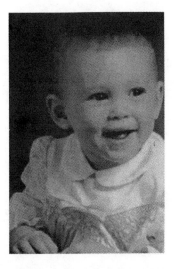

Figure 6.24. The compressed file size is now only 8,030 bytes! At this compression ration of 48:1, there is blurring of the finer detail but even now, the casual observer might not realize the image had been compressed.

6.12.   References and Related Materials

[JB] J. M. Beaumont, "Image data compression using fractal techniques," *BT Technology Journal* 9 93–109 (1991).

[FE] M. Barnsley, *Fractals Everywhere*, Academic Press, Boston (1988).

[ME] *Microsoft Encarta*, by Microsoft Corporation, Redmond, Washington (1992).

[II] *Images Incorporated*, by Iterated Systems, Inc., Norcross, Georgia (1992).

[AJ] A. Jacquin, "Image Coding Based on a Fractal Theory of Iterated Contractive Image Transformations," *IEEE Transactions on Image Processing*, 1 18–30 (1992).

[FBJ] Y. Fisher, R.D. Boss, and E. W. Jacobs, "Fractal Image Compression", to appear in *Data Compression*, R. Storer (ed.) Kluwer Academic Publishers, Norwell, MA.

[BS] M. Barnsley and A. Sloan, "Method and Apparatus for Processing Digital Data," United States Patent # 5,065,447.

[PJS] H.-0. Peitgen, H.Jürgens, and D.Saupe, *Chaos and Fractals (New Frontiers in Science)*, Springer Verlag, London (1992).

[JW] J. Waite, "A Review of Iterated Function System Theory for Image Compression," preprint. British Telecom Research Laboratories, Martlesham Heath, U.K. (1992).

A

JPEG Image Compression

A.1. Introduction

Transmission of images requires the existence of a standard agreed upon by both ends of a transmission. Using images in more than one application similarly requires a standard usable across multiple platforms. The JPEG committee image compression standard [JPG] attempts to fill this need.

The acronym JPEG stands for *Joint Photographic Experts Group*. The word "joint" comes from the fact that it is a collaborative effort between two standards committees, the CCITT (*International Telegraph and Telephone Consultative Committee*) and ISO (*International Standards Organization*). The standard is still being drafted and encompasses a variety of image formats, both lossless and lossy. There are four main kinds of JPEG compression:

1. Sequential.

2. Progressive.

3. Hierarchical.

4. Lossless.

The most widely implemented facet of the emerging JPEG standard is the baseline DCT-based sequential compression method, and this is the

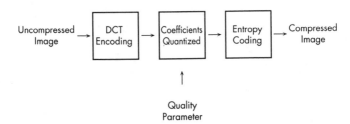

Figure A.1. Stages in JPEG encoding: a) discrete cosine transform; b) coefficients are quantized (lossy); c) coefficients and runlengths are entropy-coded (usually Huffman).

method described next. Henceforward this will be what we mean by JPEG compression.

Examples in this chapter give a qualitative description of JPEG compression. The programs give an implementation excluding header information and the final entropy coding. However, the emphasis is on clarity rather than speed.

JPEG compression involves the following steps (see Fig. A.1):

1. The image is broken into 8 × 8 blocks (Fig. A.2) and each block is transformed via the (forward) discrete cosine transform (FDCT).

2. The resulting 64 coefficients are quantized to a finite set of values. The degree of rounding depends on the specific coefficient.

3. The DC term, a DCT coefficient representing the mean pixel value for each block, is differenced from the DC term of the preceding block in scan order (Fig. A.3).

4. The remaining 63 coefficients are scanned in a zigzag fashion (Fig. A.4). Each nonzero coefficient is coded by the number of preceding zeros and its coefficient value.

5. The data stream is entropy-encoded by means of arithmetic or Huffman coding. (See Chapter 5.)

Decompression is accomplished by applying the inverse of each of the preceding steps in the opposite order (Fig. A.5). One starts with entropy decoding and proceeds to convert runlengths to a sequence of zeros and coefficients.

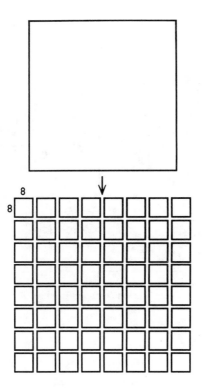

Figure A.2. The image is divided into 8 × 8 blocks.

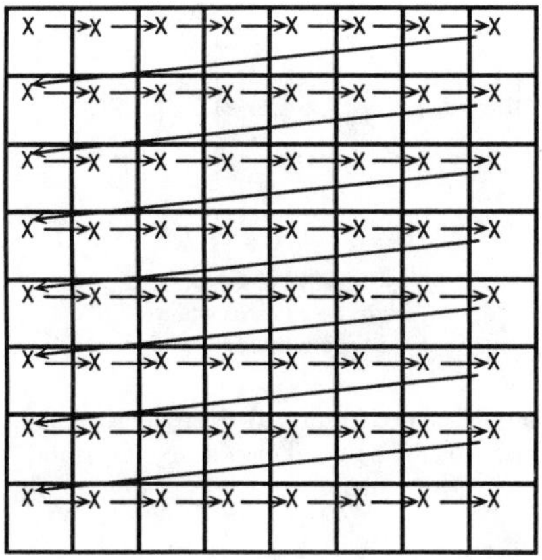

Figure A.3. DC coefficients (block means) are differenced from each other in scan order.

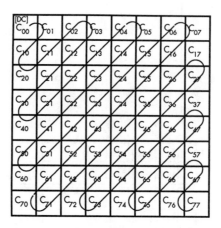

Figure A.4. The AC coefficients are encoded in zigzag order.

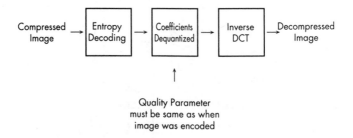

Figure A.5. Stages in JPEG decoding: a) coefficients and runlengths are entropy-decoded (Huffman or arithmetic); b) coefficients are multiplied by quantization coefficients; c) inverse discrete cosine transform.

A.2.   Discrete Cosine Transform (DCT)

The discrete cosine transform is a variant of the Fourier transform adapted
to real (as opposed to complex) data. The transform is linear; for a fixed
block size (in this case 64), the DCT can be completely specified by a
matrix.

An 8 × 8 block of pixels can be viewed as a vector in a 64-dimensional
space. Each of these blocks is transformed separately. The 64 pixel values
s_{xy} are transformed via the forward discrete cosine transform (FDCT) to
64 coordinates in this new basis. Prior to transformation, the pixel values
are shifted to center them around zero. For eight-bit data, this means
subtracting 128 from the pixel value. If the pixel data is expressed with
eight bits of precision, the transformed data is stored as a signed integer
with 11 bits of precision.

The pixel values s_{xy} and S_{uv} are related by a linear transformation described next. In theory, the entire transform could be represented by a
single 64 × 64 matrix. However, doing so would ignore the symmetries
inherent in the operation.

Forward DCT (FDCT):

$$S_{uv} = \frac{1}{4}C(u)C(v)\sum_{x=0}^{7}\sum_{y=0}^{7} s_{xy} \cos\frac{(2x+1)u\pi}{16} \cos\frac{(2y+1)v\pi}{16},$$

$$0 \le u, v \le 7. \tag{A.1}$$

Inverse DCT (IDCT):

$$s_{xy} = \frac{1}{4}\sum_{u=0}^{7}\sum_{v=0}^{7} C(u)C(v)S_{uv} \cos\frac{(2x+1)u\pi}{16} \cos\frac{(2y+1)v\pi}{16},$$

$$0 \le x, y \le 7. \tag{A.2}$$

In both equations, $C(0) = \frac{1}{\sqrt{2}}$ and $C(i) = 1$ for $1 \le i \le 7$.

In an implementation, the cosine terms are only computed once and
taken from a lookup table. Another way of viewing the DCT is to note
that the coefficients S_{uv} represent the relative contributions of the 64 basis
elements in Fig. A.6.

The discrete cosine transform is implemented in the source code at the
end of this appendix by the functions fdct() and idct(). Pixel values in
an 8 × 8 array taking values from 0 to 255 are transformed into an 8 ×
8 array of double precision floats. In practice, the cosine terms would be
taken from a table instead of computed on the fly as in this listing.

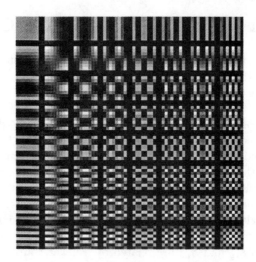

Figure A.6. The DCT basis. Every 8×8 block can be expressed as a linear combination of these 64 blocks.

A.3.   Quantization

Quantization makes JPEG encoding lossy. Each application chooses a sequence of quantization levels (in step 2) corresponding to a variety of settings on a quality–filesize curve. The highest quality corresponds to little or no rounding.

A particular choice of quantization levels corresponds to an 8×8 matrix of positive integers giving the step size for each coefficient. A step size of one means no rounding. The larger the number, the fewer bits of precision are used in this coefficient. To quantize a coefficient $a_{i,j}$, divide by the quantization coefficient, rounding to the nearest integer

$$a'_{i,j} = \text{Round}\left(\frac{a_{i,j}}{q_{i,j}}\right).$$

The coefficients in the quantization matrix are not uniform: they vary based upon the relative visual impact of errors at given frequencies; the eye is assumed to be less sensitive to errors in higher frequencies than lower ones.

Original

Quality
factor 74

Quality
factor 20

Figure A.7. A grayscale image and the result of JPEG compression and decompression for two different quality settings. As the file size decreases, one begins to notice a Gibb's phenomenon, the presence of artifacts around sharp edges. This artifact is caused by the inability of a finite combination of continuous functions to describe a jump discontinuity.

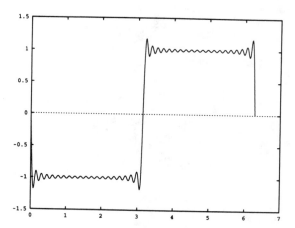

Figure A.8. The Gibb's phenomenon resulting from attempting to approximate a square wave by a trigonometric polynomial. As the number of terms is increased, the spikes become narrower but do not decrease in height.

Figure A.7 shows a grayscale image compressed with different quality settings. At low quality (high compression), artifacts start to appear. These artifacts are particularly noticeable around sharp edges. Cosine functions are continuous and a truncated sum of continuous functions cannot be expected to model a discontinuous function. The problem of approximating a step function (the one-dimensional analog of an edge) is classical and it is illustrated in Fig. A.8, which shows a truncated Fourier series expansion for a square wave.

The quantization step is illustrated by the functions `quantize()` and `dequantize()`. The specific choice of quantization values in the example given is taken from [GKW].

A.4.   Runlength Encoding

The first DCT coefficient S_{00} is proportional to the block mean, the average pixel value over the block. In the data stream, this coefficient is expressed as a difference from the preceding DC coefficient. This differencing forms the only interaction between blocks in the coding scheme.

High-frequency DCT coefficients (S_{uv} where u or v is large) tend to be smaller than lower-frequency ones for blocks taken from typical images. After quantization, many of these coefficients are rounded to zero. If we were to send the coefficients one at a time, much of the transmission time would be spent sending zeros.

Instead, zero is given a special place. The AC coefficients, all coefficients except S_{00}, are scanned in a zigzag fashion. The nonzero coefficients are coded by sending a runlength giving the number of preceding zeros, followed by the coefficient itself. There is also a code signifying the last of the nonzero coefficients.

A.5. Entropy Encoding

At this point, our data stream consists of a sequence of coefficients describing each block. An 8×8 block is encoded by sending:

1. The difference of the block mean from the preceding block mean in scan order.

2. The nonzero quantized AC coefficients preceded by a runlength indicating their position.

This compression process is completed by further encoding the data stream by an entropy coding scheme, a coding method that assigns codewords to coefficients in such a way as to assign short codewords to likely terms and longer ones to rare ones. There are two techniques for accomplishing this encoding: arithmetic coding and Huffman coding. These techniques are described in detail in Sections 5.13 and 5.10, respectively. Example source code is provided in Sections 5.14 and 5.11.

A Huffman code assigns to each coefficient a codeword with a variable number of bits in such a way that no codeword forms the prefix to another legal codeword. The stream can be broken into codewords uniquely; also, codewords can be decoded as soon as they are received. To specify a Huffman code, one needs to list the codewords. While the committee does provide a suggested list of codes, any Huffman code is legal provided it is described in the header. Issues of portability are described next.

A.6. Interchange Format

One component of the JPEG recommendations is an interchange format. Within an application, many choices can be established internally. To share data, all arbitrary choices must be explicitly spelled out. In particular, the JPEG header contains information about image dimensions, type of coding, quantization levels, and a description of the entropy-coding scheme used.

The JPEG recommendation provides a standard set of quantization levels. If an application stays within the defaults, they are not required to specify the table. However, any set of coefficients can be used provided they are inserted into the header information before exchange with another application.

The standard also provides a set of Huffman codes; the standard states that the Huffman codes must be described in the header information even if the defaults are used. Again, this only needs to be done for files to be exported to other applications. Some implementations allow one to set a flag indicating whether a file is for internal or external use.

The JPEG standards, however, do not specify a complete file format. There are, however, two current file formats available that fill this need. For simple applications, there is the JFIF format and for more complicated applications the JTIF 6.0 format. Implementation details can be found in documents provided by the Independent JPEG Group [IJG].

A.7. C Source Code Illustrating JPEG Compression

This program illustrates the stages in JPEG baseline DCT image sequential image compression. All the stages in the JPEG algorithm are implemented except entropy coding via Huffman or arithmetic codes, which have been considered in previous chapters. As is the case with many of the programs in this book, the following code is written for simplicity and not for speed. More efficient code can be found in [MN], and a complete public domain JPEG implementation is available via the Internet [IJG].

```
------------------------------------------------
FILE NAME: DCT.C
------------------------------------------------


#include <stdio.h>
#include <math.h>
/*
Sample JPEG Baseline sequential compressor/
decompressor without the entropy coding step.
The inputs to the program are:

1) An 8x8 block of pixels (values between 0 and 255)
2) The mean (DC term) of the previous block.
3) A quantization matrix.
```

The output is a stream of runlengths.

A full JPEG implementation would need to add header
information and entropy coding (Huffman or arithmetic)
of the runlengths.

```
*/

extern void read_block(char *filename),fdct(),idct(),
  print_dct(),read_quant_table(char *filename),
  print_pixels(),quantize(),dequantize(),zigzag(),
  unzigzag(),print_run_lengths();

double C(short x),round(double x);

/* pixel values */

unsigned char pixels[8][8];

/* DCT coefficients */

double dct[8][8];

/* U and V coordinates in zigzag order */

double reordered[64];

short zigzag_u[64]= {0,
    0,1,
    2,1,0,
    0,1,2,3,
    4,3,2,1,0,
    0,1,2,3,4,5,
    6,5,4,3,2,1,0,
    0,1,2,3,4,5,6,7,
    7,6,5,4,3,2,1,
    2,3,4,5,6,7,
    7,6,5,4,3,
    4,5,6,7,
    7,6,5,
    6,7,
    7};
```

```c
short zigzag_v[64]={0,
    1,0,
    0,1,2,
    3,2,1,0,
    0,1,2,3,4,
    5,4,3,2,1,0,
    0,1,2,3,4,5,6,
    7,6,5,4,3,2,1,0,
    1,2,3,4,5,6,7,
    7,6,5,4,3,2,
    3,4,5,6,7,
    7,6,5,4,
    5,6,7,
    7,6,
    7};

short quant_table[8][8];

main(int argc,char **argv)
{
  short i,previous_dc_term;
  if (argc != 4)
    {
      fprintf(stderr,
"Usage dct pixel_block quant_table"
" previous_dc_term.\n");
      exit(1);
    }

  read_block(argv[1]);

  /* START COMPRESSION */

  fdct();

  printf("ENCODE:\n\n");

  printf("\nDCT coefficients:\n");

  print_dct();

  read_quant_table(argv[2]);
```

```
  printf("\nDividing by quantization values\n"
"yields quantized coefficients:\n");

  quantize();

  print_dct();

  zigzag();

  /* The relationship of the DC term (dct[0][0]) to the
     mean pixel value is

     DC=8*(MPV-128)
     */

  previous_dc_term = atoi(argv[3]);

  printf("\nScanning coefficients in zigzag order\n"
" and runlength encoding yields:\n\n");

  print_run_lengths(previous_dc_term);

  printf("\nDECODE:\n\n");

  /* START DECOMPRESSION */

  unzigzag();

  dequantize();

  printf("Multiplying coefficients by quantization"
" values yields:\n\n");

  print_dct();

  printf("\nPerforming inverse DCT gives"
" new pixel values:\n");

  idct();

  print_pixels();
```

```
  return(0);
}

/* Perform forward discrete cosine transform */

void fdct()
{
  short x,y,u,v;
  double sum;
  for (u=0;u<8;u++)
    for (v=0;v<8;v++)
      {
sum=0.;
```

/* In an actual implementation the cosine function could
   be taken from a lookup table and not recomputed.

   Only 64 different values of the cosine are used. */

```
for (x=0;x<8;x++)
  for (y=0;y<8;y++)
    sum += (pixels[x][y]-128)*cos((2*x+1)*u*(M_PI/16.))*
      cos((2*y+1)*v*(M_PI/16.));
dct[u][v]=(0.25)*C(u)*C(v)*sum;
      }
}

/* Perform inverse discrete cosine transform. */

void idct()
{
  short x,y,u,v;
  double sum;
  for (x=0;x<8;x++)
    for (y=0;y<8;y++)
      {
sum=0.;
```

/* In an actual implementation the cosine function
   could be taken from a lookup table and not
   recomputed in the loop.

   Only 64 different values of the cosine are used. */

```
for (u=0;u<8;u++)
  for (v=0;v<8;v++)
    sum += C(u)*C(v)*dct[u][v]*cos((2*x+1)*
      u*(M_PI/16.))*
      cos((2*y+1)*v*(M_PI/16.));

/* the point 5 in 128.5 means that the double
   is converted to an integer by rounding instead
   of truncating */

pixels[x][y]=128.5+0.25*sum;
        }
}

double C(short n)
{
  if (n==0) return(1./sqrt(2.));
  else return(1.);
}

/* print an 8x8 array of doubles */

void print_dct()
{
  short i;
  putchar('\n');
  for (i=0;i<8;i++)
    printf(
      "Row %d: %5.1lf %5.1lf %5.1lf %5.1lf"
      " %5.1lf %5.1lf %5.1lf %5.1lf\n",
      i,dct[i][0],dct[i][1],dct[i][2],dct[i][3],
      dct[i][4],dct[i][5],dct[i][6],dct[i][7]);
}


/* print an 8x8 array of unsigned char */

void print_pixels()
{
  short i;
  putchar('\n');
  for (i=0;i<8;i++)
```

```
      printf(
        "Row %d: %d %d %d %d %d %d %d %d\n",
        i,pixels[i][0],pixels[i][1],pixels[i][2],pixels[i][3],
        pixels[i][4],pixels[i][5],pixels[i][6],pixels[i][7]);
}

void quantize()
{
  short i,j;
  for (i=0;i<8;i++)
    for(j=0;j<8;j++)
      dct[i][j] = round(dct[i][j]/quant_table[i][j]);
}


void dequantize()
{
  short i,j;
  for (i=0;i<8;i++)
    for(j=0;j<8;j++)
      dct[i][j] = dct[i][j]*quant_table[i][j];
}

double round(double x)
{
  if (x>0.) return((int) (x+0.5));
  else return((int) (x-0.5));
}

void read_block(char *filename)
{
  FILE *blockfile;
  short i;

  blockfile=fopen(filename,"rb");
  if (blockfile==NULL)
    {
      fprintf(stderr,"Error opening %s\n",filename);
      exit(1);
    }
  for (i=0;i<8;i++)
    fscanf(blockfile,"%d %d %d %d %d %d %d %d",
   pixels[i],pixels[i]+1,pixels[i]+2,pixels[i]+3,
```

```
    pixels[i]+4,pixels[i]+5,pixels[i]+6,pixels[i]+7);
}

void read_quant_table(char *filename)
{
  FILE *quantfile;
  short i;

  quantfile=fopen(filename,"rb");
  if (quantfile==NULL)
    {
      fprintf(stderr,"Error opening %s\n",filename);
      exit(1);
    }
  for (i=0;i<8;i++)
    fscanf(quantfile,"%d %d %d %d %d %d %d %d",
  quant_table[i],quant_table[i]+1,quant_table[i]+2,
  quant_table[i]+3,quant_table[i]+4,quant_table[i]+5,
  quant_table[i]+6,quant_table[i]+7);
}

integer_code_size(short n)
{
  if (n<0) n=-n;
  if (n==1) return(1);
  else if (n<4) return(2);
  else if (n<8) return(3);
  else if (n<16) return(4);
  else if (n<32) return(5);
  else if (n<64) return(6);
  else if (n<128) return(7);
  else if (n<256) return(8);
  else if (n<512) return(9);
  else if (n<1024) return(10);
  else
    {
      fprintf(stderr,"Illegal coefficient value %d",n);
      exit(1);
    }
  return(0); /* this statement not reached but
it keeps the compiler happy */
}
```

```
void zigzag()
{
  short i;
  for (i=0;i<64;i++)
    reordered[i]=dct[zigzag_u[i]][zigzag_v[i]];
}

void unzigzag()
{
  short i;
  for (i=0;i<64;i++)
    dct[zigzag_u[i]][zigzag_v[i]]=reordered[i];
}

void print_run_lengths(short previous_dc_term)
{
  short i,runlength=0;
  short dc_diff;
  dc_diff=((int) dct[0][0])-previous_dc_term;
  printf("(%d)(%d), ",integer_code_size(dc_diff),dc_diff);

  for (i=1;i<64;i++)
    {
      if (reordered[i]==0) runlength++;
      else
{
  printf("(%d,%d)%d, ",runlength,
 integer_code_size(reordered[i]),
 (short) reordered[i]);
  runlength=0;
}
    }
  if (reordered[63]==0) printf("(0,0)\n");
  else putchar('\n');
}
```

Compile Instructions:
This code is designed to be compiled using Turbo C 1.0 by Borland. To produce the executable function DCT.EXE, enter the Turbo C command line:

```
tcc -ms -v DCT.C
```

Running Instructions:
To run DCT.EXE, enter the DOS command line:

```
DCT PIXEL.DAT QTABLE.DAT LAST_MEAN
```

Here, PIXEL.DAT and QUANT.DAT are ascii files containing eight rows of eight numbers from 0–255 (pixel values) delimited by spaces, and LAST_MEAN is a number between 0 and 255.

Sample Run:
The file PIXEL.DAT contains:

```
139 144 149 153 155 155 155 155
144 151 153 156 159 156 156 156
150 155 160 163 158 156 156 156
159 161 162 160 160 159 159 159
159 160 161 162 162 155 155 155
161 161 161 161 160 157 157 157
162 162 161 163 162 157 157 157
162 162 161 161 163 158 158 158
```

The file QTABLE.DAT contains:

```
16 11 10 16 24 40 51 61
12 12 14 19 26 58 60 55
14 13 16 24 40 57 69 56
14 17 22 29 51 87 80 62
18 22 37 56 68 109 103 77
24 35 55 64 81 104 113 92
49 64 78 87 103 121 120 101
72 92 95 98 112 100 103 99
```

The command:

```
DCT PIXEL.DAT QTABLE.DAT 128
```

produces the output:

ENCODE:

DCT coefficients:

```
Row 0: 235.6  -1.0 -12.1  -5.2   2.1  -1.7  -2.7   1.3
Row 1: -22.6 -17.5  -6.2  -3.2  -2.9  -0.1   0.4  -1.2
Row 2: -10.9  -9.3  -1.6   1.5   0.2  -0.9  -0.6  -0.1
Row 3:  -7.1  -1.9   0.2   1.5   0.9  -0.1  -0.0   0.3
Row 4:  -0.6  -0.8   1.5   1.6  -0.1  -0.7   0.6   1.3
Row 5:   1.8  -0.2   1.6  -0.3  -0.8   1.5   1.0  -1.0
Row 6:  -1.3  -0.4  -0.3  -1.5  -0.5   1.7   1.1  -0.8
Row 7:  -2.6   1.6  -3.8  -1.8   1.9   1.2  -0.6  -0.4
```

Dividing by quantization values
yields quantized coefficients:

```
Row 0:  15.0   0.0  -1.0   0.0   0.0   0.0   0.0   0.0
Row 1:  -2.0  -1.0   0.0   0.0   0.0   0.0   0.0   0.0
Row 2:  -1.0  -1.0   0.0   0.0   0.0   0.0   0.0   0.0
Row 3:  -1.0   0.0   0.0   0.0   0.0   0.0   0.0   0.0
Row 4:   0.0   0.0   0.0   0.0   0.0   0.0   0.0   0.0
Row 5:   0.0   0.0   0.0   0.0   0.0   0.0   0.0   0.0
Row 6:   0.0   0.0   0.0   0.0   0.0   0.0   0.0   0.0
Row 7:   0.0   0.0   0.0   0.0   0.0   0.0   0.0   0.0
```

Scanning coefficients in zigzag order
and runlength encoding yields:

(7)(-113), (1,2)-2, (0,1)-1, (0,1)-1, (0,1)-1, (2,1)-1,
(0,1)-1, (0,0)

DECODE:

Multiplying coefficients by quantization values yields:

```
Row 0: 240.0   0.0 -10.0   0.0   0.0   0.0   0.0   0.0
Row 1: -24.0 -12.0   0.0   0.0   0.0   0.0   0.0   0.0
Row 2: -14.0 -13.0   0.0   0.0   0.0   0.0   0.0   0.0
Row 3: -14.0   0.0   0.0   0.0   0.0   0.0   0.0   0.0
Row 4:   0.0   0.0   0.0   0.0   0.0   0.0   0.0   0.0
Row 5:   0.0   0.0   0.0   0.0   0.0   0.0   0.0   0.0
Row 6:   0.0   0.0   0.0   0.0   0.0   0.0   0.0   0.0
Row 7:   0.0   0.0   0.0   0.0   0.0   0.0   0.0   0.0
```

Performing inverse DCT gives new pixel values:

```
Row 0: 142 144 147 150 152 153 154 154
Row 1: 149 150 153 155 156 157 156 156
Row 2: 157 158 159 161 161 160 159 158
Row 3: 162 162 163 163 162 160 158 157
Row 4: 162 162 162 162 161 158 156 155
Row 5: 160 161 161 161 160 158 156 154
Row 6: 160 160 161 162 161 160 158 157
Row 7: 160 161 163 164 164 163 161 160
```

A.8. References

[JPG] *Digital Compression and Coding of Continuous-tone Still Images, Part 1: Requirements and guidelines*, Number: ISO/IEC CD 10918-1, Alternate Number: SC2 N2215.

[IJG] *Independent JPEG Group* software available by anonymous ftp from wuarchive.wustl.edu (in the file `/graphics/jpegsrc.v3.tar.Z`). The independent JPEG group can be contacted at `jpeg-info@uunet.uu.net`.

[GKW] G. K. Wallace, "The JPEG Still Picture Compression Standard," *Comm. of the ACM*, Volume 34, Number 4 (1991). A revised version has been submitted to *IEEE Transactions on Consumer Electronics*.

[MN] M. Nelson, *The Data Compression Book*. M & T Books, Redwood City, CA (1991).

Index